IB Economics in a Nutshell

Exam study guide

Ellie Tragakes

Noema Press

Acknowledgment

The author would like to express her immense gratitude to Peter Rock-Lacroix, who made all the diagrams in this book, and who offered countless and most helpful suggestions for improvements in both the diagrams and in the text.

IB Economics in a Nutshell

Noema Press
e-mail: noemapress@gmail.com

Diagrams digitized as scalable vector graphic (SVG) files using Inkscape on Trisquel. Both Inkscape and Trisquel are free/libre software, available at inkscape.org and trisquel.info.

Cover photos are from Wikimedia Commons.
Design by Developnet, Athens, Greece.
Printed and bound by Typoshop, Athens, Greece.

Noema (νόημα) is the Greek word for meaning, thought, concept, perception.

ISBN 978-960-93-5931-3

Introduction

This short guidebook is intended to help you review all the topics of the syllabus before tests and exams. It is not a textbook and cannot be used as such. It should be used as a supplement to your textbook, where you will find more in-depth explanations of syllabus topics.

Key to symbols

In the interests of brevity, and to make cause-and-effect relationships clear, the following symbols are sometimes used.

⇑   increases

⇓   decreases

⇒   therefore, it follows that

☑   advantage, positive characteristic, positive consequence

☒   disadvantage, negative characteristic, negative consequence

✔   important point to note

blue bold words and phrases   syllabus terms and concepts

Note

This book

✔ covers all the topics in the IB Economics syllabus in summary form,

✔ includes key definitions, diagrams and theories you need to know,

✔ contains a glossary of important terms.

You can use it to

✔ review the main points of each topic as you cover it in class and in your studies of economics,

✔ review quickly and thoroughly before tests and exams,

✔ make sure you have covered all the topics in the syllabus that you will be examined on.

Note also that

✔ HL material appears against a light peach background,

✔ the numbering of topics in this book follows the numbering of the IB economics syllabus,

✔ diagrams use **green** lines to show an initial situation and **brown** lines to show any change, with the exception of externality diagrams where **green** lines show the social optimum, **red** lines show the suboptimal (socially inefficient) outcome due to market failure, and **blue** lines show the policy outcome.

Contacting the author

✔ If you have any questions or require any clarifications,

✔ If you have spotted any errors you would like to report,

✔ If you have any other comments,

please write to the author at ellie.nutshell@gmail.com

Contents

FOUNDATIONS OF ECONOMICS

Economics as a social science

social science = any discipline that studies aspects of human society, including economics, anthropology, sociology, political science, psychology

The social scientific method
This is the same as the scientific method and consists of the following steps:

1. Make observations about a question of interest.	2. Identify important variables needed to answer the question.
3. Formulate a hypothesis about how the variables are related.	4. Conduct tests to see if the hypothesis is supported by the data.
5. If the data support the hypothesis, then the hypothesis is accepted (not refuted) and can be used in building theories.	6. If the data do not support the hypothesis, this is rejected and a search begins for a new hypothesis.

Some features of the method of Economics

Economists build **models** in order to simplify the complexities of the real world and highlight the more important relationships between variables. Many of the relationships included in models are based on hypotheses that are supported by empirical data.	The **ceteris paribus** assumption is very important in Economics. It means that when we study economic theory, we change only one variable at a time, in order to be able to study the variable's effects, on the assumption that **all other variables remain constant and unchanging**.
Positive versus normative statements **positive statement** = a statement about something that **is**, **was**, or **will be**; it may be true or false; ex "the rate of inflation is 5%" (this may or may not be true). Positive statements are used to describe events, and make hypotheses and theories. **normative statement** = a statement about something that **ought to be**, expressing a subjective opinion or value judgment; it cannot be true or false; ex "the rate of inflation is too high" is based on an opinion of what is "too high". Normative statements are used to determine the goals of economic policies.	An important assumption in economics is that of **rational economic decision-making** = decision-makers (consumers, firms, workers and all resource-owners) behave according to their best self-interest, and try to get more rather than less (more benefits from consumption, more profit from production, higher wages and more income from selling labor and other resources, and so on).

Factors of production and scarcity

factors of production = **resources** = inputs used to produce all goods and services that people need and want; there are four types of resources:

land = all natural resources that are above the ground (ex forests, rivers, agricultural land, fish in the sea) and all natural resources that are under the ground (ex oil, natural gas, minerals)	**capital** (also known as **physical capital**) = machines, tools, equipment, factories, all construction; it differs from the other three because it is itself a **produced** factor of production
labor = all human effort, or work, that goes into producing goods and services (ex the work done by teachers, builders, lawyers, plumbers)	**entrepreneurship** = the human effort used to organize the other three factors, as well as risk-taking, innovation, management

scarcity = the condition of being limited in relation to the needs and wants of human beings; factors of production are **scarce** while human needs and wants are infinite; since there are not enough resources to produce everything needed and wanted by human beings, goods and services are also scarce

Three basic questions

Scarcity forces all economies, regardless of their form of organization, to answer three basic questions:

What to produce?	How to produce?	For whom to produce?
What goods and services will be produced by the available resources, and in what quantities will they be produced?	What factors of production will be used to produce the goods and services, and in what combinations and quantities?	How will the goods and services produced be distributed among their potential users; who will get what, and in what quantities?

Choice and opportunity cost

The scarcity of resources means that **choices have to be made**: the questions **what to produce** and **how to produce** involve choices that relate to **resource allocation** (explained below). (The question **for whom to produce** involves choices that relate to **income distribution**; see p 55.)

resource allocation = assigning particular resources to the production of particular goods and services **overallocation of resources** = too many resources are assigned to the production of particular goods and services; there is **overproduction** **underallocation of resources** = too few resources are assigned to the production of particular goods and services; there is **underproduction**	**reallocation of resources** = changing the allocation of resources, and hence the combination and quantities of goods and services produced, so that different amounts of resources are assigned to each good and service **misallocation of resources** = assigning the wrong amount of resources to the production of particular goods and services, resulting in **overallocation** or **underallocation**

opportunity cost = the value of the next best alternative that is sacrificed as a result of making a choice; this concept is **central to economics**, because **scarcity necessitates choice**, and **choice most often involves an opportunity cost**. Ex if you choose to study for your exams, the opportunity cost of your choice is the sacrifice of what you mostly preferred to do instead of studying. If society chooses to produce good A, the opportunity cost of this choice is the sacrifice of the most preferred alternative good that could have been produced with the same resources.

The production possibilities model: scarcity, choice and opportunity cost

The **production possibilities curve (frontier) (PPC or PPF)** shows the maximum quantities of two goods, ex potatoes and bicycles (or two groups of goods, ex agricultural products and manufactured goods) that can be produced by an economy with its available resources and technology. To produce on the PPC (at points such as a or b) the economy must:
- use its resources fully; there must be **full employment** of all resources;
- use all its resources **efficiently**, so that there is no resource waste.

If either one or both of these conditions do not hold, the economy will produce at a point inside the PPC, such as point c: at c, either the economy does not have full (or maximum) employment, or it is producing inefficiently, or both.

The PPC model shows the following:
✔ Due to **scarcity**, it is impossible to produce outside the PPC: point d is **unattainable**, meaning it is not possible to produce that combination of goods.
✔ Due to **scarcity, it is necessary to make choices**: the economy that has full employment and is efficient must choose its point of production; ex point a or b or any other point on the PPC.
✔ **Choice gives rise to opportunity cost**: It is not possible to increase production of one good without decreasing production of the other good.

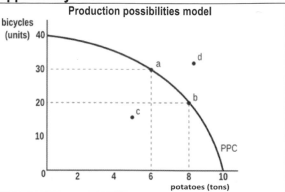

Production possibilities model

At point a, the economy produces 30 bicycles and 6 tons of potatoes. At point b, the economy produces 20 bicycles and 8 tons of potatoes.
✔ To move from point a to point b, the economy must **sacrifice 10 bicycles** in order to gain 2 tons of potatoes. **The 10 bicycles are the opportunity cost** of increasing the quantity of potatoes by 2 tons.
✔ The movement from point a to point b involves a **reallocation of resources**.

Central themes

Economic growth versus economic development

A main goal of governments around the world is **economic growth** (growth in output produced). Yet economic growth on its own may not ensure the achievement of **economic development** (increases in standards of living in the broader population of a country). Important questions to consider are: How do we measure economic development? What factors prevent economic development from occurring? Under what conditions does economic development take place? What kinds of policies should be pursued to ensure that economic growth translates into economic development?

The threat to sustainability

Environmental **sustainability** (the use of resources at a pace and in ways that do not decrease the quantity or destroy the quality of resources available for future generations) is threatened by production based on the use of fossil fuels, as well as by numerous other activities that destroy or degrade natural resources, including forests, wildlife, sea life, the global climate and many more. Important questions are: What kinds of activities lead to unsustainability? Does economic growth necessarily lead to unsustainable development? What kinds of policies can be pursued to promote sustainability and prevent environmental degradation and destruction?

How much should governments intervene in markets

All economies in the world work through a mixture of government activities based on the **command method** (where the government uses its authority to make laws and regulations that all economic decision-makers, including firms and consumers, must abide by) and private sector activities based on the **market method** (where all economic decision-makers interact in markets and respond to prices determined in markets). Important questions are: What are the benefits and disadvantages of government intervention in markets? What are the benefits and disadvantages of freely functioning markets with no government intervention? How much, and in what ways should governments intervene in markets?

Economic efficiency versus equity: conflicting or consistent objectives

Economic efficiency (the use of resources in the best possible way so as to avoid resource waste) and **equity** (the state of being fair, usually interpreted to mean **equality in income distribution**) are two important economic objectives. Important questions to consider are: Under what conditions are efficiency and equity achieved? What kinds of policies are appropriate for achieving greater efficiency, and what policies for achieving greater equity? Are efficiency and equity conflicting objectives as some economists believe? Are there certain conditions under which efficiency and equity are consistent and complement each other? Are there policies that can be used to promote both?

1.1 COMPETITIVE MARKETS: DEMAND AND SUPPLY

Competitive markets

market = any arrangement that allows buyers and sellers to come together and make an exchange (ex a physical meeting place as a fish market or a shop, or classified ads, internet, etc)	**competitive market** = a market where the price of a good, service, or factor of production is determined through the interactions of **many small buyers and sellers**, so that no one can influence the price

Demand

Understanding demand

demand (D) = the quantity of a good that buyers (consumers) are **willing and able** to buy at various prices over a time period, ceteris paribus

The law of demand	Demand curves: Individual demand and market demand
law of demand = a law stating that there is a negative causal relationship between **price (P)** and **quantity (Q)** of a good demanded: the higher the price, the lower the quantity demanded; the lower the price, the greater the quantity demanded. The law of demand is illustrated by the **demand curve**, which is downward sloping.	**individual demand** = the demand of a single buyer **market demand** = the demands of all the buyers in a market, found by adding up all the individual demands for each price. In a market with two buyers, market demand, D_m = D of Buyer 1 + D of Buyer 2.
Why the demand curve is downward sloping Consumers derive **benefits** from buying/consuming goods and services. The additional benefits derived from buying/consuming one more unit of a good are called **marginal benefits (MB)**. As we buy more and more units of a good, the marginal benefits we enjoy decrease (ex the more sodas you drink, the less benefits you get from each additional soda, therefore MB⇓). Since MB⇓ as Q consumed ⇑, consumers will be willing to buy more and more units of a good only if its price falls. Therefore as P⇓, Q demanded⇑, and vice versa. **For these reasons, the demand curve is also known as a marginal benefits (MB) curve.**	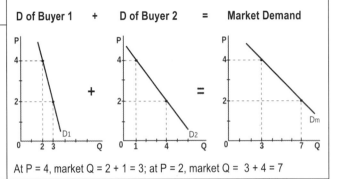 At P = 4, market Q = 2 + 1 = 3; at P = 2, market Q = 3 + 4 = 7

Distinguishing between a movement along a demand curve and a shift of the demand curve

Movement along a demand curve (change in Q demanded)	Shift of a demand curve (change in demand)
A movement along the demand curve for a good can be caused **only by a change in the price of the good**. According to the **law of demand**, if P⇑, Q⇓ and there is an upward movement (b ⟹ a); if P⇓, Q⇑ and there is a downward movement (a ⟹ b). The change in Q due to the change in P is called a **change in quantity demanded**.	A shift of the demand curve for a good can be caused **only by a change in any of the non-price determinants of demand** (see below). A rightward shift indicates an increase in demand and a leftward shift indicates a decrease in demand. The change in Q due to the shifts in D is called a **change in demand**.
Demand curve showing changes in Q demanded 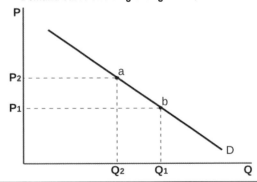	**Demand curve shifts: changes in demand** 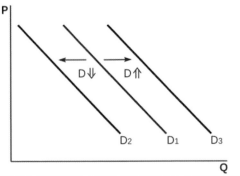

Non-price determinants of demand (causes of demand curve shifts)

Demand changes (and the demand curve shifts) in response to **four main factors**:

Changes in tastes and preferences When tastes and preferences of consumers change in favor of a good, D increases (shifts right); if preferences change against a good, D decreases (shifts left)	**Changes in the number of buyers (demographic changes)** If the number of buyers in a market increases, D increases (shifts right); if the number of buyers decreases, D decreases (shifts left)
Changes in income The effects on D depend on whether the good is: (i) **normal** = demand for the good increases as consumer income increases; most goods are normal: as income rises, D increases (shifts right); as income falls, D falls (shifts left) (ii) **inferior** = demand for the good decreases as consumer income increases; ex lower-price goods like used cars, used clothes, margarine (as opposed to butter): as income rises, D falls (shifts left); as income falls, D increases (shifts right)	**Changes in prices of related goods** The effects on D depend on whether the related goods are: (i) **substitutes** = goods that satisfy a similar need, ex meat and fish; as P of good A (ex meat) increases, D for good B (ex fish) increases (shifts right); as P of good A falls, D for good B falls (shifts left) (ii) **complements** = goods that are used together, ex tennis balls and tennis rackets; as P of good A increases, D for good B decreases (shifts left); as P of good A decreases, D for good B increases (shifts right)

Supply

Understanding supply

supply (S) = the quantity of a good that sellers (firms) are **willing and able** to produce and sell at various prices over a time period, ceteris paribus

The law of supply **law of supply** = a law stating that there is a positive causal relationship between **price (P) and quantity (Q)** of a good supplied: the higher the price, the higher the quantity supplied; the lower the price, the lower the quantity supplied. The law of supply is illustrated by the **supply curve**, which is upward sloping.	**Individual supply and market supply** **individual supply** = the supply of a single seller (firm) **market supply** = the supplies of all the sellers in a market, found by adding up all the individual supplies for each price. In a market with two sellers, market supply, S_m = S of Seller 1 + S of Seller 2.
Why the supply curve is upward sloping The price at which the firm sells its good determines the revenue of the firm (the money it receives from its sales). As the price of a good increases, the firm receives more revenue, production of the good becomes more profitable, therefore it is in firms' interests to increase the quantity they produce. The reason for greater profitability is that as price and revenue increase, firms are better able to cover the higher costs of production that arise from increased quantity produced. Therefore as P⇑, Q supplied ⇑, and vice versa.	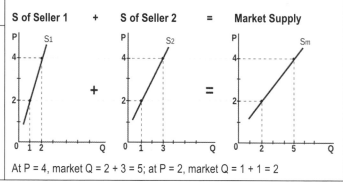 At P = 4, market Q = 2 + 3 = 5; at P = 2, market Q = 1 + 1 = 2

Distinguishing between a movement along a supply curve and a shift of the supply curve

Movement along a supply curve (change in Q supplied) A movement along the supply curve for a good can be caused **only by a change in the price of the good**. According to the **law of supply**, if P⇑, Q⇑ and there is an upward movement (b ⇒ a); if P⇓, Q⇓ and there is a downward movement (a ⇒ b). The change in Q due to the change in P is called a **change in quantity supplied**.	**Shift of a supply curve (change in supply)** A shift of the supply curve for a good can be caused **only by a change in the non-price determinants of supply** (see below). A rightward shift indicates an increase in supply and a leftward shift indicates a decrease in supply. The change in Q due to the shifts in S is called a **change in supply**.
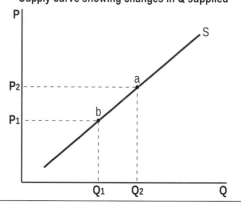	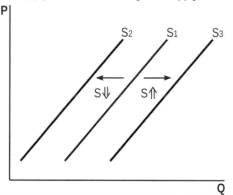

Non-price determinants of supply (causes of supply curve shifts)

Supply changes (and the supply curve shifts) in response to **seven main factors**:

Changes in costs of production (factor prices) If prices of factors of production (labor, land, capital, entrepreneurship) increase, S falls (shifts left); if factor prices decrease, S increases (shifts right)	**Changes in an indirect tax** (= tax on spending to buy goods and services paid indirectly to the government); if an indirect tax increases, S falls (shifts left); if an indirect tax falls, S increases (shifts right)
Changes in the number of firms in the market If the number of firms in a market increases, S increases (shifts right); if the number of firms in a market falls, S decreases (shifts left)	**Changes in a subsidy** (= payment by the government to firms in order to lower costs and price, and increase supply); if a subsidy on the product of a firm increases, S increases (shifts right). If a subsidy ⇓, S⇓ (shifts left)
Technological changes If there is a technological improvement, S increases (shifts right); if there is technological worsening (less likely to occur) S decreases (shifts left)	**Changes in expectations** If firms expect the future price of their product to increase, they supply less in the market in the present so they can sell more in the future at the higher price ⇒ S falls (shifts left). If firms expect the price to fall, they supply more in the present ⇒ S rises (shifts right)

Changes in prices of related goods The effects on supply depend on whether the related goods are in:
(i) **joint supply** = when two or more goods, ex butter and skim milk, are derived from a single product (whole milk), it is not possible to produce **more** of one, ex butter, without producing **more** of the other, ex skim milk. If the price of butter rises, Q of butter produced increases (upward movement along the butter S curve) and S of skim milk increases (S curve for skim milk shifts right). If the price of butter falls, Q of butter produced decreases (downward movement along the butter S curve) and S of skim milk falls (S curve for skim milk shifts left).
(ii) **competitive supply** = when two goods use the same resources, ex onions and potatoes grown on the same agricultural land, it is not possible to produce **more** of one without producing **less** of the other. If the price of potatoes increases, the Q of potatoes produced increases (upward movement along the potato S curve) and the S of onions falls (S curve for onions shifts left). If the price of potatoes decreases, the Q of potatoes falls (downward movement along the potato S curve) and the S of onions increases (S curve for onions shifts right).

Market equilibrium

Equilibrium

Market equilibrium is a position of balance between demand and supply, and occurs when **quantity demanded is equal to quantity supplied**. In the diagram, this point of equality is where the D and S curves cross each other, determining **equilibrium price**, Pe, and **equilibrium quantity**, Qe. At every price other than Pe, there is **market disequilibrium**.

If P > Pe ⇒ **excess supply = surplus** ⇒ **Q demanded < Q supplied**.
If P < Pe, ⇒ **excess demand = shortage** ⇒ **Q demanded > Q supplied**.

✔ In a free, competitive market, where there is no interference with the forces of supply and demand, P and Q will always settle at their equilibrium values.
✔ If there is a shortage, the excess demand will ensure that P⇑ to Pe.
✔ If there is a surplus, the excess supply will ensure that P⇓ to Pe.

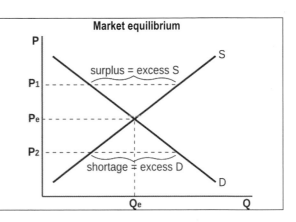

Market equilibrium

Changes in market equilibrium

Market equilibrium can change only if there is a change (shift) in demand (D) or in supply (S), arising from any of their non-price determinants. Any such shift leads to excess demand or excess supply, resulting in a new market equilibrium.

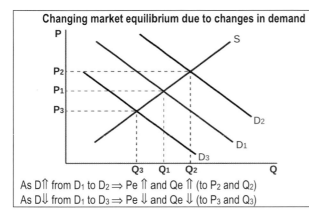

Changing market equilibrium due to changes in demand

As D⇑ from D₁ to D₂ ⇒ Pe ⇑ and Qe ⇑ (to P₂ and Q₂)
As D⇓ from D₁ to D₃ ⇒ Pe ⇓ and Qe ⇓ (to P₃ and Q₃)

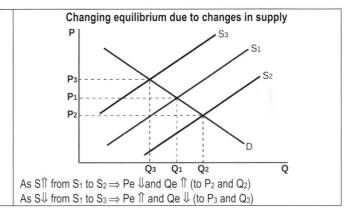

Changing equilibrium due to changes in supply

As S⇑ from S₁ to S₂ ⇒ Pe ⇓ and Qe ⇑ (to P₂ and Q₂)
As S⇓ from S₁ to S₃ ⇒ Pe ⇑ and Qe ⇓ (to P₃ and Q₃)

The role of the price mechanism

Resource allocation

Resource allocation = assigning specific resources to the production of specific goods and services

Scarcity, choice and opportunity cost (see p 1 - 2)
✔ Resources are **scarce** (= limited in quantity in relation to people's needs and wants for them) therefore **societies must make choices** on how to best **allocate** resources to avoid resource waste.
✔ **Scarcity** means production cannot occur outside the PPC (point x).
✔ A **choice** must be made on how many resources to allocate to bread (symbolizing food) or to guns (symbolizing defense); **this is a choice answering the what to produce and how to produce questions of resource allocation**.
✔ Scarcity means that a choice of more bread production necessarily involves less gun production (and vice versa).
✔ Every choice involves an **opportunity cost** (= the value of the next best alternative foregone or sacrificed): moving from **a** to **b** involves an increase in bread production of B₂ – B₁ with an opportunity cost of G₁ – G₂ (guns foregone).

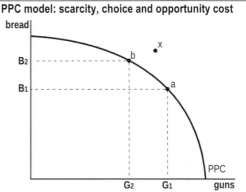

PPC model: scarcity, choice and opportunity cost

Signaling and incentive functions of price in resource allocation
Prices determined in markets play a crucial role in allocating resources to the production of specific goods. The economy is initially at P₁ and Q₁.
Suppose D⇑ from D₁ to D₂ (due to a change in a non-price determinant). At the initial price, P₁, there is excess demand (= Q₂ – Q₁) ⇒ **P begins to ⇑** acting as:
(i) a **signal** to producers and consumers that there is a shortage; i.e. the rising P provides information about the shortage to producers and consumers; and
(ii) **an incentive to producers to produce more Q**, leading to an upward movement along the S curve (Q supplied increases) because of firms' greater willingness and ability to produce as P⇑; and **an incentive to consumers to buy less Q than Q₂**, leading to an upward movement along the D₂ curve (Q demanded decreases) because of consumers' lower willingness and ability to buy as P⇑.
✔ The new market equilibrium settles at price P₂ and quantity Q₃.
✔ **Resource reallocation** has occurred, as some resources were taken out of production of other goods and brought into production of this good (Q₃ > Q₁).

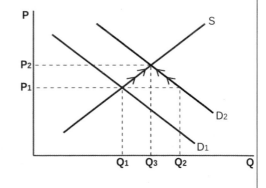

Price as a signal and incentive in resource allocation

Market efficiency

Consumer and producer surplus, social surplus and allocative efficiency

consumer surplus = the benefit received by consumers who buy a good at a lower price than the price they are willing to pay = the area under the demand curve up to the equilibrium price, Pe, shown by the blue area. ✔ In a free competitive market, consumer surplus is maximum.
producer surplus = the benefit received by producers who sell a good at a higher price that the price they are willing to receive = the area above the supply curve up to the equilibrium price, Pe, shown by the orange area. ✔ In a free competitive market, producer surplus is maximum.
social surplus = the sum of producer and consumer surplus ✔ In a free competitive market, social surplus is maximum.
allocative efficiency = best allocation of resources from society's point of view, occurring in a free, competitive market (with no externalities; see p 19). **marginal benefit (MB)** = the extra benefit to consumers from consuming one more unit of a good, equal to the demand curve **marginal cost (MC)** = the extra cost to producers of producing one more unit of a good, equal to the supply curve.

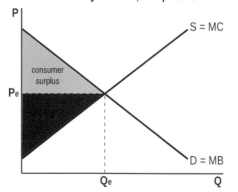

Consumer and producer surplus, social surplus and allocative efficiency in a free, competitive market

At equilibrium there is allocative efficiency because:
✔ social surplus is maximum (the greatest it can be); and
✔ marginal benefit = marginal cost (MB = MC)

HL topics on demand, supply and market equilibrium

Demand

A linear (= straight-line) demand (D) curve is given by $Qd = a - bP$, where

Qd = quantity demanded (dependent variable)	P = price (independent variable)	a = Q intercept (the point on the horizontal axis cut by the demand curve)	$-b$ = the slope of the D curve, defined as $-\Delta Qd/\Delta P$ (where b is a positive number)

Plotting a demand curve
Plot the demand equation $Qd = 12 - 2P$, where Qd is in kg of apples and P is in €.
Step 1: label the vertical axis of your graph as **P (€)** and the horizontal axis **Q (kg of apples)**.
Step 2: To find two points on the D curve in the simplest way: set P = 0 $\Rightarrow$ **Qd = 12**. This is the **Q intercept** (the point on the horizontal or Q axis cut by the demand curve), giving the point (12,0)
Step 3: set Qd = 0 $\Rightarrow$ 0 = 12 −2P $\Rightarrow$ 2P =12 $\Rightarrow$ P = 12/2 $\Rightarrow$ **P = 6**. This is the **P intercept** (the point on the vertical or P axis cut by the D curve) giving the point (0,6).
These are the end-points of the D curve (the **green** line).

Alternatively, you can set P (or Q) equal to any reasonable value (within the range of the D curve) and solve:
Ex set P = 1 $\Rightarrow$ Qd = 12 − 2(1) $\Rightarrow$ Qd = 12 − 2 $\Rightarrow$ **Qd =10**. You have now found the point (10,1)

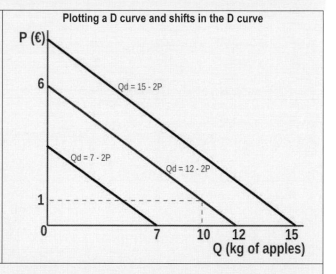

Plotting a D curve and shifts in the D curve

Shifting the demand curve
Any parallel shift in the demand curve, due to a change in any non-price determinant, appears as a change in "a" in the equation $Qd = a - bP$.
✔ If a increases, the D curve shifts right; if a decreases, the D curve shifts left.
In the demand equation $Qd = 12 - 2P$, the Q of apples demanded increases by 3 kg at each price. Find the new demand equation and plot it.
Step 1: Since a = 12 in the initial equation, a = 12 + 3 = 15 in the new equation, which becomes $Qd = 15 - 2P$.
Step 2: To plot the new D curve, simply shift the initial D curve 3 units (kg) to the right.
If the Q of apples demanded decreases by 5 kg at each price, the new demand equation is $Qd = 7 - 2P$, and D shifts 5 units (kg) to the left.

Changing the steepness of the demand curve
In the demand equation $Qd = a - bP$, the steepness of the curve is determined by the value of " $-b$ ", which is the **slope** = $-\Delta Qd/\Delta P$ (= change in the dependent variable divided by change in the independent variable):

✔ The larger the absolute value of the slope, the flatter the D curve.

Given $Qd = 12 - 2P$, suppose -2 changes to -4. The new demand curve, given by $Qd = 12 - 4P$, becomes **flatter** as shown in the diagram.

✔ Note that the slope here is "**run over rise**" rather than "**rise over run**", due to the reversal of the axes of the dependent and independent variables.

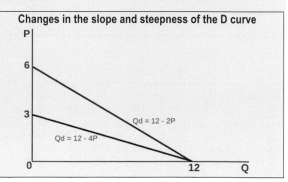

Changes in the slope and steepness of the D curve

Supply

A linear supply (S) curve is given by **Qs = c + dP**, where

Qs = quantity supplied (dependent variable)	**P** = price (independent variable)	**c = Q intercept** (the point on the horizontal axis cut by the supply curve)	**d** = the slope of the S curve, defined as $\Delta Qs/\Delta P$ (where d is a positive number)

Plotting a supply curve

Plot the supply equation **Qs = 2 + 3P**, where Qs is in kg of apples and P is in €.

Step 1: label the vertical axis of your graph as **P (€)** and the horizontal axis **Q (kg of apples)**

Step 2: set P = 0 $\Rightarrow$ **Qs = 2**. This is the **Q intercept** (the point on the horizontal or Q axis cut by the supply curve), giving the point (2,0).

Step 3: If you now set Q = 0 (as you did with the D curve), you will find that P < 0 (a negative number), which is not in the permissible range of the S curve. To get around this, you can set Q equal to another value (> 2 that you found above). So let Q = 8 $\Rightarrow$ 8 = 2 + 3P $\Rightarrow$ 6 = 3P $\Rightarrow$ **P = 2**, so you have the point (8,2).

You now have two points that you can join together to find the S curve.

✔ If the value of **c** in **Qs = c + dP** is negative, for example, Qs = -6 + 3P, then setting P = 0 will give you Q < 0, which is not in the permissible range of the S curve. Here you can set Q = 0 to find the P intercept $\Rightarrow$ 0 = -6 + 3P $\Rightarrow$ P = 2, or the point (0,2). (Note: This is not shown in the diagram.)

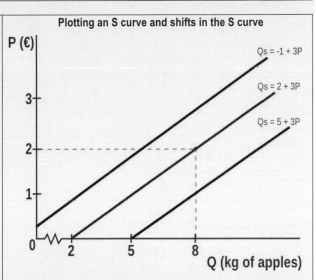

Plotting an S curve and shifts in the S curve

Shifting the supply curve

Any parallel shift in the supply curve, due to a change in any non-price determinant, shows as a change in "**c**" in the equation **Qs = c + dP**.

✔ If c increases, the S curve shifts right; if c decreases, the S curve shifts left.

In the supply equation **Qs = 2 + 3P**, the Q of apples supplied increases by 3 kg at each price. Find the new supply equation and plot it.

Step 1: Since c = 2 in the initial equation, c = 2 + 3 = 5 in the new equation, which becomes **Qs = 5 + 3P**.

Step 2: To plot the new S curve, simply shift the initial S curve 3 units (kg) to the right.

If the Q of apples supplied decreases by 3 kg at each price, the new supply equation is **Qs = - 1 + 3P**, and S shifts 3 units (kg) to the left.

Changing the steepness of the supply curve

In the supply equation **Qs = c + dP**, the steepness of the curve is determined by the value of "**d**", which is the **slope = $\Delta Qd/\Delta P$** (= change in the dependent variable divided by change in the independent variable):

✔ The larger the value of the slope, the flatter the S curve.

Given **Qs = 2 + 3P**, suppose 3 changes to 2. The new supply curve, given by **Qs = 2 + 2P**, becomes **steeper** as shown in the diagram.

✔ As in the D curve, the slope is "**run over rise**" rather than "**rise over run**", due to the reversal of the axes of the dependent and independent variables.

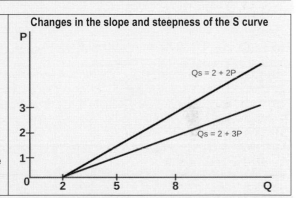

Changes in the slope and steepness of the S curve

Market equilibrium

Solving equations to find equilibrium P and Q

Given the demand curve **Qd = 12 – 2P** and the supply curve **Qs = 2 + 3P**, where Qd and Qs are in kg of apples and P is in €, calculate the equilibrium price and quantity.

Step 1: Since at equilibrium Qd = Qs $\Rightarrow$ 12 – 2P = 2 + 3P

Step 2: Solving for P: 5P = 10 $\Rightarrow$ **P = €2**

Step 3: Substituting P = 2 into the demand (or supply) equation: Qd = 12 – 2(2) $\Rightarrow$ Qd = 12 – 4 $\Rightarrow$ **Q = 8 kg**

✔ Do not forget the labels: € for P and **kg** for Q.

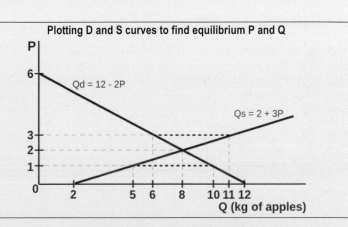

Plotting D and S curves to find equilibrium P and Q

Calculating excess demand using the example above	Calculating excess supply using the example above
Excess demand arises for any P < Pe = €2, where Qd > Qs.	**Excess supply** arises for any P > Pe = €2, where Qd < Qs.
Supposing P = €1, use this value for P to solve for Qd and Qs:	Supposing P = €3, use this value for P to solve for Qd and Qs:
Qd = 12 – 2P = 12 – 2 = **10 kg.** Qs = 2 + 3P = 2 + 3 = **5 kg.**	Qd = 12 –2(3) = 12 – 6 = **6 kg.** Qs = 2 + 3(3) = 2 + 9 = **11 kg.**
Excess demand = Qd – Qs = 10 – 5 = **5 kg.**	Excess supply = Qs – Qd = 11 – 6 = **5 kg.**
✔ This excess demand can be seen as the **brown** dotted line above.	✔ This excess supply can be seen as the **orange** dotted line above.

1.2 ELASTICITY

Price elasticity of demand (PED)

PED and how to calculate it

According to the law of demand, an increase in P gives rise to a decrease in Q demanded, and vice versa. Now we ask, given a change in P, does Q demanded change a lot or a little? The concept of PED addresses this question.

| PED = responsiveness of Q demanded to changes in P = % change in Q demanded divided by % change in P $$= \frac{\%\Delta Q}{\%\Delta P} = \frac{\frac{\Delta Q}{Q} \times 100}{\frac{\Delta P}{P} \times 100} = \frac{\frac{\Delta Q}{Q}}{\frac{\Delta P}{P}}, \text{ where}$$ ΔQ = $Q_{final\ value} - Q_{initial\ value}$
 Q = initial Q value
 ΔP = $P_{final\ value} - P_{initial\ value}$
 P = initial P value | **The value of PED**
 Because of the law of demand, stating the inverse relationship between P and Q, **PED has a negative value**: as P ⇑ Q ⇓ and vice versa.

 ✔ However, PED is treated **as if it were positive** (absolute value).

 ✔ PED measures **responsiveness of Q along a given D curve**. | **Calculating PED**
 Suppose the price of pizzas increases from $4 per pizza to $6 per pizza and the quantity demanded falls from 200 pizzas to 150 pizzas. **Calculate the PED for pizzas.**

 $$\frac{\%\Delta Q}{\%\Delta P} = \frac{\frac{\Delta Q}{Q}}{\frac{\Delta P}{P}} = \frac{\frac{150-200}{200}}{\frac{6-4}{4}} = \frac{\frac{-50}{200}}{\frac{2}{4}} = \frac{-200}{400} = -\tfrac{1}{2} \Rightarrow \tfrac{1}{2}$$
 ✔ Note that whereas the value of PED is negative, it is treated as if it were positive. |

Price elastic and price inelastic demand

Price elastic demand **PED > 1**: %ΔQ > %ΔP = the percentage change in Q demanded is greater than the percentage change in P (the change in Q is proportionately larger than the change in P). **Price inelastic demand** **0 < PED < 1**: %ΔQ < %ΔP = the percentage change in Q demanded is smaller than the percentage change in P (the change in Q is proportionately smaller than the change in P) ✔ PED is measured between two points on a D curve. In a diagram with two intersecting D curves, **the flatter curve has the more elastic D for the same ΔP**: D_1 is more elastic than D_2 since $\Delta Q >$ for D_1 than for D_2.	**Steepness of the D curve and PED** 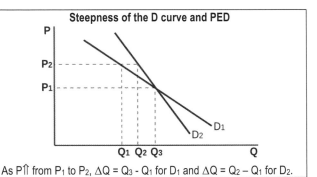 As P⇑ from P_1 to P_2, $\Delta Q = Q_3 - Q_1$ for D_1 and $\Delta Q = Q_2 - Q_1$ for D_2.

A straight-line negatively-sloped demand curve has variable (changing PED)

Variable (changing) PED along the D curve Along a straight-line negatively-sloped D curve illustrating the law of demand, PED changes along the length of the curve, continuously falling as P⇓ and Q⇑. In the northwest part of the D curve PED > 1, in the southeast part PED < 1, and at the midpoint of the D curve PED = 1. **Why PED differs from the slope** The slope of the D curve = -ΔQ/ΔP. By contrast, $$PED = -\frac{\Delta Q / Q}{\Delta P / P} = -\frac{\Delta Q}{\Delta P} \cdot \frac{P}{Q} \quad \Rightarrow \quad \textbf{PED = slope x P/Q.}$$ The slope of a straight line is always constant, therefore PED = a constant number x P/Q which is continuously changing (decreasing) as P⇓ and Q⇑ along the D curve. Therefore PED ⇓ as P⇓ and Q⇑.	**Variable (changing) PED along the D curve** 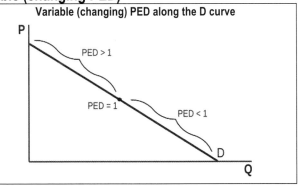

Special cases of constant (unchanging) PED

Perfectly elastic demand	**Perfectly inelastic demand**	**Unit elastic demand**
PED = ∞: the percentage change in Q demanded resulting from a change in P is infinitely large; this is a special case used in economic theory to illustrate demand in perfect competition (HL topic, see p 30). ✔ When demand is perfectly elastic, the demand curve is horizontal. **Perfectly elastic demand: PED = ∞** 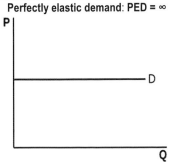	**PED = 0**: the percentage change in Q demanded is zero; no matter how high P rises, Q demanded does not respond; this situation might be approached in cases of drug addiction. ✔ When demand is perfectly inelastic, the demand curve is vertical. **Perfectly inelastic demand: PED = 0** 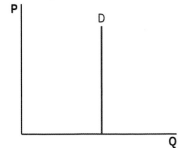	**PED = 1**: the percentage change in Q demanded is equal to the percentage change in P (change in Q is proportionately equal to change in P); this is a theoretical idea that is unlikely to be found often in the real world. ✔ When demand is unit elastic, the demand curve is a rectangular hyperbola. **Unit elastic demand: PED = 1**

The determinants of PED

Number and closeness of substitutes	Proportion of income spend on the good
substitute goods = two or more goods that satisfy a similar need. The more close substitutes a good has, the more elastic its demand = the greater its PED. Ex if P of apples ⇑ consumers can switch to other fruits (substitutes to apples) ⟹ high responsiveness (drop) of Q of apples demanded. But if P of gasoline ⇑ consumers have few alternatives ⟹ low responsiveness (drop) of Q of gasoline demanded. Apples have price-elastic D; gasoline has price-inelastic D.	The greater the proportion of income spent on a good, the more elastic its demand = the greater its PED. Ex Comparing televisions to ice cream: since a television takes up a larger proportion of consumer income than an ice cream, an ⇑ in the P of televisions will be felt more strongly by consumers than an ⇑ in the P of ice cream, leading to a greater responsiveness (drop) in the Q of televisions demanded. PED for televisions > PED for ice cream.
Degree of necessity and degree of addiction	**Time**
necessity = a good that is necessary to a consumer (to be contrasted with a **luxury** = a good that is not essential) The more necessary a good, or the more addictive it is, the less elastic its demand = the lower its PED. Ex food is a necessity people cannot live without ⟹ if P of food ⇑, the Q of food demanded will drop proportionately less. PED for necessities < PED for luxuries.	The more time a consumer has available to make a decision to buy a good, the more elastic the demand. Ex if P of gasoline ⇑, over a short time there will be a small drop in Q demanded, but over longer periods consumers can switch to other forms of transportation than cars, or can buy more fuel-efficient cars ⟹ larger drop in Q demanded.

Applications of PED 1: PED and total revenue of firms

total revenue (TR) = P x Q = a firm's total earnings from selling its output. As P changes, TR may ⇑, or ⇓, or stay unchanged, **depending on PED**:

PED > 1 (price elastic D) ⟹ %ΔQ > %ΔP ⟹ P and TR change in opposite directions: if P⇑ ⟹ TR⇓. Reason: if P⇑, Q⇓ proportionately more ⟹ since the % decrease in Q is larger than the % increase in P, TR⇓. if P⇓ ⟹ TR⇑. Reason: if P⇓, Q⇑ proportionately more ⟹ since the % increase in Q is larger than the % decrease in P, TR⇑. In the diagram, ΔP is in the elastic part of the D curve. When P = P₁, TR = P₁ x Q₁ = yellow + orange areas. When P⇑ to P₂, TR = P₂ x Q₂ = = yellow + blue areas. Since blue < orange, TR⇓ as P⇑.	**ΔP in elastic part of D curve: P and TR change in opposite directions** 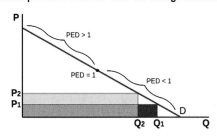
PED < 1 (price inelastic D) ⟹ %ΔQ < %ΔP ⟹ P and TR change in the same direction: if P⇑ ⟹ TR⇑. Reason: if P⇑, Q⇓ proportionately less ⟹ since the % increase in P is larger than the % decrease in Q, TR⇑. if P⇓ ⟹ TR⇓. Reason: if P⇓, Q⇑ proportionately less ⟹ since the % decrease in P is larger than % increase in Q, TR⇓. In the diagram, ΔP is in the inelastic part of the D curve. When P = P₁, TR = P₁ x Q₁ = yellow + orange areas. When P⇑ to P₂, TR = P₂ x Q₂ = yellow plus blue areas. Since blue > orange, TR⇑ as P⇑	**ΔP in inelastic part of D curve: P and TR change in same direction** 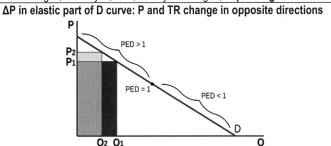

PED = 1 (unit elastic demand) ⟹ %ΔQ = %ΔP so the change in P has an equal (and opposite) effect on TR as the change in Q. Therefore: **as P⇑ or ⇓, TR remains unchanged.** In both diagrams, orange area = blue area.

ΔP at point of straight-line D curve where PED = 1	**Unit elasticity throughout the range of the D curve**
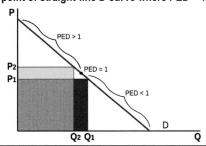	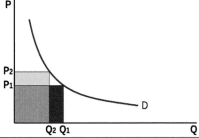

Role of PED to firms making pricing decisions If a firm wants to increase its total revenue, it must know the PED for its product since increasing or decreasing its P will have a different impact on TR depending on the PED, and on where on the D curve it is located. ✔ Therefore, falling PED along the D curve affects the firm's TR. TR increases as the firm lowers its P from P₁ to P₂ (P₂ being at the midpoint of the D curve, where PED = 1). At P₂, **where PED = 1, TR is maximum**; if P falls below P₂, TR begins to decrease since here PED < 1. ✔ **Summary of PED and TR** **PED > 1:** P and TR change in opposite directions; as P⇓, TR⇑ **PED < 1:** P and TR change in the same direction; as P⇓, TR⇓ **PED = 1:** changes in P leave TR unchanged	**PED in relation to TR** 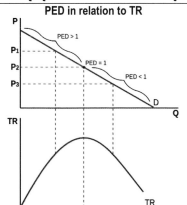

Applications of PED 2: PED for primary commodities and manufactured products

primary commodities (or products) = goods arising from the factor of production **land**, including all agricultural products as well as fishing, forestry and extractive products (ex oil and minerals from the earth)	Most primary commodities have a low PED (inelastic demand) because they do not have close **substitutes**, and they are **necessities**. Manufactured products usually are not as necessary as primary goods, and they generally do have substitutes, due to product differentiation; therefore they have a higher PED (more elastic demand).

Applications of PED 3: PED and indirect taxes

indirect taxes = taxes on spending to buy particular goods, paid indirectly to the government through the seller of the good

When an indirect tax is imposed on a good, the firm's supply curve shifts to the left (which is equivalent to an upward shift), with the vertical difference between the two supply curves = tax per unit. After the tax is imposed, **the equilibrium P and Q change to P_c = price paid by the consumer and Q_1 = new quantity produced**, while **P_p = price received by the producer**. The difference $P_c - P_p$ = tax per unit = government revenue per unit, and the yellow area ($P_c - P_p$) x Q_1 = total tax collected = total government revenue from the tax. As the diagrams show: **the lower the PED, i.e., the more inelastic the D (the steeper the D curve), the greater the government revenue**. Reason: as P paid by the consumer ⇑, the more inelastic the D, the smaller the responsiveness (drop) in Q demanded, and so the higher the tax revenue.

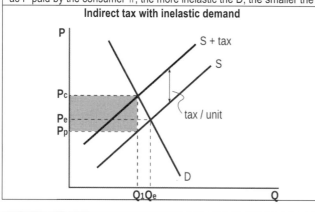
Indirect tax with inelastic demand

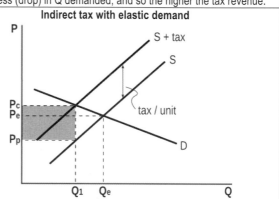
Indirect tax with elastic demand

HL topic Applications of PED 4: PED and tax incidence

In the case of an indirect tax on a good, if PED < PES the incidence of the tax (the tax burden) is greater on consumers than on producers; if PED > PES the incidence of the tax is greater on producers (to be explained more fully on p 15).

Cross price elasticity of demand (XED)

XED and how to interpret it

If there are two goods, X and Y, a change in the price of one may lead to a change in demand for the other. Given a change in the price of good Y (P_Y), how and how much will demand for good X (Q_X) change? The concept of XED addresses these questions.

XED = responsiveness of demand for good X to changes in price of good Y = % change in Q_X demanded divided by % change in P_Y	**The meaning of a positive XED**	**The meaning of a negative XED**
$$=\frac{\%\Delta Q_X}{\%\Delta P_Y}=\frac{\frac{\Delta Q_X}{Q_X}\times100}{\frac{\Delta P_Y}{P_Y}\times100}=\frac{\frac{\Delta Q_X}{Q_X}}{\frac{\Delta P_Y}{P_Y}},\text{ where}$$ $\Delta Q_X = Q_X$ final value $- Q_X$ initial value Q_X = initial Q_X value $\Delta P_Y = P_Y$ final value $- P_Y$ initial value P_Y = initial P_Y value ✔ XED involves **responsiveness of D** and hence **a shift of the D curve**.	If XED > 0 ⟹ X and Y are **substitutes** (p 3): Q_X and P_Y change in the same direction. Ex Desktops and laptops: if P of desktops ⇑, Q demanded of desktops ⇓ (due to the law of demand) and consumers switch to buying more laptops ⟹ D for laptops ⇑ (D curve shifts right). **Substitutes: D for laptops** 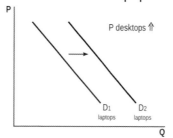	If XED < 0 ⟹ X and Y are **complements** (p 3): Q_X and P_Y change in opposite directions. Ex Coffee and sugar: if the P of coffee ⇑, Q demanded of coffee ⇓ (due to the law of demand) and consumers therefore also buy less sugar ⟹ D for sugar ⇓ (D curve shifts left). **Complements: D for sugar** 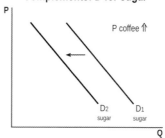
The meaning of a zero XED If XED = 0, there is no responsiveness of good X to the price of good Y: the goods are unrelated. Ex hotdogs and shoes.	✔ **The greater the value of the positive XED, the greater the substitutability of X and Y**: apples and pears are likely to have a higher XED than apples and ice cream.	✔ **The greater the absolute value of the negative XED, the greater the complementarity of X and Y**: tennis balls and rackets have a higher XED than milk and cereal.

Calculating XED

The P of pizzas ⇑ by 10% and the Q bought of cokes ⇓ by 5%. Calculate the XED and identify the relationship between pizzas and cokes. $$\text{XED}=\frac{\%\Delta Q_c}{\%\Delta P_p}=\frac{-5\%}{10\%}=-1/2;$$ **since XED < 0, pizzas and cokes are complements**.	The P of pizzas ⇓ by 15% and the Q bought of hotdogs ⇓ by 10%. Calculate the XED and identify the relationship between pizzas and hotdogs. $$\text{XED}=\frac{\%\Delta Q_h}{\%\Delta P_p}=\frac{-10\%}{-15\%}=2/3;$$ **since XED > 0, pizzas and hotdogs are substitutes**.

Applications of XED: implications for businesses

The case of substitutes	The case of complements
• **A single firm producing substitute products** PepsiCo produces both Pepsi and 7UP. If it lowers its price for Pepsi, what will happen to its sales of 7UP? **If XED is high**: a fall in $P_{Pepsi} \Rightarrow$ a large fall in sales of 7UP; an increase in $P_{Pepsi} \Rightarrow$ a large increase in sales of 7UP. **if XED is low**: a change in $P_{Pepsi} \Rightarrow$ a small impact on sales of 7UP. • **Rival firms producing substitute products** Adidas and Nike are two firms producing substitute products. Knowledge of XED for their products allows Adidas to predict changes in its sales due to changes in Nike prices, and vice versa. • **Mergers between firms producing substitute products** Two rival firms producing substitutes with a high XED may want to **merge** (= join together) to eliminate competition between them (though this may be illegal).	Knowledge by a firm of the XED of complementary products produced by other firms can be useful because if a complement's price rises, this may result in a drop in demand for the firm's product, while a decrease in the complement's price could result in greater demand for the product. Such information can lead to collaboration between firms, such as charter flights and hotels, where both may gain from a lower price. Information on XED can also be useful in predicting effects of indirect taxes on specific products. Ex gasoline taxes lower the demand for cars, especially large cars (gasoline and cars are complementary goods).

Income elasticity of demand (YED)

YED and how to interpret it

Changes in income lead to changes in demand. How, and how much does demand change? The concept of YED addresses these questions.

YED = responsiveness of demand for good X to changes in income (abbreviated as Y) = % change in Q demanded divided by % change in Y $= \dfrac{\%\Delta Q}{\%\Delta Y} = \dfrac{\frac{\Delta Q}{Q} \times 100}{\frac{\Delta Y}{Y} \times 100} = \dfrac{\frac{\Delta Q}{Q}}{\frac{\Delta Y}{Y}}$, where $\Delta Q = Q_{final\ value} - Q_{initial\ value}$ Q = initial Q value $\Delta Y = Y_{final\ value} - Y_{initial\ value}$ Y = initial Y value ✔ YED involves **responsiveness of D** and hence **a shift of the D curve**.	YED can be used to distinguish between two different sets of goods:
	(i) YED is positive or negative: • if YED > 0 (positive) $\Rightarrow$ **normal good** (p 3) $\Rightarrow$ as income ⇑, D for the good ⇑ (D shifts right); if income ⇓, D for the good ⇓ (D shifts left) • if YED < 0 (negative) $\Rightarrow$ **inferior good** (p 3) $\Rightarrow$ as income ⇑, D for the good ⇓ (D shifts left)); if income ⇓, D for the good ⇑ (D shifts right). ✔ Positive YED: the good is normal; negative YED: the good is inferior.
	(ii) YED is less than or greater than one: • if YED < 1 $\Rightarrow$ the good is a **necessity** (p 9) because % ΔQ < % ΔY. Ex medicines are a necessity, so if income ⇓, there will be a proportionately **smaller fall in medicines demanded** (relatively small leftward shift of D). • If YED > 1 $\Rightarrow$ the good is a **luxury** (p 9) because % ΔQ > % ΔY. Ex brand-name clothes are a luxury (for many consumers), so if income ⇓, there will be a proportionately **larger fall in brand-name clothes demanded** (relatively large leftward shift in D). ✔ YED < 1: the good is a necessity; YED > 1: the good is a luxury.

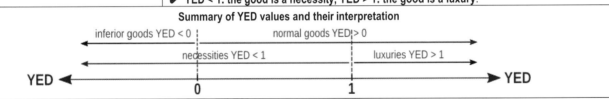

Summary of YED values and their interpretation

inferior goods YED < 0   normal goods YED > 0

necessities YED < 1   luxuries YED > 1

YED ◀ ————— 0 ————— 1 ————— ▶ YED

Calculating YED

Income increases from $1000 to $1200 per month, and the number of steaks bought per month increases from 5 to 7, the quantity of chicken increases from 8 to 9, while the number of hotdogs bought falls from 15 to 12. Calculate the YED for each of the three goods, and identify what type of good each one is.	income ⇑ by 20% steaks ⇑ by [(7-5) / 5] x 100 = 40% chicken ⇑ by [(9-8) / 8] x 100 = 12.5% hotdogs ⇓ by [(12-15) / 15] x 100 = -20%	YED for steaks = 40% / 20% = 2 $\Rightarrow$ normal, luxury YED for chicken = 12.5% / 20% = 0.62 $\Rightarrow$ normal, necessity YED for hotdogs = -20% / 20% = -1.00 $\Rightarrow$ inferior, necessity

Applications of YED: Implications for producers and the economy

Implications for producers	Implications for the economy
Producers may be interested in knowing the YED of their product as this affects how rapidly demand for it will grow as incomes change. In a growing economy with increasing incomes, the industries or goods and services with high YEDs will experience the most rapid increases in demand, and this information is useful for new firms making a decision on which line of production to go into, as well as for existing firms planning investments for the future. In an economy that is experiencing recession and falling incomes, goods and services with negative YEDs (inferior goods) may experience rapid growth. Ex in Greece, which has had a very deep, ongoing recession, there has been a major growth in inexpensive fast food restaurants (an inferior good) as consumers with falling incomes switch to these and away from ordinary restaurants (a normal good).	**Primary products** (= goods arising from the factor of production **land**), which include agriculture and food, usually have a low YED (food is a necessity), while **manufactured products** usually have higher YEDs, and **services** as a group have the highest of all (YED>1). These differing YED values have meant that in many countries around the world there is a change in the structure of economies over time: countries usually begin with very large primary sectors, but with economic growth and growth in incomes, manufacturing and services become increasingly important, as the primary sector shrinks in relative importance. This changing structure is the result of relatively more rapid growth in manufacturing and even faster growth of services, while the primary sector experiences slowest growth of all.

HL topic Implications for economically less developed countries
Low YEDs for primary products, sometimes forming the bulk of exports of poor countries, in combination with higher YEDs for manufactured products, forming the bulk of exports of more developed countries, have important implications for the value of exports and imports of less economically developed countries, in some cases forming a barrier to their development prospects due to deteriorating **terms of trade** (see p 76).

Price elasticity of supply (PES)

PES and how to calculate it

According to the law of supply, an increase in P gives rise to an increase in Q supplied, and vice versa. Now we ask, given a change in P, does Q supplied change a lot or a little? The concept of PES addresses this question.

PES = responsiveness of Q supplied to changes in P = % change in Q supplied divided by % change in P $$= \frac{\%\Delta Q}{\%\Delta P} = \frac{\frac{\Delta Q}{Q} \times 100}{\frac{\Delta P}{P} \times 100} = \frac{\frac{\Delta Q}{Q}}{\frac{\Delta P}{P}}, \text{ where}$$ $\Delta Q = Q_{\text{final value}} - Q_{\text{initial value}}$ Q = initial Q value $\Delta P = P_{\text{final value}} - P_{\text{initial value}}$ P = initial P value ✔ PES measures **responsiveness of Q along a given S curve**.	**Calculating PES** Suppose the price of pizzas increases from \$4 per pizza to \$6 per pizza and the quantity supplied increases from 2,000 pizzas to 2,400 pizzas. **Calculate the PES for pizzas**. $$\frac{\%\Delta Q}{\%\Delta P} = \frac{\frac{\Delta Q}{Q}}{\frac{\Delta P}{P}} = \frac{\frac{2400-2000}{2000}}{\frac{6-4}{4}} = \frac{\frac{400}{2000}}{\frac{2}{4}} = \frac{1600}{4000} = 0.4$$

Price elastic and price inelastic supply

Price elastic supply **PES > 1**: $\%\Delta Q > \%\Delta P$ = percentage change in Q supplied is greater than the percentage change in P (change in Q proportionately larger than the change in P). **Price inelastic supply** **0 < PES < 1**: $\%\Delta Q < \%\Delta P$ percentage change in Q supplied is smaller than the percentage change in P (change in Q proportionately smaller than the change in P) ✔ PES is measured between two points on the S curve. In a diagram with two intersecting S curves, the flatter curve has the more elastic S: S_1 is more elastic than S_2 since as P changes, $\Delta Q >$ for S_1 than for S_2. ✔ You can see if supply is elastic or inelastic by just looking at the S curve. If the S curve crosses the vertical axis (ex S_1), PES >1 (elastic supply). If the S curve crosses the horizontal axis (ex S_2), PES <1 (inelastic supply).	**Steepness of the S curve and PES** 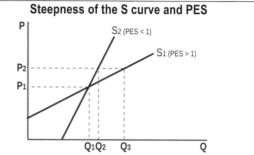 As P⇑, $\Delta Q = Q_3 - Q_1$ for S_1 and $\Delta Q = Q_2 - Q_1$ for S_2.

Special cases of constant (unchanging) PES

Perfectly elastic supply	Perfectly inelastic supply	Unit elastic supply
PES = ∞: the percentage change in Q supplied resulting from a change in P is infinitely large; this is a special case used in economic theory to illustrate world supply in international trade (see p 64). ✔ PES = ∞ ⇒ horizontal S curve. **Perfectly elastic supply : PES = ∞** 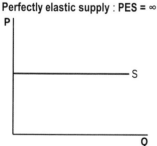	**PES = 0**: the percentage change in Q supplied is zero; no matter how high P rises, Q supplied does not respond; ex original antique furniture has such a zero responsiveness. ✔ PES = 0 ⇒ vertical S curve. **Perfectly inelastic supply: PES = 0** 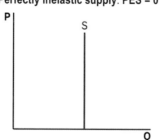	**PES = 1**: the percentage change in Q supplied is equal to the percentage change in P (change in Q is proportionately equal to change in P); this is a theoretical idea that is unlikely to be found often in the real world. ✔ PES = 1 ⇒ S curve cuts the origin. **Unit elastic supply: PES = 1** 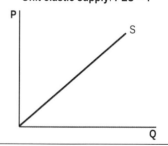

The determinants of PES

Time The longer the time period a producer has to respond to price changes, the more elastic the supply. In a short period of time the producer may be unable to obtain all necessary resources and technology in order to increase output in response to a price increase. As more time passes, it becomes easier to do so, therefore responsiveness (PES) increases.	**Unused capacity of firms** If firms have machines, equipment, or labor that are not being fully used, then it is easier to expand production in the event that price increases, simply by making use of the idle resources, and therefore the more elastic the supply.
Mobility of factors of production The more quickly and easily necessary resources can be moved from one type of production to another where they are needed, the more elastic the supply.	**Ability to store stocks** If a firm can store stocks easily and inexpensively, then in the event of a price increase it is more likely to have available stock that can be sold in the market, and the more elastic the supply.

Applications of PES 1: PES for primary commodities and manufactured products

primary commodities (or products) = goods arising from the factor of production **land**. Most primary commodities have a low PES (inelastic supply), and lower than the PES of manufactured products, mainly because they need more time than manufactured products to be produced or extracted (mined). Agricultural products need to go through their natural growing time. Forestry needs an especially long time for trees to grow, and other primary products, ex minerals, require a long time and high costs for exploration into the earth, drilling and mining.

HL topic Applications of PES 2: PES and tax incidence

In the case of an indirect tax on a good, if PES < PED the incidence of the tax (the tax burden) is greater on producers than on consumers; If PES > PED the incidence of the tax is greater on consumers (to be explained on p 15)

Summary of elasticities

Price elasticity of demand = PED

PED formula	Possible values	What this means	How to interpret it	Examples
$$\frac{\%\Delta Q}{\%\Delta P} = \frac{\dfrac{\Delta Q}{Q}}{\dfrac{\Delta P}{P}}$$ Though PED is negative, it is treated as if it were positive (absolute value)	Usual cases			
	PED < 1	change in Q is proportionately smaller than change in P	inelastic demand	gasoline, cigarettes, food
	PED > 1	change in Q is proportionately larger than change in P	elastic demand	expensive holidays, yachts,
	Special cases			
	PED = 1	change in Q is proportionately equal to change in P	unit elastic demand	concept used in economic theory
	PED = 0	Q does not change at all in response to change in P	perfectly inelastic demand	concept used in economic theory
	PED = ∞	Q has an infinitely large response to change in P	perfectly elastic demand	concept used in economic theory

Cross-price elasticity of demand = XED

XED formula for two goods X and Y	Possible values	What this means	How to interpret it	Examples
$$\frac{\%\Delta Q_x}{\%\Delta P_y} = \frac{\dfrac{\Delta Q_x}{Q_x}}{\dfrac{\Delta P_y}{P_y}}$$	XED > 0	positive XED ⟹ If P of good X ⇑ then D of good Y ⇑	goods X and Y are substitutes	oranges and pears, laptops and desktops
	XED < 0	negative XED ⟹ If P of good X ⇑ then D of good Y ⇓	goods X and Y are complements	sugar and coffee, tennis balls and tennis rackets
	XED = 0	zero XED ⟹ D of good Y is unchanged as P changes	goods X and Y are unrelated	computers and shoes, pizzas and pencils

Income elasticity of demand = YED

YED formula	Possible values	What this means	How to interpret it	Examples
$$\frac{\%\Delta Q}{\%\Delta Y} = \frac{\dfrac{\Delta Q}{Q}}{\dfrac{\Delta Y}{Y}}$$	YED < 0	negative YED ⟹ if income ⇑ then D for good ⇓	inferior good	used cars, used clothes
	YED > 0	positive YED ⟹ If income ⇑ then D for good ⇑	normal good	new cars, new clothes
	YED < 1	change in D is proportionately smaller than change in income	necessity	food, medicines
	YED > 1	change in D is proportionately larger than change in income	luxury	expensive cars and clothes, many services

Price elasticity of supply = PES

PES formula	Possible values	What this means	How to interpret it	Examples
$$\frac{\%\Delta Q}{\%\Delta P} = \frac{\dfrac{\Delta Q}{Q}}{\dfrac{\Delta P}{P}}$$	Usual cases			
	PES < 1	change in Q is proportionately smaller than change in P	inelastic supply	oil and gasoline, some agricultural products
	PES > 1	change in Q is proportionately larger than change in P	elastic supply	any good that can be produced quickly
	Special cases			
	PES = 1	change in Q is proportionately equal to change in P	unit elastic supply	concept used in economic theory
	PES = 0	Q does not change at all in response to change in P	perfectly inelastic supply	concept used in economic theory
	PES = ∞	Q has an infinitely large response to change in P	perfectly elastic supply	concept used in economic theory

Summary of determinants

✔ Remember the difference between the **non-price determinants of demand and supply**, and the **determinants of PED and PES**.

Non-price determinants of demand and supply

Determinants of demand shift the D curve (p 3)	Determinants of supply shift the S curve (p 4)	
changes in tastes and preferences	changes in costs of factors of production	changes in a subsidy
changes in income (normal and inferior goods)	changes in the number of firms in the market	changes in technology
changes in the number of buyers	changes in expectations	changes in prices of related goods (joint supply and competitive supply)
changes in prices of related goods (complements and substitutes)	changes in an indirect tax	

Determinants of PED and PES

Determinants of PED show if D is elastic or inelastic (p 9)	Determinants of PES show if S is elastic or inelastic (p 12)
number and closeness of substitutes	mobility of factors of production
degree of necessity and degree of addiction	unused capacity
proportion of income spent on the good	ability to store stocks
time	time

1.3 GOVERNMENT INTERVENTION

Indirect taxes

indirect taxes (= excise taxes) = taxes on spending to buy particular goods and services, paid indirectly to the government by the seller

Why governments impose indirect taxes

Indirect taxes provide governments with revenues needed to finance various government expenditures.	Indirect taxes can be used to improve the allocation of resources when there are negative externalities (see p 19).
Indirect taxes on goods that are harmful (ex cigarettes) can be used to decrease consumption of those goods.	Indirect taxes can be used to reduce the quantity of imports into a country (tariffs; see p 64)

The difference between specific and ad valorem taxes

specific tax = the tax is a specific amount imposed per unit of the good, and results in a parallel shift of the S curve to the left or upward; the vertical distance between the initial S curve, S, and the after-tax S curve, "S + tax" is equal to the amount of the tax per unit.	ad valorem tax = the tax is a percentage of the price of the good, and results in a new S curve "S + tax'' that is steeper than the original S curve, because the amount of tax increases as P increases.

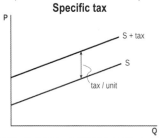
Specific tax

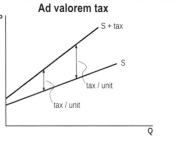
Ad valorem tax

Market outcomes and effects of an indirect tax on stakeholders

The initial equilibrium (before the tax) is at P_1 and Q_1. After the tax:

Market outcomes:
- new equilibrium Q is lower at Q_2
- new equilibrium P, **which is the P paid by the consumer**, is higher at P_c
- new P received by the producer is lower at P_p

Effects on stakeholders:
- consumers lose: they pay a higher P and buy a lower Q
- producers lose: they receive a lower P and sell a lower Q (their revenues fall from $P_1 \times Q_1$ to $P_p \times Q_2$)
- workers lose: less is produced, therefore some lose their jobs
- the government gains tax revenue = yellow shaded area = tax per unit x Q_2 (the new quantity produced and sold)
- society loses: there is resource misallocation (underallocation and underproduction since $Q_2 < Q_1$) and welfare loss = brown triangle

✔ An ad valorem tax has same market outcomes and effects on stakeholders.

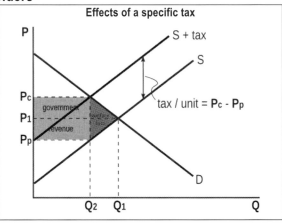
Effects of a specific tax

HL topics on indirect taxes
Effects of indirect taxes using linear demand and supply functions

In a free market with no government intervention, demand is given by **Qd = 16 – 2P**, and supply by **Qs = -8 + 4P**, where Qd and Qs are in units of good Z per day and P is in $. The government imposes an indirect tax on good Z of $3 per unit. Using this information, calculate the market outcomes and effects on stakeholders of this tax.

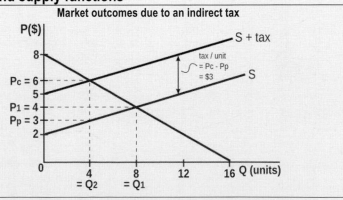
Market outcomes due to an indirect tax

Market outcomes

Find equilibrium P and Q before the tax:	Find after-tax equilibrium Q, P paid by consumers (Pc), and P received by producers (Pp)
(i) plot D and S curves and find their point of intersection;	(ii) plot new S curve by shifting S upward by $3 (= tax per unit); find the new point of intersection;
(ii) mathematically, using the D and S equations:	(ii) mathematically, using the rule: after-tax Qs = c + d (P – t), where t = tax per unit:
$16 – 2P = -8 + 4P \Rightarrow$ **P = $4, Q = 8 units**	after-tax Qs = -8 + 4 (P – 3) $\Rightarrow$ **after-tax Qs = -20 +4P**
	Using the D equation and the new S equation: $16 – 2P = -20 + 4P \Rightarrow$ **P = $6, Q = 4 units**
	New price paid by consumers, **Pc = $6** (= new equilibrium P)
	New price received by producers, **Pp = $3** (= Pc – t = $6 - $3)

14

Effects on stakeholders

Consumer expenditure: Before the tax: $4 x 8 units = $32; after the tax: $6 x 4 units = $24 Consumer expenditure **decreased by $8** (= $24 - $32 = - $8)	Producer revenue: Before the tax: $4 x 8 units = $32; after the tax: $3 x 4 units = $12 Producer revenue **decreased by $20** (= $12 - $32 = - $20)

Government tax revenue:
Government tax revenue = tax per unit x number of units sold = $3 x 4 = $12. The government **gained $12 of revenue (yellow rectangle)**

<table>
<tr>
<td>

Consumer surplus (= area under D curve above P paid by consumers):

Before the tax: $\dfrac{(\$8-\$4) \times 8 \text{ units}}{2} = \dfrac{4 \times 8}{2} = \dfrac{32}{2} = \$16$

After the tax:

$\dfrac{(\$8-\$6) \times 4 \text{ units}}{2} = \dfrac{2 \times 4}{2} = \dfrac{8}{2} = \$4$ **(blue triangle)**

Consumer surplus decreased by $12 (= $4 - $16 = - $12); **consumers are worse off**.

Producer surplus (= area above S curve under P received by producers):

Before the tax: $\dfrac{(\$4-\$2) \times 8 \text{ units}}{2} = \dfrac{2 \times 8}{2} = \dfrac{16}{2} = \$8$

After the tax: $\dfrac{(\$3-\$2) \times 4 \text{ units}}{2} = \dfrac{4}{2} = \$2$ **(orange triangle)**

Producer surplus decreased by $6 (= $2 - $8 = $6); **producers are worse off**.

</td>
<td>

Consumer surplus, producer surplus and welfare loss due to an indirect tax

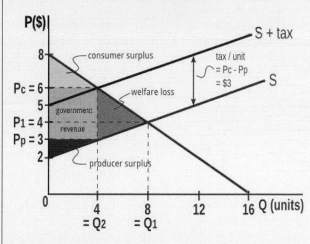

</td>
</tr>
</table>

Welfare loss = (deadweight loss) = benefits lost by society because of resource misallocation
Welfare loss can be calculated by $[(Pc – Pp) \times (Q_1 – Q_2)] / 2 = [(6 – 3) \times (8 – 4)] / 2 = (3 \times 4) / 2 =$ **$6 = brown triangle**.
Note that welfare loss = [pre-tax consumer surplus + producer surplus] minus [after tax consumer surplus (blue), producer surplus (orange) and government tax revenue (yellow)]:
Consumer and producer surplus before the tax: $24 (= $16 + $8); consumer and producer surplus after the tax: $6 (= $4 + $2); government tax revenue: $12.
Welfare loss = $24 - $6 - $12 = $6 shown by the **brown triangle; society is worse off.**

Tax incidence

tax incidence = the particular group bearing the burden of a tax, i.e. the group paying all or a portion of a tax.

The incidence of indirect taxes is usually shared between consumers and producers; both pay a portion of the tax. However, the share paid by each group is determined by the **relative sizes of PED and PES**.	**If PED = PES, tax incidence is the same on consumers and producers**. **If PED > PES, tax incidence is greater on producers.** **If PED < PES, tax incidence is greater on consumers**.

PED = PES: same tax incidence D is equally elastic as S: consumers' incidence = producers' incidence: $(Pc – P_1) \times Q_2$ (green) $= (P_1 – Pp) \times Q_2$ (red)	**PED > PES: producers pay more** D is more elastic than S: consumers' incidence < producers' incidence: $(Pc – P_1) \times Q_2$ (green) $< (P_1 – Pp) \times Q_2$ (red)	**If PED < PES: consumers pay more** D is less elastic than S: consumers' incidence > producers' incidence: $(Pc – P_1) \times Q_2$ (green) $> (P_1 – Pp) \times Q_2$ (red)
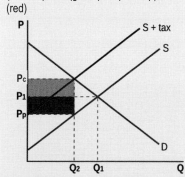		

✔ The group with the lower responsiveness to price (lower price elasticity) pays the larger share of the tax (= has a higher tax incidence).

Subsidies

subsidy = payment by the government to firms in order to lower costs and price, and increase supply

Why governments grant subsidies

Subsidies can be used to increase firms' revenues (ex subsidies on agricultural products to support farmers).	Subsidies can be used to encourage consumption of goods and services that are considered to be desirable for society (ex education).
Subsidies can be used to support particular firms or industries (ex firms using or producing clean (or green) technologies).	Subsidies can be used to lower the price of particular goods in order that they sell more in export markets (see p 64).
Subsidies can be used to lower the prices of particular goods or services for consumers (ex food prices to help low-income people).	Subsidies can be used to improve the allocation of resources when there are positive externalities (see p 21-22).

Market outcomes and effects of a subsidy on stakeholders

A subsidy results in a parallel shift of the S curve to the right or downward; the vertical distance between the initial S curve, S, and the after-subsidy S curve, "S with subsidy" = subsidy per unit.
The initial equilibrium (before the subsidy) is at P_1 and Q_1. After the subsidy:

Market outcomes:
- new equilibrium Q is higher at Q_2
- new equilibrium P, **which is P paid by the consumer**, is lower at P_c
- new P received by the producer is higher at P_p

Effects on stakeholders:
- consumers gain: they pay a lower P and buy a higher Q
- producers gain: receive a higher P and sell a higher Q (revenues ⇑)
- workers gain: more is produced therefore some unemployed find jobs
- the government loses: it must pay the subsidy = bold red rectangle = subsidy per unit x Q_2, with negative effects on the government budget
- society loses: (i) high-cost producers are protected by the higher price, leading to inefficiency; (ii) government spending on the subsidy has opportunity costs; (iii) there is resource misallocation (overallocation and overproduction since $Q_2 > Q_1$) and welfare loss = brown triangle

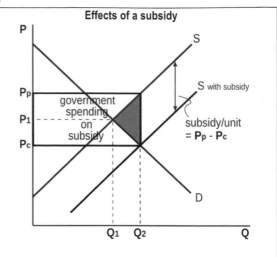

Effects of a subsidy

HL topics on subsidies
Effects of subsidies using linear demand and supply functions

In a free market with no government intervention, demand is given by **Qd =16 – 2P**, and supply by **Qs = -20 + 4P**, where Qd and Qs are in units of good Y per day and P is in €. The government imposes a subsidy on good Y of €3 per unit. Using this information, calculate the market outcomes and effects on stakeholders of this subsidy.

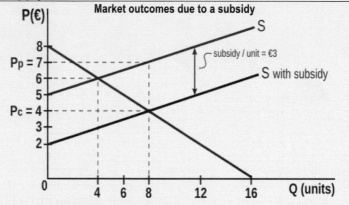

Market outcomes due to a subsidy

Market outcomes:
Find equilibrium P and Q before the subsidy:
(i) plot D and S curves and find their point of intersection;
OR
(ii) mathematically, using the D and S equations:
$16 - 2P = -20 + 4P \Rightarrow$ **P = €6, Q = 4 units**

Find the after-subsidy equilibrium Q, P paid by consumers (Pc), and P received by producers (Pp)
(ii) plot new S curve by shifting S downward by €3 (= subsidy per unit); find the new point of intersection; OR
(ii) mathematically, using the rule: after-subsidy Qs = c + d (P + s), where s = subsidy per unit:
after-subsidy Qs = -20 + 4 (P + 3) $\Rightarrow$ **after-subsidy Qs = -8 +4P**
Using the D equation and the new S equation: $16 - 2P = -8 + 4P \Rightarrow$ **P = €4, Q = 8 units**
New price paid by consumers, **Pc = €4** (= new equilibrium P). New price received by producers, **Pp = $7** (= Pc + s) = €4 + €3

Effects on stakeholders:

Consumer expenditure:	Producer revenue:
Before subsidy: €6 x 4 units = €24; after subsidy: €4 x 8 units = €32 Consumer expenditure ⇑ by €8 (= €32 - €24)	Before the subsidy: €6 x 4 units = €24; after the subsidy: €7 x 8 units = €56. Producer revenue ⇑ by €32 (= €56 - €24)

Government spending on the subsidy:
Government spending = subsidy per unit x number of units sold = €3 x 8 = €24 (**bold red rectangle below**)

Consumer surplus (= area under D curve and above P paid by consumers):

Before the subsidy: $\dfrac{(€8-€6) \times 4 \text{ units}}{2} = \dfrac{2 \times 4}{2} = \dfrac{8}{2} = €4$

After the subsidy: $\dfrac{(€8-€4) \times 8 \text{ units}}{2} = \dfrac{4 \times 8}{2} = \dfrac{32}{2} = €16$

Consumer surplus increased by €12 (= €16 - €4); **consumers are better off**. The **gain** in consumer surplus is shaded **blue**.

Producer surplus (= area above S curve under P received by producers):
Before the subsidy: [(€6 - €5) x 4] / 2 = 4 / 2 = €2.

After the subsidy: $\dfrac{(€7-€5) \times 8 \text{ units}}{2} = \dfrac{2 \times 8}{2} = \dfrac{16}{2} = €8$

Producer surplus increased by €6 (= €8 - €2); **producers are better off**. The **gain** in producer surplus is shaded **orange**.

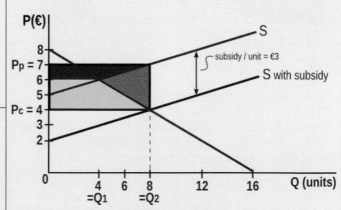

Consumer surplus, producer surplus and welfare loss due to subsidy

Welfare loss can be calculated by [(Pp – Pc) x (Q_2 – Q_1)] / 2 = [(7 – 4) x (8 – 4)] / 2 = (3 x 4) / 2 = **€6 = brown triangle**.
Note that welfare loss arises because the gain in consumer and producer surplus of €18 (= €12 + €6) is smaller than the loss to society of government spending on the subsidy (= €24). Therefore €24 - €18 = €6 = welfare loss, shown by the **brown triangle; society is worse off.**

Price controls

price controls = government intervention in the market involving the setting of **price ceilings (maximum prices)** or **price floors (minimum prices)**, thus preventing the market from reaching a market-clearing equilibrium price.

Price ceilings (maximum prices)

Price ceiling = a maximum price on a good set by the government that is below the equilibrium price of the market, resulting in a **shortage**

Why governments impose price ceilings	Price ceiling and welfare effects
The maximum P that can be legally charged, Pcl, is below equilibrium P (Pe); it is set by governments to make some necessities affordable to poor people: • **food price controls** (ceilings) for particular food products (bread, milk, wheat, rice and other staples) • **rent controls** (ceilings), which specify a maximum rent that can be charged for specific housing. Consequences of price ceilings for the market and the economy: • **Shortages (excess demand)** The price ceiling does not let P adjust to its equilibrium value, Pe, and results in a shortage (= excess demand), since at Pcl, Q demanded > Q supplied (Qd > Qs). • **Non-price rationing mechanisms** Since price no longer fulfills its signaling and incentive functions, methods other than price are needed to ration (= distribute) the good to buyers, such as waiting lines, first-come first-served, favoritism (ex selling the good to friends) • **Underground/parallel markets** Since there are unsatisfied buyers at Pcl, some people buy the good at Pcl and illegally re-sell it at a higher price	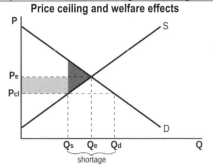 • **Inefficient resource allocation** Underallocation of resources since less is produced than Qe • **Welfare losses for society** Welfare loss = brown shaded triangle, since only Qs of the good is produced and consumed, rather than Qe. Also, the blue shaded area is a gain in consumer surplus (due to the fall in price from Pe to Pcl) at the expense of producer surplus

Consequences of price ceilings for stakeholders

• **Consumers** Consumers who buy the good at the lower P **gain**: those who want to buy it but cannot due to the shortage **lose**. This can be seen from the welfare analysis, which shows the gain by consumers of a portion of producer surplus due to the lower P paid (the blue area), and the loss of a portion of consumer surplus due to welfare loss (the consumer surplus part of the brown shaded area). • **Workers** Some workers lose their jobs due to lower output produced.	• **Producers** Producers lose because they sell a lower Q (Qs) rather than Qe, and because they receive a lower P (Pcl) rather than Pe. This can be seen from the welfare analysis, showing the loss of the blue area of producer surplus to consumers, and the loss of a portion of producer surplus due to welfare loss. • **Government** There are no economic gains nor losses, but the government may gain politically from increased popularity.

Price floors (minimum prices)

Price floor = a minimum price on a good set by the government that is above the equilibrium price of the market, resulting in a **surplus**

Why governments impose price floors	Price floor	Welfare effects of a price floor
The minimum P that can be legally charged, Pfl, is above the equilibrium P (Pe). This is done by governments to: • support farmers' incomes by increasing the price they receive for their products • support the wages of low-skilled workers by increasing them above their market-equilibrium level.	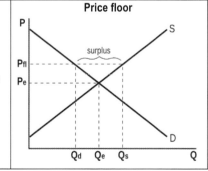	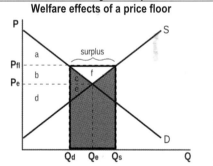

Agricultural price floors: consequences for the economy

• **surpluses (excess supply)** The price floor does not let P adjust to its equilibrium value, Pe, and results in a surplus (= excess supply), since at Pfl, Q demanded < Q supplied (Qd < Qs). • **Inefficient firms** The higher price provided by the floor allows firms with high costs of production (inefficient firms) to survive and not try to cut costs. • **Government measures to dispose the surplus** Governments buy the surplus, as this is the only way the price floor can be maintained at the higher than equilibrium price; this involves budget expenditures with opportunity costs. Governments must then decide what to do with it: store it (involving storage costs); export it (requiring subsidies to cover the higher price); destroy it (which involves waste of the resources used to produce it).	• **Inefficient resource allocation** More is produced than consumers want, so there is resource overallocation. • **Welfare losses for society** Welfare loss is shown by the brown shaded area. After the price floor is imposed, consumer surplus is reduced to area a (under the D curve up to Pfl), and producer surplus increases to include b+c+d+e+f (above the S curve up to Pfl). Social surplus appears to have increased, however from this total it is necessary to subtract government spending to buy the excess supply, equal to the red bold rectangle. The net welfare loss is the brown shaded area.

Agricultural price floors: consequences for stakeholders

• **Consumers** lose as they pay a higher price for a lower quantity purchased; this can also be seen in the welfare analysis above. • **Producers** gain because they receive a higher price and sell a larger quantity; this can also be seen in the welfare analysis above. • **Workers** gain because more output is produced therefore there will be an increase in employment.	• **The government** loses as it must pay for the purchase of the surplus out of its budget, and may additionally have to pay storage costs or subsidies on exports of the surplus quantity; this can also be seen in the welfare analysis above. • **Stakeholders in other countries** lose if the excess supply is exported, leading to increased global supply and hence lower global prices, hurting farmers in countries where there are no price floors.

Minimum wages

minimum wage = a minimum price of labor usually set by the government to protect **low-skilled workers** and ensure they can achieve a minimum standard of consumption; it is an application of a minimum price in the labor market The wage is the price of labor. The D curve shows the demand for labor by firms, and the S curve shows the supply of labor by workers. The minimum wage, Wm, does not allow the price of labor to adjust to its equilibrium value, We, and results in a surplus of labor (excess supply), since at Wm, Q of labor demanded < Q of labor supplied (Qd < Qs). This excess supply of labor is **unemployed labor**.	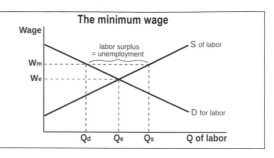

Consequences of minimum wages for the economy	Consequences of minimum wages for stakeholders
• **Illegal workers** Some workers may accept to work for wages below the legal minimum. • **Misallocation of resources in the labor market** The price of labor works as a signal and incentive in the labor market; the minimum wage may prevent the efficient allocation of labor resources. • **Misallocation of resources in product markets** Firms using unskilled labor have higher production costs due to the minimum wage; this may affect resource allocation in the product market.	• **Workers** Those who receive the minimum wage benefit, however those who become unemployed due to the minimum wage lose. • **Firms** Firms hiring unskilled labor and paying the minimum wage may be worse off due to higher costs of production. • **Consumers** Higher costs of production of firms that pay the minimum wage mean a leftward shift of the S curves of their products, resulting in a higher P and lower Q produced, therefore consumers are worse off.

HL Topics on price controls

Price ceilings

Given the demand function Qd = 10 – 2P and supply function Qs = -2 + 2P, where P is in $ and Q is in 1000 kg (a) calculate the excess demand (shortage) resulting from a price ceiling of $2; (b) calculate the change in consumer expenditure and firm revenue. (a) To find the shortage, substitute the ceiling price in the demand and supply equations: Qd = 10 – 2(2) = 6; Qs = -2 + 2(2) = 2. Shortage = Qd – Qs = 6000 kg – 2000 kg = **4000 kg** (b) To calculate the change in consumer expenditure and firm revenue, find equilibrium P and Q before the price ceiling: Setting Qd = Qs ⇒ 10 – 2P = -2 + 2P ⇒ 12 = 4P ⇒ P = 3; Q = 10 – 2P = 10 – 2(3) = 4; **equilibrium P = $3 and equilibrium Q = 4000 kg**. Consumer expenditure before the price ceiling = P paid x Q purchased = $3 x 4000 kg = **$12,000**. Consumer expenditure after price ceiling = P paid x Q purchased = $2 x 2000 kg = **$4000**. Consumer expenditure **fell by $8000** (= $4000 - $12,000 = - $8000)	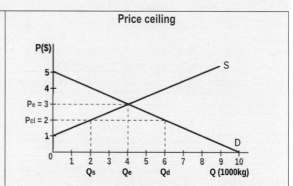 ✔Note that Q purchased is the **Q that is produced** at the ceiling price, not Q demanded. ✔Firm revenue fell by **the same amount as consumer expenditure**, because P and Q are the same for firms and consumers both before and after the price ceiling is imposed.

Price floors

Given the demand function Qd = 10 – 2P and supply function Qs = -2 + 2P, where P is in $ and Q is in 1000 kg, calculate (a) the excess supply (surplus) resulting from a price floor of $4 (b) the change in consumer expenditure (c) the change in firm revenue (d) government expenditure needed to purchase the surplus	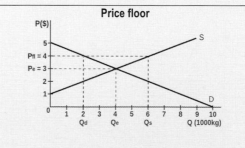
(a) To find the surplus, substitute the floor price in the demand and supply equations: Qd = 10 – 2(4) =2; Qs = -2 + 2(4) = 6. Surplus = Qs – Qd = 6000 kg –2000 kg = **4000 kg**	

| (b) To calculate the change in consumer expenditure, find equilibrium P and Q before the price floor is imposed:
setting Qd = Qs ⇒ 10 – 2P = -2 + 2P ⇒ 12 = 4P ⇒ P = 3; Q = 10 – 2P = 10 – 2(3) = 4; therefore **at equilibrium P = $3 and Q = 4000 kg**.

Consumer expenditure before the price floor = price paid x quantity purchased = $3 x 4000 kg = **$12,000**.

Consumer expenditure after the price floor = price paid x quantity purchased = $4 x 2000 kg = **$8000**.

Consumer expenditure **fell by $4000** (= $8000 - $12,000 = - $4000). | (c) To calculate the change in firm revenue, compare firm revenue before and after the price floor. Revenue before the price floor is found using the equilibrium P and Q you found above (it is the same as consumer expenditure) = **$12,000**.
Firm revenue after the price floor = price received x quantity sold = $4 x 6000 kg = **$24,000**.
Therefore firm revenue **increased by $12,000** (= $24,000 - $12,000).

(d) Government expenditure to purchase the surplus = price floor x amount of the surplus = $4 x 4000 kg = **$16,000**. |

1.4 MARKET FAILURE

market failure = the failure of the market to allocate resources efficiently, resulting in overallocation, underallocation or no allocation of resources to the production of a good or service relative to what is socially most desirable

Externalities

externality = positive effect (benefit) or negative effect (cost) for third parties who are not part of a transaction and whose interests are not taken into account; the market fails to achieve allocative efficiency, because **marginal social benefits (MSB) ≠ marginal social costs (MSC)**

marginal private benefits (MPB) = additional benefits for **consumers** arising from consumption of an additional unit of a good **marginal social benefits (MSB)** = additional benefits for **society** arising from consumption of an additional unit of a good **marginal private costs (MPC)** = additional costs to **producers** arising from production of an additional unit of a good **marginal social costs (MSC)** = additional costs to **society** arising from production of an additional unit of a good	**When there is no externality** • With no externality, D = MPB = MSB and S = MPC = MSC • At market equilibrium, where D = S, **MSB = MSC, indicating there is allocative efficiency** • Qopt represents the socially optimum quantity and Popt the socially optimum price (the "best" quantity and "best" price from the point of view of what is most desirable from society's point of view)	**Allocative efficiency with no externality** 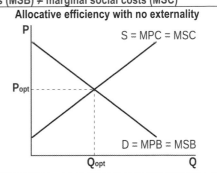

Externality diagrams: points to note

✔ Qm and Pm show the **market outcome**, found by the **intersection of MPC with MPB**	✔ **Negative externalities**: the market always **overallocates** resources: too much is produced relative to the social optimum, therefore **Qm > Qopt**
✔ Qopt and Popt show the **socially optimum** (or "best") outcome, found by the **intersection of MSC with MSB**	✔ **Positive externalities**: the market always **underallocates** resources: too little is produced relative to the social optimum, therefore **Qm < Qopt**
✔ Resource misallocation (overallocation or underallocation) leads to **welfare loss** (deadweight loss) for society = brown shaded triangle	

Negative externalities: imposition of external costs on society

Negative externality of production 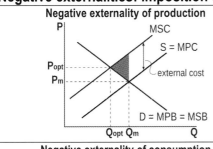	**Producers impose external costs on society**: social costs of production are greater than private costs, therefore **MSC > MPC**: MSC curve lies above MPC curve. • Vertical difference between MSC and MPC curves = value of external costs. • Demand is not affected therefore D = MPB = MSB. • Qm > Qopt: the market overallocates resources: too much is produced. • Welfare loss (deadweight loss) is the brown shaded triangle. • Example: production of goods by use of fossil fuels leading to carbon emissions, hence there are external costs including pollution of clean air, rivers, lakes, etc, and negative effects on human health.
Negative externality of consumption 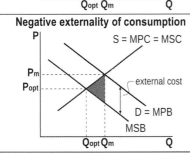	**Consumers impose external costs on society**: private consumption creates negative effects on others, therefore **MSB < MPB**: MSB curve lies below MPB curve. • Vertical difference between MPB and MSB curves = value of external costs. • Supply is not affected therefore S = MPC = MSC. • Qm > Qopt: the market overallocates resources: too much is produced. • Welfare loss (deadweight loss) is the brown shaded triangle. • Examples: smoking (cigarette consumption), where external costs include negative health effects on non-smokers and increased health care costs; use of cars using gasoline (a fossil fuel), where external costs include pollution of clean air.

Positive externalities: creation of external benefits for society

Positive externality of production 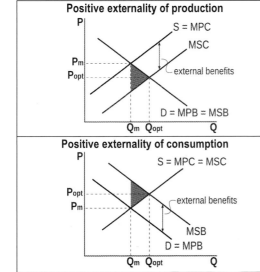	**Producers create external benefits for society**: their production activities are beneficial for third parties, therefore **MSC < MPC**; MSC curve lies below MPC curve. • Vertical difference between MPC and MSC curves = value of external benefits. • Demand is not affected therefore D = MPB = MSB. • Qm < Qopt: the market underallocates resources: too little is produced. • Welfare loss (deadweight loss) is the brown shaded triangle. • Examples: research by private firms leads to development of new technologies that benefit the whole of society (termed "technology spillovers"); training for workers provided by a firm which benefit other firms once the worker changes job.
Positive externality of consumption	**Consumers create external benefits for society**: private consumption is beneficial for third parties, therefore **MSB > MPB**; MSB curve lies above MPB curve. • Vertical difference between MSB and MSC curves = value of external benefits. • Supply is not affected therefore S = MPC = MSC. • Qm < Qopt: the market underallocates resources: too little is produced. • Welfare loss (deadweight loss) is the brown shaded triangle. • Examples: consumption of education leads to benefits for society including lower unemployment, increased productivity, lower crime rates, higher economic growth; similar external benefits arise from consumption of health care.

19

How to correctly draw any externality diagram without memorizing: four rules and how to use them

The rules	How to use the rules
✔ Production externality: the S curve splits into two; consumption externality: the D curve splits into two. ✔ Supply reflects **costs**; demand reflects **benefits**. ✔ Negative externality Qm > Qopt; positive externality Qm < Qopt. ✔ The point of the welfare loss triangle always looks toward Qopt.	1. Draw a demand and supply diagram and label the axes "P" and "Q". 2. For a production externality draw two S curves; for a consumption externality draw two D curves. In each case find the two corresponding equilibrium quantities on the Q axis. 3. In a negative externality, since Qm > Qopt, label the larger quantity Qm and the smaller quantity Qopt; in a positive externality the larger quantity is Qopt and the smaller quantity Qm. 4. Qm corresponds to **private** costs and benefits, therefore to **MPC** in a production externality and to **MPB** in a consumption externality, while Qopt corresponds to **social** costs and benefits and so to **MSC** or **MSB**; you can now label all the curves. 5. Find the triangle that points toward Qopt and shade it; this is welfare loss.

Merit and demerit goods

merit goods = goods whose consumption creates **positive consumption externalities**; are socially desirable but **underprovided by the market and underconsumed**; require government policies to increase their provision (production) and consumption. Ex education, health care, infrastructure (roads, sanitation, sewerage systems).	demerit goods = goods whose consumption creates **negative consumption externalities**; are socially undesirable but are **overprovided by the market and overconsumed**; require government policies to reduce their provision (production) and consumption. Ex cigarettes, gasoline (as fuel for cars).

Policy responses to externalities and their evaluation

Government command approaches (based on the use of government authority to make decisions; see p 2) include regulations, legislation, advertising, education, and direct government provision.	**Market-based policies** use methods that change relative prices (such as **indirect taxes** and **subsidies**) and therefore change the incentives facing decision-makers and hence their behavior.

✔ In the diagrams below, the blue lines represent the result of government policies to correct the externality.

Negative production externalities: policy responses	
Command approaches include legislation, regulations and advertizing that aim at directly reducing emissions and/or environmental damage: Ex: • Impose restrictions on emissions • Limit the amount of output produced • Force firms to install non-polluting technologies • Ban dangerous substances (ex asbestos) • Create protected areas forbidding industrial or agricultural activities • Restrictions on logging, fishing and hunting • Negative advertising to influence consumers to avoid purchasing products of highly polluting firms	**Evaluation of legislation, regulations and advertizing** ☑ Simpler to implement compared to market-based policies. ☑ Effective in at least partially achieving their objectives. ☑ In some cases are more appropriate than market solutions. ☒ Involve costs of monitoring and enforcement. ☒ Are inefficient, as they do not differentiate between firms with higher or lower costs of reducing pollution/environmental harm. ☒ Do not provide incentives for switching to cleaner technologies ☒ Face incomplete knowledge on extent of damage done by various pollutants and therefore on how much to restrict activities.
Market-based policies change the price incentives faced by firms: • **An indirect tax on output** causes the supply curve to shift **from MPC toward MSC** causing P to increase and Q to fall; if the tax is exactly equal to the value of the external cost, MPC will reach MSC and the externality is eliminated: the new equilibrium is given by MSC = MSB resulting in Qopt and Popt, and welfare loss is eliminated. • **An indirect tax on emissions** (pollutants) also causes the supply curve to shift **from MPC toward MSC**, leading to Qopt and Popt; this works by creating incentives for firms to reduce emissions and shift to **clean technologies** (= technologies that reduce negative environmental effects) in order to avoid paying the tax. The more the pollutants emitted, the greater the tax, therefore the greater the incentives to switch to clean technologies. Ex the **carbon tax** = tax on carbon emissions of fossil fuels. **Negative production externality:** **indirect tax on output or emissions** 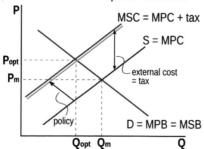 • **Tradable permits** (= cap and trade schemes) = a maximum permissible amount of a particular pollutant is determined, and permits to emit this pollutant are distributed to firms by the government (or international body), which can be bought and sold in a market. These offer the incentive to switch to **clean technologies**. Ex European Union Emissions Trading System covering power and heat generation, oil refineries, metals, pulp and paper, and energy intensive industries.	**Evaluation of market-based policies** ☑ Can internalize the externality = make producers pay for the external cost. ☑ Greater efficiency (lower cost) in reducing pollution than government regulations. ☑ The most efficient policies are (a) taxes on emissions and (b) tradable permits. Firms that can reduce emissions at a lower cost face the incentive to lower emissions and (a) pay a lower tax or (b) sell permits for a profit; firms facing high costs of reducing emissions can (a) pay the tax or (b) buy permits. The result is a reduction of emissions at a lower overall cost to society. ☑ Taxes on emissions and tradable permits create incentives to switch to clean technologies. ☑ A switch to cleaner technologies causes MSC to shift to the right, reducing the size of the externality and welfare loss. ☒ For both taxes and tradable permits, difficulties in identifying the most harmful pollutants and the value of external costs. ☒ In the case of taxes, difficulties in identifying the value of tax that will equal the value of the harm (the external cost). ☒ For tradable permits, there are difficulties in determining the correct amount of overall permissible pollution (the "cap" of cap and trade schemes). ☒ For tradable permits, there are difficulties in determining how to distribute the permits among firms. ☒ For both indirect taxes and tradable permits, there are difficulties in ensuring compliance and enforcement. ✔ Carbon taxes are often preferred to tradable permits because • they make energy prices more predictable • they can be used for all fossil fuel emissions • they are easier to design, implement and enforce ✔ Tradable permits may be preferred because carbon taxes • cannot set a limit to the permissible level of carbon • are **regressive** (since they are an indirect tax; see p 56)

Negative consumption externalities: policy responses

Command approaches include legislation, advertizing and educating the public in order to influence the behavior of consumers and reduce demand so that the **MPB curve shifts toward MSB**, leading to Qopt and Popt:
- Legislation, ex no smoking in public places; no drinking and driving;
- Negative advertising to change consumers' preferences, ex informing consumers about the dangers of smoking
- Education of consumers, ex encouraging the use of public transportation rather than cars (to reduce fossil fuel emissions)

Negative consumption externality: legislation, advertising, education

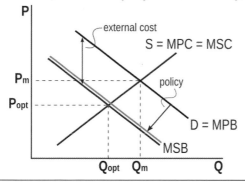

Evaluation of legislation, advertising and education
☑ Simple to implement compared market-based policies.
☑ Effective at least partially in reducing demand for the good causing the negative externality.
☑ In some cases are more appropriate than market solutions (ex banning smoking in public places).

☒ Are very unlikely to reduce demand to the required level (MPB unlikely to shift all the way to MSB); Q unlikely to reach Qopt and so can only partly eliminate the externality.
☒ Advertizing and education of consumers have opportunity costs as funds are diverted from other objectives.
☒ Difficulties of compliance and enforcement and costs of ensuring that the regulations are being followed.

Market-based policies change price incentives of firms and consumers:
- **An indirect tax on the good causing the negative externality** causes the supply curve to shift **from MPC to MPC+tax**, causing P to increase and Q to fall. If the tax is exactly equal to the value of the external cost, "MPC + tax" will intersect MPB at the level of Qopt; the externality and welfare loss are eliminated, and a higher price, Pc is charged.

Negative consumption externality: indirect tax

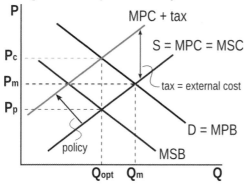

Evaluation of market-based policies
☑ Can internalize the externality = make consumers pay for the external cost.
☑ Can be more efficient than government regulations because they are based on the price mechanism, using price incentives for consumers to respond to.
☑ If the good being taxed has inelastic demand (PED < 1; see below) the tax will result in high tax revenues that can be used to finance government advertising and education programs.

☒ Difficulties in measuring the value of the external costs.
☒ Difficulties in determining the size of the tax that will be equal to the external costs.
☒ If demand for the good that is taxed is inelastic (PED < 1: percentage fall in Q demanded < percentage increase in P), the tax is unlikely to result in a significant fall in Q produced and consumed, and hence will not be very effective in eliminating the externality.
☒ Indirect taxes are regressive (see p 56) affecting poor people more strongly, sometimes causing them to switch to lower quality substitutes that may be more harmful.

Positive production externalities: policy responses

Command approaches aim at directly increasing provision:
- **Direct government provision**, such as in the case of research and development (R&D) for the development of new scientific knowledge, new technologies, new products; this has the effect of shifting the **MPC curve toward the MSC curve** (= "S with government provision or subsidy"), reaching the socially optimum quantity Qopt and price Popt.

Market-based policies change incentives faced by producers:
- **Provision of subsidies** by the government to private firms, universities and other organizations involved with research and development (R&D); this also has the effect of **shifting the MPC curve toward the MSC curve** (= "S with government provision or subsidy") and the socially optimum quantity Qopt.

Positive production externality: direct government provision or subsidy

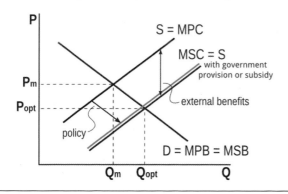

Evaluation of direct government provision and subsidies
☑ Are highly effective in increasing the amount of R&D carried out.

☒ Difficulties in estimating the value of the external benefits.
☒ Difficulties in determining the size of the subsidy or the funds that should be allocated toward direct provision, in order to match the value of the external benefits.
☒ Involve use of government funds that have opportunity costs
☒ Difficulties faced by the government in determining which particular activities (of the numerous activities that compete for public funding) should be supported, and by how much.
☒ The government's selection process on what activities to support is often subject to political pressures with choices made on political rather than economic grounds.

Positive consumption externalities: policy responses

Command approaches include legislation, advertising and education that aim at influencing the behavior of consumers to increase demand so that the **MPB curve shifts toward MSB**, reaching Qopt and Popt:
- Legislation forcing increased consumption, ex making primary school education compulsory for all children
- Advertizing and education encouraging consumption, ex encouraging parents to vaccinate their children; encouraging health check-ups

Positive consumption externality: legislation, advertizing, education

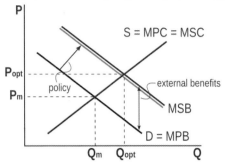

- Direct government provision, ex education, health care, infrastructure (clean water supplies, sewerage systems), which has the effect of **shifting the S curve to "S with government provision or subsidy"** and reaching the socially optimum quantity Qopt and the lower price, Pc for consumers (see diagram below).

Market-based policies change price incentives of firms and consumers:
- Provision of subsidies by the government, with the effect of shifting the **S curve to "S with government provision or subsidy"**, resulting in the socially optimum quantity Qopt and the lower price, Pc for consumers.

**Positive consumption externality:
direct government provision or subsidy**

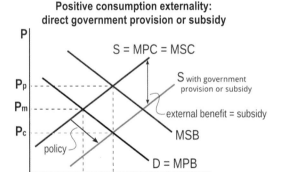

Evaluation of legislation, advertizing and education
- ☑ Simple to implement.
- ☑ Effective at least partially in increasing demand for the good causing the positive externality, especially in the cases of laws making education compulsory.

- ☒ Advertizing and education alone are unlikely to increase demand to the required level (MPB unlikely to shift all the way to MSB); Q unlikely to reach Qopt and so can only partly eliminate the externality.
- ☒ Advertizing and education have opportunity costs as funds are diverted from other objectives.
- ☒ Difficulties of compliance and enforcement of legislation (ex children in low-income countries may be sent out to work rather than to school).
- ☒ Increase in demand leads to a higher P, possibly making goods unaffordable to low-income groups; must therefore be used together with subsidies or free government provision (ex free education, health care services).

Evaluation of direct government provision and subsidies
- ☑ Are highly effective in increasing the Q supplied and consumed, and are therefore very common in correcting these externalities.
- ☑ Subsidies and/or free government provision are key factors in making these affordable to all (ex free education, free health care services).

- ☒ Difficulties in measuring the value of the external benefits.
- ☒ Difficulties in determining the amount of government provision and/or subsidy that will be equal to the external benefits.
- ☒ Opportunity costs of government spending on direct provision and/or subsidy.
- ☒ Difficulties faced by the government in making choices on what to support and by how much in view of the very many competing claims on the government budget.

Common access resources and the threat to sustainability

common access resources = natural resources without ownership, that are not traded in a market, have no price, and can therefore be used freely by anyone; they are **non-excludable** (people cannot be excluded from using them because it is not possible to charge a price for their use) yet **rivalrous** (their use by one person makes them less available for use by someone else). Ex forests, rivers, lakes, the oceans, soil quality, biodiversity and even the ozone layer	**sustainability** = the use of natural resources at a rate that allows them to reproduce themselves, thus resulting in environmental preservation over time, so that future generations will be able to use them to satisfy their needs and wants. Arises from the concept of **sustainable development** = "Development which meets the needs of the present without compromising the ability of future generations to meet their own needs." (Brundtland Commission)

The lack of a pricing mechanism for common access resources and the threat to sustainability

The unique nature of common access resources, namely their **non-excludability**, arising from being freely available for use by anyone without a price, together with their **rivalry** so that their use by one reduces availability for others, poses a serious threat to sustainability. The threat arises because since these resources can be freely used, they may be **overused**, **depleted** (= reduced in quantity) and **degraded** (= reduced in quality).

Example 1 A forest with no ownership can be used by anyone to chop down trees for use as timber and for clearing land for agriculture. This poses a **threat to sustainable use of forests**: if trees are chopped down more quickly than new trees can grow, forests become **depleted** (reduced in quantity), while the environment is **degraded** (reduced in quality) due to loss of natural habitat of forest animals, loss of biodiversity, and global warming.	**Example 2** Fish in oceans, rivers and lakes have no ownership and can be fished by anyone. This poses a **threat to sustainable use of fish resources**: if fish are fished faster than they can reproduce themselves, they become **depleted** (reduced in quantity), while the oceans, rivers and lakes are **degraded** (reduced in quality) as their ecosystem is disrupted.
✔ In both examples, resources are being used **unsustainably**, leaving behind fewer and lower-quality resources for use by future generations.	

Use of fossil fuels as a threat to sustainability	Poverty as a threat to sustainability
The use of fossil fuels in production (an energy input for industry and agriculture) and consumption (an energy input for the use of cars and heating systems) creates negative externalities of enormous proportions. These externalities can be seen as resulting from overuse, depletion and degradation of common access resources (clean air, oceans, rivers, sea life), giving rise to external costs that include climate change, depletion of the ozone layer, acid rain, and a vast amount of health problems and related health care costs. ✔ You can use a **negative production externality** diagram or a **negative consumption externality** diagram to illustrate and explain the threats to sustainability posed by use of fossil fuels.	In economically less developed countries, poverty often leads people to use open access resources unsustainably as they **make an effort to survive on extremely low incomes**. High population growth exerts additional pressures on unsustainable resource use. Examples include deforestation (cutting down forests) to clear land for agriculture or to obtain firewood; soil degradation (depletion of the soil's nutrients) as farmers cannot afford inputs to maintain soil fertility and as they move to new pasture lands for their animals; soil erosion as people move to fragile lands on mountains.

Evaluation of government responses to threats to sustainability

Legislation and regulations There are many kinds of legislation/regulations that can be used to deal with threats to sustainability posed by negative production and consumption externalities. See p 20 - 21 for a list of examples and evaluation.	**Funding for clean technologies**, or technologies that reduce negative environmental effects (due to negative externalities), ex wind and solar power, biofuels and geothermal energy. According to the World Bank, both private and public funding for clean technologies fall far short of what is needed.
Carbon taxes are taxes on emissions of carbon dioxide arising from the use of fossil fuels. The higher the emissions the greater the amount of tax paid, thus creating incentives for firms to switch to clean technologies. Ex Denmark, Finland, France, Ireland, Poland and Sweden have implemented carbon taxes. See p 20 for diagram and evaluation.	**Cap and trade schemes** (= **tradable permits**) involve setting a maximum amount of pollutant (usually carbon dioxide) that can be emitted, and distributing permits to firms to release the pollutant (by a government or international body); the permits can then be traded in a market. Ex European Union Emissions Trading System. See p 20 for discussion and evaluation.
Elimination of environmentally harmful subsidies Many countries subsidize fossil fuel production or consumption, resulting in lower costs of production of fossil fuels for firms and lower prices for consumers, thus encouraging their production and consumption. Such subsidies should be eliminated. The World Bank estimates that global subsidies for petroleum products are nearly ten times global funding for energy R&D.	**Government subsidies for the development of clean technologies** Governments may provide subsidies to government agencies or private firms that conduct R&D for the development of clean technologies. This has the effect of increasing the supply of clean technologies and lowering their price to buyers of these technologies (see p 16), while at the same time reducing the use of technologies based on fossil fuels and therefore reducing the size of negative production externalities.
Need for international collaboration Negative environmental externalities (both of production and consumption) extend far beyond national boundaries, and therefore require international collaboration for their solution. Ozone depletion and global climate change, for example, are global issues for which all countries, to a greater or lesser degree, are responsible. There cannot be a solution to such issues in the absence of effective international agreements. Ex the Kyoto Protocol.	

Lack of public goods

private good = a good that is **rivalrous** (its use by one makes it less available for use by others) and **excludable** (people can be excluded, i.e. prevented from using it by charging a price). Private goods include any good that can be sold in a market for a price; ex cars, computers, houses, education, health care services, i.e. goods that are produced by private firms or by the government for which **a price is charged**	**public good** = a good that is **non-rivalrous** (its use by one does not make it less available for use by others) and **non-excludable** (**It is not possible to charge a price** and therefore exclude people from using the good). Ex national defense, the police force, lighthouses, knowledge, street lights

Why public goods are a type of market failure: the free rider problem

free rider problem = occurs when people use a good without paying for it; it is closely related to non-excludability. When it is not possible to exclude people from using a good (ex a lighthouse) by charging a price for it, they take a "free ride", i.e. they use it without having to pay for its use.	**Public goods represent market failure** because of the free rider problem. Since it is not possible to charge a price for the good, private firms will not produce it, even though it may be socially desirable and consumers may have a demand for it. Firms will not produce it because without a price it will be impossible for them to cover their costs. Public goods are therefore a type of market failure because the market (i.e. private firms) fail to produce it at all.

quasi-public goods = goods that are non-rivalrous but are excludable; the free rider problem does not hold because it is possible to exclude users by charging a price. Ex toll roads (whoever is not willing or able to pay the toll will be excluded from its use)

Direct provision of public goods by the government

Since the market fails to allocate any resources to the production of public goods, and since public goods are socially desirable, they are directly provided by the government and financed (paid for) by government tax revenues. In view of the opportunity costs of government spending, and the many competing uses of government funds, governments face the difficulties of deciding what particular public goods to provide and in what quantities. Political pressures on the government may also come into play, resulting in choices made on political rather than (or in addition to) economic grounds.

Summary of different kinds of goods based on rivalry and excludability

	rivalrous	non-rivalrous
excludable	**private goods** = goods with or without positive and negative externalities (both production and consumption) sold for a price; merit goods (as long as they are produced by the market) and demerit goods Ex cars, bicycles, clothes, education, gasoline (petrol)	**quasi-public goods** = goods that do not fall neatly into the other three categories; often (but not always) have large positive externalities and so **may** be provided by the government Ex un-crowded toll roads, museums and public swimming pools that charge entrance fees, cable TV
non-excludable	**common access resources** = natural resources that are not owned by anyone, not sold in markets and not having a price; their lack of a price makes them subject to overuse (i.e. unsustainable use), depletion and degradation Ex forests, rivers, lakes, soil quality, fish in the oceans	**public goods** = socially desirable goods not produced by private firms because it is not possible to charge a price; subject to **the free rider problem**: people use them without having to pay; since they are socially desirable they are produced by the government and provided free of charge Ex national defense, roads, street lighting, lighthouses

HL topic Asymmetric information

asymmetric information = a type of market failure occurring when one party to a transaction (buyer or seller) has more information than the other party, leading to allocative inefficiency

When sellers have more information than buyers

Ex Sellers of used cars know more about the car's condition than the buyer; sellers of food and medicines (or in general, items important to human health) know more about the products they are selling than buyers; sellers of legal and medical services (lawyers and doctors) know more about the nature of the service they are providing than buyers.
In a free, unregulated market, these knowledge asymmetries usually result in an **underallocation of resources** to the production of the good or service, because buyers try to protect themselves against the risk of purchasing a good or service that is not in their best interests.
Possible government responses:
Legislation and regulations:
☑ Health and safety standard and quality controls protect consumers against the risks of purchasing inferior or dangerous products.
☒ Are time-consuming processes causing delays in economic activity.
☒ Large opportunity costs in terms of implementation and monitoring
Provision of information to consumers:
☑ Ex Information about the quality of medical services, nutrition information on food products, information on health hazards of products help consumers make informed purchasing decisions.
☒ Information collection is complicated and costly; may be inaccurate.
☒ Some information is impossible to provide to buyers (ex specialized legal or medical knowledge).
Licensure:
☑ Requirement that professionals have a license (doctors, lawyers).
☒ May be used to restrict the number of professional in a market and create monopoly power.

When buyers have more information than sellers

Arises most often in the case of **buyers of insurance**, leading to two kinds of problems:
1. The problem of adverse selection: the buyer of health insurance knows more about the condition of his/her health that the seller; this results in an underallocation of resources to health insurance, as sellers try to protect themselves against high-risk (i.e. unhealthy) insurance buyers, and also results in high prices for health insurance policies.
Government responses to adverse selection in insurance:
☑ Correction of underallocation of resources to health insurance by covering everyone in a population through social health insurance, or direct government provision of health care services at a zero/low price.
☒ Opportunity costs of spending from the government budget or social insurance budget
2. The problem of moral hazard: the buyer of insurance changes his/her behavior after the purchase of insurance, increasing the chances of risky behavior. Ex the purchase of car theft insurance may make the buyer less careful about locking his/her car.
Responses to moral hazard in insurance:
☑ The problem is usually dealt with by the seller of insurance, who may force the buyer to share in the payment of damages (ex if the car is stolen, the owner must pay a part of the cost of replacing the car); this decreases the car owner's risky behavior.
☒ Unequal effects on low-income versus high-income people

HL topic Abuse of monopoly power

monopoly power = the ability of a firm to influence the price of the good that it produces and sells; it is type of market failure because it results in an underallocation of resources to the production of the good in question, and hence in allocative inefficiency and welfare loss

Monopoly power is discussed at length on p 32 - 34. It is associated with all market structures except perfect competition, **but is mainly found in monopoly and oligopoly** and is undesirable from the point of view of society because it results in:

☒ higher prices and lower quantities than in a competitive market	☒ productive inefficiency (production at higher than minimum AC)
☒ allocative inefficiency (P > MC)	☒ welfare loss

Possible government responses to monopoly power (see p 34)

Legislation may include anti-monopoly laws intended to prevent the formation of monopolies or to break up monopolies, thus encouraging competitive behavior.	**Nationalization** = the transfer of ownership from the private to the public sector (the opposite of **privatization**, see p 61), as an alternative to **regulation of** natural monopolies (see p 34.
Government regulation often used in the case of natural monopolies (see p 33 - 34) to bring about an outcome that is more favorable to consumers, meaning lower prices and higher quantities than would result in a private unregulated monopoly.	**Trade liberalization** = removal of barriers to trade (see p 63), resulting in larger quantities of imports entering a country, which create competition for existing firms that must now compete with products from abroad.

1.5 HL TOPIC THEORY OF THE FIRM AND MARKET STRUCTURES

1.5.1 Production and costs

Distinction between the short run and the long run in microeconomics

short run = period of time when **at least one factor of production is fixed** (unchanging) and all other factors are variable (changing)	**long run** = period of time when **all factors of production are variable** (changing); there are no fixed factors
fixed factors of production (inputs) = factors of production (inputs) that are not easily changed in quantity over short periods of time, such as capital (machinery, factories, etc) or land	**variable factors of production (inputs)** = factors of production (inputs) that are changed in quantity easily over short periods of time, such as labor, office supplies, electricity use

Production in the short run: diminishing returns

total product (TP) = the total quantity of output produced	**average product (AP)** = total quantity of output produced on average by each unit of variable input, ex labor: $$AP = \frac{TP}{\text{units of labor input}}$$	**marginal product (MP)** = additional output produced by one additional unit of variable input, ex labor: $$MP = \frac{\Delta TP}{\Delta \text{ units of labor input}}$$

law of diminishing returns = as more and more units of a variable input (ex labor) are added to a fixed input (ex capital), the marginal product of the variable input (labor) at first increases, reaches a maximum, and then begins to fall; diminishing returns occur in **the short run** when at least one input is fixed. Ex a pizza restaurant has a kitchen with ovens and workspace that are fixed over the short run; as more cooks and pizza ingredients (flour, cheese, etc.) are used, the marginal product of each worker at first increases but at some point it will start to fall and will eventually become negative, due to overcrowding. This law forms **the basis of costs of production in the short run**.

Calculations and diagrams based on total, average and marginal product data

You are given data on "Total product (TP)" and "Units of variable input (labor)" in the table below. Using the formulas for AP and MP given above, calculate AP and MP. (The answers are shown in bold.)

Total product TP (units)	Units of variable input (labor)	Marginal product MP (units)	Average product AP (units)
0	0	-	-
2	1	**2**	**2**
5	2	**3**	**2.50**
9	3	**4**	**3**
12	4	**3**	**3**
14	5	**2**	**2.80**
15	6	**1**	**2.50**
15	7	**0**	**2.14**
14	8	**-1**	**1.75**

The total, marginal and average product curves have these general shapes and are related to each other as shown:

✔ The TP curve rises, reaches a maximum, and then begins to fall.

✔ The MP curve is the slope of the TP curve (slope = $\Delta TP/\Delta$labor units):
- MP increases as the TP curve becomes steeper,
- MP begins to fall when the TP curve begins to get flatter,
- MP is equal to zero when TP is maximum, and
- MP is negative when TP falls.

✔ **The MP curve intersects the AP curve at the maximum of AP.**

✔ **The MP curve illustrates the law of diminishing returns**.

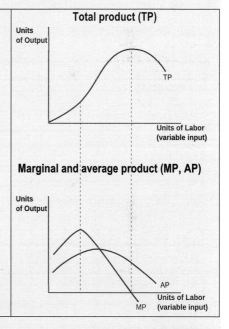

Total product (TP)

Marginal and average product (MP, AP)

Introducing costs of production

explicit cost = a cost involving payment of money made by a firm to obtain a factor of production (input) for use in production. Ex payment for labor services (wages paid to workers)	**implicit cost** = a cost involving sacrificed income for the use of a factor of production (input) that is owned by the firm for use in production. Ex the income sacrificed for work put into one's own business; rental income sacrificed for using a self-owned building; includes the value of entrepreneurship that is used by the firm
economic costs = the sum of explicit and implicit costs; in economics when we refer to "costs" we mean **economic costs**	✔ All costs of production are **opportunity costs** (see p 1). In the case of explicit costs, opportunity costs are the value of the best alternative that was not purchased; in the case of implicit costs, opportunity costs are the sacrificed income.

Costs of production in the short run

fixed costs = costs that do not vary with output: as output increases or decreases, fixed costs are constant; they must be paid even when output is zero. They appear as a horizontal line. Ex payment of rent, payment of insurance (abbreviated as **TFC** = total fixed costs)	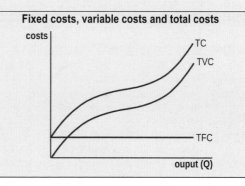 **Fixed costs, variable costs and total costs**
variable costs = costs that vary with output: as output increases, variable costs increase; variable costs are zero when output is zero. Ex payment of wages for labor services (abbreviated as **TVC** = total variable costs)	
total costs = the sum of fixed and variable costs (abbreviated as **TC** = total cost). The TC curve is the vertical sum of the TFC and TVC curves: **TC = TFC + TVC**	

average costs = costs per unit of output (Q)

average fixed costs (AFC) = total fixed costs per unit of output (Q):

$$AFC = \frac{TFC}{Q}$$

average variable costs (AVC) = total variable costs per unit of output (Q):

$$AVC = \frac{TVC}{Q}$$

average total costs (ATC) = total costs per unit of output (Q):

$$ATC = \frac{TC}{Q}$$

✔ Note that just as TC = TFC + TVC, so also **ATC = AFC + AVC.**

marginal costs (MC) = the extra costs of producing an additional unit of output (Q):

$$MC = \frac{\Delta TC}{\Delta Q}$$

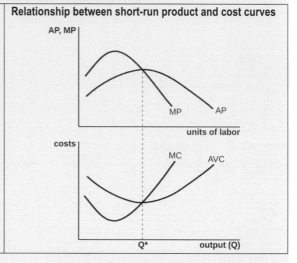

Average costs (AFC, AVC, ATC) and marginal costs (MC)

✔ The ATC curve is the vertical sum of the AFC and AVC curves. Therefore **the difference between ATC and AVC is equal to AFC.**
✔ Note that the **MC curve cuts the AVC and ATC curves at their minimum points**.

The relationship between the product curves and the cost curves in the short run

The short-run cost curves owe their shape to **the law of diminishing returns**, which explains why the product curves and the cost curves are mirror images of each other:

When the marginal product of labor increases, this means that the extra output produced by each additional unit of labor is increasing, and that therefore the extra cost of producing each additional unit of output (= MC) is falling.

When diminishing returns set in, and the marginal product of labor begins to fall, this means that the extra output produced by each additional unit of labor is decreasing, and that therefore the extra cost of producing each additional unit of output (= MC) is rising.

The same ideas account for the relationship between the AP and AVC curves.

✔ Therefore, when MP is maximum, MC is minimum, and when AP is maximum, AVC is minimum (AFC is ignored because fixed costs are constant).

✔ MP intersects AP at its maximum, and MC intersects AVC at its minimum.

Relationship between short-run product and cost curves

Calculating short-run costs

In the table below, you are given data on total product (TP or Q) and total cost (TC). Calculate (a) TFC, (b) TVC, (c) AFC, (d) AVC, (e) ATC, and (f) MC. (The answers are shown in bold.)

Total product (TP or Q)	Total fixed cost (TFC) £	Total variable cost (TVC) £	Total cost (TC) TC=TFC+TVC £	Average fixed cost (AFC) AFC=TFC/Q £	Average variable cost (AVC) AVC=TVC/Q £	Average total cost (ATC) ATC=AFC+AVC £	Marginal cost (MC) MC=ΔTC/ΔQ £
0	50	0	50	-	-	-	-
2	50	150	200	25	75	100	75
5	50	300	350	10	60	70	50
9	50	450	500	5.56	50	55.56	37.50
12	50	600	650	4.17	50	54.17	50
14	50	750	800	3.57	53.57	57.14	75
15	50	900	950	3.33	60	63.33	150

(a) TFC is found through the information in the TC column. Since TC = £ 50 when TP = 0 ⇒ £ 50 = fixed cost, and is constant for all levels of output	(c) Use the formula AFC = TFC/Q
	(d) Use the formula AVC = TVC/Q
	(e) Use the formula ATC = AFC + AVC (alternatively, ATC = TC/Q)
(b) Since TC = TFC + TVC ⇒ TVC = TC – TFC	(f) Use the formula MC = ΔTC/ΔQ

✔ You should be able to graph all of the above curves. The cost curves follow the same general shapes shown in the corresponding diagrams.

Production in the long run: returns to scale

In the long run, all factors of production (inputs) are **variable**. What happens to output (in the long run) given a change in all inputs? Ex:

There are two inputs: labor (workers) and capital (machines), which are doubled after a period of time:	Units of output produced with constant returns to scale	Units of output produced with increasing returns to scale	Units of output produced with decreasing returns to scale
number of workers number of machines			
Period 1 10 3	1000	1000	1000
Period 2 20 6	2000	2300	1700

constant returns to scale = as inputs increase, output increases in the same proportion: inputs doubled and output also doubled
increasing returns to scale = as inputs increase, output increases more than in proportion: inputs doubled and output more than doubled
decreasing returns to scale = as inputs increase, output increases less than in proportion: inputs doubled and output less than doubled

Costs of production in the long run: economies and diseconomies of scale

Explaining the long-run average total cost curve (LRATC)

In the short-run, a firm faces a short-run ATC curve, or SRATC (described above). When it increases its size by increasing all its inputs (in the long run), its SRATC shifts to the right. At first, this rightward shift is also downward; later it is rightward and horizontal, and even later it is rightward and upward. The pattern traced out by these rightward shifts of a series of SRATC curves provides the **long-run average total cost curve**, or **LRATC**. **long-run average total cost curve** = a cost curve showing the relationship between average cost of a firm and quantity of output it produces as it increases in size by varying all its inputs (in the long run); it is made up of a series of short-run average total cost curves.	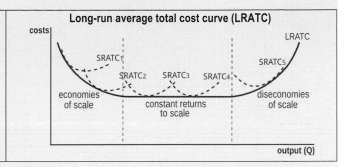 **Long-run average total cost curve (LRATC)**

Explaining the shape of the LRATC curve

economies of scale = increases in the size of a firm (in the long run) lead to **falling costs per unit of output = falling average costs**. Economics of scale arise because larger firms are better able to take advantage of: • Specialization of labor or management, leading to greater efficiency • Efficiency of larger machines that can be afforded by larger firm • Spreading of marketing, advertising and R&D (research and development) costs over larger quantities of output • Indivisibilities of machines or production processes; they cannot be "divided" into smaller sizes for use by small firms • Bulk buying of inputs, or buying large quantities of inputs by larger firms that need large supplies, offered at lower prices per unit • Lower-cost financing, or borrowing at lower interest rates and better terms, often available for larger firms	**diseconomies of scale** = increases in the size of a firm (in the long run) lead to **rising costs per unit of output = rising average costs**. If a firm becomes too large there may be • Management problems due to poor coordination and monitoring of firms activities • Communication difficulties resulting in inefficiencies • Low worker morale and motivation if they are an unimportant part of a very large firm Firms need not always experience economies or diseconomies of scale; in the event of **constant returns to scale** they will experience constant costs per unit of output = constant average costs.

The relationship between production and costs in the long run

Falling ATC due to **economies of scale** correspond to **increasing returns to scale in production**: as inputs double, output more than doubles ⇒ cost per unit of output (ATC) must be falling.	Increasing ATC due to **diseconomies of scale** correspond to **decreasing returns to scale in production**: as inputs double, output less than doubles ⇒ cost per unit output (ATC) must be rising.

1.5.2 Revenues

total revenue (TR): $TR = P \times Q$	average revenue (AR) = revenue per unit of output : $AR = TR / Q$ Since $TR / Q = P \Rightarrow AR = P$	marginal revenue (MR) = extra revenue arising from the sale of one more unit of output: $MR = \Delta TR / \Delta Q$

Revenues of firms with no influence over price	**Revenues of firms with influence over price**
✔ Such firms are found only in **perfect competition** (p 30). ✔ For these firms **P = AR = MR**.	✔ Such firms are found in **monopoly** (p 32), **monopolistic competition** (p 35) and **oligopoly** (p 35). ✔ MR = slope of TR curve ⇒ when TR is maximum, MR is zero.

Q	P = AR = TR / Q ($)	TR ($)	MR = ΔTR/ΔQ ($)
0	-	-	-
1	5	5	5
2	5	10	5
3	5	15	5
4	5	20	5

Q	P = AR = TR/Q ($)	TR ($)	MR = ΔTR/ΔQ ($)
0	-	-	-
1	8	8	8
2	7	14	6
3	6	18	4
4	5	20	2
5	4	20	0
6	3	18	-2
7	2	14	-4

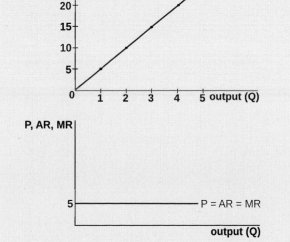

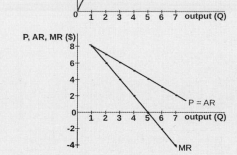

1.5.3 Profit and goals of firms

economic profit = total revenue (TR) minus economic costs (explicit + implicit costs); economic profit may be positive, zero or negative	**normal profit** = **zero economic profit**, arising when total revenue (TR) = economic costs
abnormal profit = **positive economic profit**, arising when total revenue (TR) > economic costs; it is profit over and above **normal profit**	**loss** = **negative economic profit**, arising when total revenue (TR) < economic costs

The importance of normal profit

Normal profit, arising when economic profit is zero, is the amount of revenue required by a firm to just keep it in business. The firm that earns zero economic profit will not shut down, because its revenue is sufficient to cover all of its costs, including its implicit costs, which cover payment for the entrepreneurship that is used in the firm, as well as the opportunity costs of all other self-owned factors of production (ex rental income sacrificed through the use in the firm of a self-owned building).

Profit maximization as a goal of firms

Standard economic theory assumes that firms are driven by their goal to maximize profit, where profit is interpreted to mean **economic profit**. There are two methods used to maximize profits: the **TR – TC method** and the **MR = MC method**:

✔ Using the **TR – TC method**, profit is maximum at **the level of output where TR – TC is greatest**.	✔ Using the **MR = MC method**, profit is maximum at **the level of output where MR = MC**.

Calculating profit-maximizing output and amount of profit: firms with no influence over price

You are given data on Q, TR and TC. Find profit-maximizing level of output, Q, and the amount of profit earned, (a) by using the TR – TC method and (b) by using the MR = MC method. In both cases verify your results graphically. (c) How can you tell that this firm has no influence over price?

(a) Calculate TR-TC for each level of output (shown in bold); identify the largest value, which is 7 (If TR-TC = the same value twice, choose the one corresponding to the larger Q). This gives an output level of Q* = **5 units**, and to **profit = $7**.

(b) Calculate MR and MC (shown in bold); find where they are equal: MR = MC = 7, corresponding to output of Q* = **5 units** (cannot find profit from MR = MC alone).

(c) The firm has no influence over price because MR is constant at P = $7.

✔ Note that both approaches give the identical results.

Q (units)	TR ($)	TC ($)	TR-TC ($)	MR ($)	MC ($)
0	0	9	-9	-	-
1	7	13	-6	7	4
2	14	15	-1	7	2
3	21	17	4	7	2
4	28	21	7	7	4
5	35	28	7	7	7
6	42	39	3	7	11
7	49	55	-6	7	16

✔ When TR – RC < 0, the firms make a loss.

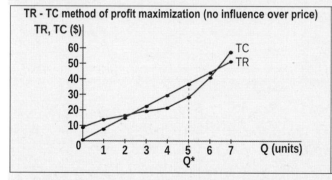

TR - TC method of profit maximization (no influence over price)

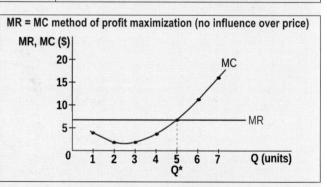

MR = MC method of profit maximization (no influence over price)

Calculating profit-maximizing output and amount of profit: firms with influence over price

You are given data on Q, P, and TC. Find profit-maximizing level of output, Q, and the amount of profit earned, (a) by using the TR – TC method and (b) by using the MR = MC method. In both cases verify your results graphically. (c) How can you tell that this firm has some influence over price?

(a) Calculate TR, and TR-TC for each level of Q (shown in bold); identify the largest TR-TC, which is 7 (If TR-TC = the same value twice, choose the one corresponding to the larger Q). This gives an output level of Q* = **4 units**, and **profit = $7**.

(b) Calculate MR and MC (shown in bold); find where they are equal: MR = MC = 4, corresponding to output of Q* = **4 units** (cannot find profit from MR = MC alone).

(c) Firm has some influence over price because P is falling and TR is non-linear.

✔ Note that both approaches give the identical results.

Q (units)	P ($)	TR ($)	TC ($)	TR-TC ($)	MR ($)	MC ($)
0	11	0	9	-9	-	-
1	10	10	13	-3	10	4
2	9	18	15	3	8	2
3	8	24	17	7	6	2
4	7	28	21	7	4	4
5	6	30	28	2	2	7
6	5	30	39	-9	0	11
7	4	28	55	-27	-2	16

✔ When TR – RC < 0, the firms make a loss.

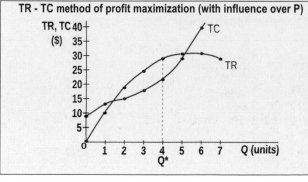

TR - TC method of profit maximization (with influence over P)

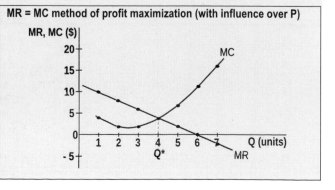

MR = MC method of profit maximization (with influence over P)

Understanding why MR = MC gives rise to maximum profit

Consider the diagrams above, showing the MR = MC method of profit maximization (for firms both with and without influence over P).

For any Q < Q*, MR > MC, meaning that the extra revenue of producing one more unit of output is greater than the cost of producing that same unit, therefore it is worthwhile for the firm to produce more.	For any Q > Q*, MC > MR, meaning that the extra cost of producing one more unit of output is greater than the revenue obtained from that same unit, therefore the firms should produce less.
At Q*, where MR = MC, it is not possible for the firm to change its output level to improve its position, therefore profit is maximized.	

Alternative goals of firms

Growth maximization Firms may be interested in maximizing growth (in terms of the quantity of output produced) rather than profits (i.e. give up some profit for the sake of more growth). Advantages of greater growth include achievement of greater economies of scale hence lower average costs, greater diversification into other products, greater market power (= ability to influence price) and lower risk of take-overs by other firms.	**Revenue maximization** Firms may be interested in maximizing revenues (TR = P x Q) rather than profits for several reasons, such as the impression of success of a firm with large sales, and the relative ease that revenues can be measured (as compared with profits). **TR is maximum at Q*, where MR = 0** (can be seen in diagram p 27); this leads to a higher Q and lower P than in the case of profit maximization (see p 32).	**Revenue maximization** 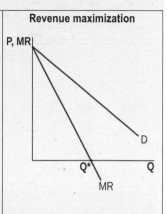
Managerial utility maximization Large firms run by managers who are not owners may try to maximize their personal utility (satisfaction) by giving themselves larger benefits, such as higher salaries, use of luxurious company cars and expense accounts, all of which may work to reduce profits.		
Satisficing This is an alternative to maximizing behavior. Firms have many different goals, some of which may conflict, and they may not want to "maximize" anything (profit, revenue, growth, managerial utility) that could give rise to a significant sacrifice of something else. They may prefer a strategy that makes compromises among different objectives and achieves a **satisfactory outcome** with respect to all the important goals.	**Corporate social responsibility** This involves avoidance of activities that may lead to negative production externalities (such as pollution or environmental degradation) or other undesirable activities (such as use of child labor or hazardous working conditions), all of which may create a negative image with consumers. Such firm behavior is encouraged by consumers who prefer to buy goods and services from socially responsible firms.	

Summary of product, cost, revenue and profit terms

Product terms

total product (TP)	= total quantity of output produced by a firm	
average product (AP)	= total product per unit of labor input	= TP / units of labor
marginal product (MP)	= extra product produced by an additional unit of labor	$= \Delta TP / \Delta$ units of labor

Cost terms

implicit costs	= sacrificed income for the use of a factor of production (input) that is owned by the firm for use in production
explicit costs	= payment of money by a firm to obtain a factor of production (input) for use in production
economic costs	= explicit costs + implicit costs

total fixed costs (TFC)	= costs that do not vary with output
total variable costs (TVC)	= costs that vary with output
total costs (TC)	= TFC + TVC

average fixed costs (AFC)	= fixed costs per unit of output (Q)	= TFC / Q
average variable costs (AVC)	= variable costs per unit of output (Q)	= TVC / Q
average total costs (ATC)	= total costs per unit of output (Q)	= AFC + AVC = TC / Q

marginal costs (MC) = extra cost of producing one more unit of output $= \Delta TC / \Delta Q$

long run average total cost (LRATC) curve = a cost curve showing the relationship between average cost of a firm and the quantity of output it produces as it increases in size by varying all its inputs (in the long run)

Revenue terms

total revenue (TR)	= price x quantity (= P x Q)	
average revenue (AR)	= total revenue per unit of output (Q)	= TR / Q (= P)
marginal revenue (MR)	= extra revenue from the sale of an extra unit of output $= \Delta TR / \Delta Q$	

Profit terms

economic profit	= total revenue minus economic costs	= TR – TC
abnormal profit	= positive economic profit	= TR – TC when TR > TC
normal profit*	= zero economic profit	= TR – TC when TR = TC
loss	= negative economic profit	= TR – TC when TR < TC

*normal profit = the amount of revenue needed to keep a firm in business, which just covers all its explicit and implicit costs, including payment for entrepreneurship

1.5.4 Perfect competition

Assumptions of the model

There is a **large number of small firms**, each of which acts independently and is unable to influence the price of its product.	There is **freedom of entry and exit**, so that any firm can freely enter and exist an industry without restrictions of any kind.
All firms sell a **homogeneous (or identical) product**, so that it is not possible to distinguish the product of different producers.	There is **perfect information**, so that all firms and consumers have all necessary information on price and output to make decisions.
There is **perfect resource mobility**, so that resources (factors of production) can be moved freely and without cost from one firm to another.	

The perfectly competitive firm as a price taker

price taker = a firm that sells all the output it wants at the P determined in the market; the firm has no ability to influence P, because of its small size, and because it sells a homogeneous product; therefore the demand curve facing the firm is perfectly elastic at Pe determined by D and S.

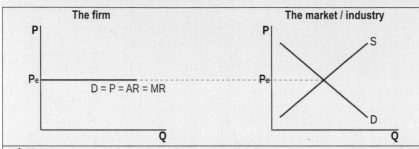		In the market (industry), demand (D) and supply (S) determine an equilibrium price, Pe. This price is accepted by each individual firm in the industry. If a firm tries to increase its price, it will lose all customers to other firms, since the product they all sell is identical. While the firm could lower its price below Pe, it would be foolish to do so since it can sell all it wants at Pe.

✔ The revenue curves facing the perfectly competitive firm can be seen on p 27 under "Revenues of firms with no influence over price", where it was noted that **P = AR = MR**. Since the demand curve facing the firm is perfectly elastic (horizontal) at Pe, it follows that **D = P = AR = MR**.

Short-run profit maximization in perfect competition (MR = MC method)

In the short run, the perfectly competitive firm may make **abnormal profit**, **normal profit**, or **loss**.

How to find the profit-maximizing (or loss-minimizing) equilibrium, and amount of profit or loss of the firm:

1. Find Q where MR = MC; this is $Q\pi$ if the firm earns abnormal or normal profit, and Q_{loss} if it makes a loss.	2. Draw a line upward to P (= D) or to ATC (whichever is higher).
3. Compare P with ATC to find which is larger: **P > ATC ⇒ abnormal profit; P = ATC ⇒ normal profit; P < ATC ⇒ loss**.	4. Multiply the vertical difference between P and ATC by Q produced ($Q\pi$ or Q_{loss}) to find total abnormal profit or total loss.

Abnormal profit (positive economic profit)	Normal profit (zero economic profit)	Loss (negative economic profit)
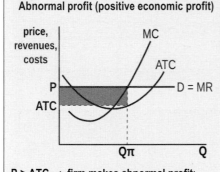	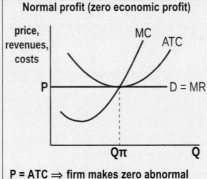	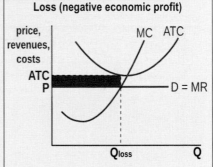
P > ATC ⇒ firm makes abnormal profit; (P - ATC) x $Q\pi$ = abnormal profit (green area).	**P = ATC ⇒ firm makes zero abnormal profit or loss; it earns normal profit.**	**P < ATC ⇒ firm makes a loss;** (ATC - P) x Q_{loss} = loss (red area).

✔ The cost curves are identical in each of the three cases. What differs is the P, which is determined in the market and which the firm "takes".

Shutting down in the short run: break-even price and shut-down price

break-even price = the price at which the firm makes normal profit, i.e. P = minimum ATC, meaning that P (= revenue per unit) = cost per unit
shut-down price = the price at which the firm will shut down; in the short run it is where P = minimum AVC

In the short run, a loss-making firm tries to minimize its losses. Since it is in the short run, it has at least one fixed input, and therefore has fixed costs. If it shuts down, its losses will equal its fixed costs. If it can make losses smaller than its fixed costs by continuing to produce, it should continue to produce.
✔ Remember that the difference between ATC and AVC = AFC.
At P_1 (= break-even price where the firm earns normal profit), P is sufficient to cover all of AVC and all of AFC (i.e. all of ATC).
At P_2 (where the firm is making a loss), P is sufficient to cover all of AVC and a portion of AFC; **the firm will produce because its loss < fixed costs**.
At P_3 (where the firm again is making a loss) P is sufficient to cover only AVC and none of AFC; **the firm is indifferent between producing and not producing** because in both cases loss = fixed costs; this is the shut-down price.
At P_4 (where the firm again is making a loss) P is covers only a part of AVC and none of AFC; **the firm will not produce** because for any P < P_3, loss > fixed costs.

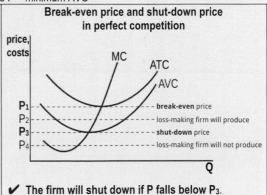

Break-even price and shut-down price in perfect competition

✔ The firm will shut down if P falls below P_3.

✔ The perfectly competitive firm's **short-run supply curve is its MC curve up to the point of minimum AVC** (= shut-down price).

In long-run equilibrium all firms earn normal profit (zero economic profit)

From abnormal profit in the short run to normal profit in the long run	The firms in the industry are initially accepting price P_1 determined in the market, earning abnormal profits (green area) in the short run. When the industry goes into the long run, outsider firms attracted by profits enter the industry, causing the market supply curve to shift to the right and the price to fall. Market supply increases until the new supply curve S_2 gives a price of P_2, where the abnormal profits are eliminated; **all firms in the industry earn normal profit, where P = minimum ATC.**
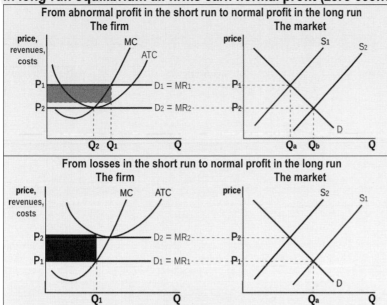	

From losses in the short run to normal profit in the long run	The firms in the industry are initially accepting price P_1 determined in the market, making losses (red area) in the short run. When the industry goes into the long run, some of the loss-making firms leave the industry, causing the supply curve to shift to the left and the price to increase. Market supply decreases until the new supply curve S_2 gives a price of P_2, where the losses have been eliminated among the remaining firms in the industry; **all remaining firms earn normal profit, where P = minimum ATC.**
The firm — The market	

✔ Note the difference between the shut-down price in the short run and in the long run:

Short-run shut-down price is where **P = minimum AVC**. If P falls below this level, the firm will make losses larger than its fixed costs and so is better of stopping production and closing down (see p 30).	**Long-run shut-down price** is where **P = minimum ATC**. If P falls below this level, the firm has no reason to continue to produce as in the long run all its inputs are variable and it can leave the industry.

✔ The **break-even price**, where **P = minimum ATC** and the firm makes normal profit, is the same in the short run and in the long run. (Note that the break-even price and the long-run shut-down price are the same.)

Productive and allocative efficiency in perfect competition

productive efficiency = producing at the lowest possible cost; **occurs where production takes place at minimum ATC**
allocative efficiency = producing the combination of goods and services that consumers mostly want; **occurs when P = MC**

Long-run equilibrium in perfect competition: productive and allocative efficiency	The firm in long-run equilibrium earns normal profit, since P = ATC. This equilibrium allows the firm to achieve both productive efficiency, since output Qe is where ATC is minimum, and allocative efficiency, since P = MC.
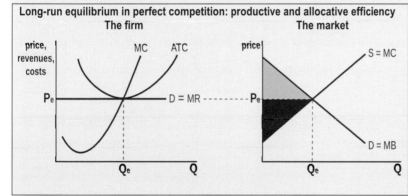	In the perfectly competitive market, equilibrium occurs where **MB = MC**, and **social surplus (the sum of consumer and producer surplus) is maximum, indicating allocative efficiency** (as explained on p 6).
	✔ The significance of these efficiency conditions is that **there is no resource waste.**

Productive and allocative efficiency in the short –run

The perfectly competitive firm always achieves allocative efficiency, both in the short and long run, because since P = MR, profit maximization occurring at MR = MC means that P = MC where profit is maximum. However, the firm that earns abnormal profit in the short run does not achieve productive efficiency, since production takes place at Q where ATC is not minimum. You can check these points by examining the diagrams above.

Evaluation of perfect competition

☑ Achievement of productive efficiency (in the long run) means that there is no resource waste in production.	☒ The model is based on unrealistic assumptions and there are few if any real-world markets that it accurately describes.
☑ Achievement of allocative efficiency means there is no resource waste on account of producing goods not wanted/valued by society.	☒ Because of the small size of firms, they cannot grow large enough to enjoy **economies of scale** (see p 27).
☑ Because of the above efficiencies, perfect competition becomes a standard for assessing the extent of inefficiencies in other market structures.	☒ As firms open and close continuously, there may be a waste of resources involved as factors of production move from one firm/industry to another (this is assumed away by the model).
☑ Competition leads firms to lower their costs of production and higher-cost firms are forced out of the market.	☒ Homogeneous products mean that consumers cannot enjoy any product variety.
☑ Consumers benefit from low prices arising from competition and lack of abnormal profits in the long run.	☒ Since firms do not earn abnormal profits in the long run, they are unlikely to engage in research for new product development.
☑ Consumers decide what and how much will be produced, because the market responds immediately to changes in consumer tastes and preferences, and also because firms have no power to influence consumers through advertising as all goods are homogeneous.	☒ The model cannot guarantee that there will not be any **externalities of production or consumption** (see p 19), in which case if these occur (as they are likely to) allocative efficiency will no longer be achieved.

1.5.5 Monopoly

Assumptions of the model

There is a **single firm, or a dominant firm** in the market. The single firm represents the entire market or industry.	The firm produces a good that has **no close substitutes** (if there were close substitutes, it would not be a monopoly).
There are **high** barriers to entry = factors that prevent or make it very difficult for other firms to enter the industry and begin production.	

Understanding barriers to entry

Barriers to entry are important features of both **monopoly** and **oligopoly**. Examples include:

Large **economies of scale**, causing average costs to fall as output increases in the long run (p 27); entry of new firms is difficult as entering on a smaller scale would mean high average costs, high prices, and therefore inability to compete with the existing firm.	**Legal barriers**, created by legislation, include **patents** (= rights given to firms to be sole producers of a new product for a period of time), **copyrights** (= rights to authors to be sole producers of written work), **tariffs** and **quotas** (= trade barriers restricting imports; see p 64). ·
Natural monopoly, where a single firm can cover the needs of an entire market at a lower average cost that two or more firms (see p 33); new firms are strongly discouraged from entering due to very low average costs of the natural monopolist.	**Aggressive tactics** = methods used by existing firms to prevent outside firms from entering, such as by lowering price to make it difficult for a new firm to compete, or by threatening the new firm by a take-over.
Branding, which involves advertising to create a unique product image and name, attracting consumer loyalty; firms may be unable to break into markets with strong brands due to consumer loyalty toward the already existing products.	**Control of necessary resources** involves ownership or control of essential resources involved in production, such as control of oil reserves or diamond mines.

The monopolist's demand and revenues in relation to price elasticity of demand (PED)

The monopolist's revenues and revenue curves were explained on p 27 ("Revenues of firms with influence over price"). Since **P = AR**, it follows that the **AR curve is also the demand (D) curve facing the monopolist**. The AR=D and MR curves are shown here in relation to PED.

Monopoly AR = D and MR curves in relation to PED	The monopolist does not produce in the inelastic part of the D curve
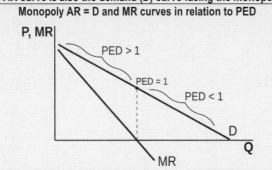	In the upper left portion of the D curve PED >1, at the midpoint of the D curve PED = 1, and at the bottom right portion PED < 1 (p 8 – 9 and p 27). When PED > 1, MR is positive (TR increases) When PED = 1, MR = 0 (TR is maximum) When PED < 1, MR is negative (TR decreases) This means that **the monopolist will not produce in the portion of the D curve where PED < 1** (TR decreases). This can be seen from the profit maximizing condition MC = MR; since MC is always positive, it cannot be equal to MR at any negative MR value. Another way to see this is to note that as Q produced increases, TC increases, but if TR decreases (as it does when MR < 0) $\Rightarrow$ profit must be falling, which firm will not accept.

Monopolist profit maximization

The monopolist faces the same cost curves as the perfectly competitive (or any other) firm. What differs is the shape of the D = AR and MR curves, which are added to the cost curves to find profit-maximizing equilibrium.
1. Find profit-maximizing Q (= $Q\pi$) by MR = MC.
2. Find the corresponding P (= $P\pi$) by drawing a vertical line to the D = AR curve and across to the vertical axis.
3. Draw a line from the point of ATC to the vertical axis.
4. Profit (positive economic or abnormal profit since **P > ATC**) is found by ($P\pi$ – ATC) x $Q\pi$ = green area.

How the monopolist maximizes profit

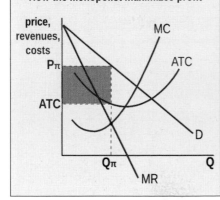

Monopolist loss minimization

The monopolist may also make a loss (negative economic profit); this happens when P < ATC. Loss is minimized the same way that profit is maximized:

1. Find loss-minimizing Q (= Q_{loss}) by MR = MC.
2. Find the corresponding P (= P_{loss}) by drawing a vertical line to the D = AR curve and across to the vertical axis.
3. Continue the vertical line upward to ATC and draw a ine from the point of ATC to the vertical axis.
4. Loss is found by (ATC – P_{loss}) x Q_{loss} = red area.

How the monopolist minimizes loss

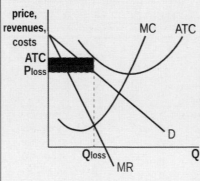

Monopolist revenue maximization

Revenue maximization is an alternative goal to profit maximization, which may at times be pursued by firms (see p 29).
Revenue is maximized at the level of output where MR = 0, corresponding to maximum total revenue (TR) (as seen in the diagram on p 27).
1. Find revenue maximizing Q (= Qr) at the point where MR = 0.
2. Find the corresponding P (= Pr) by drawing a vertical line to the D = AR curve and across to the vertical axis.
The diagram also shows profit-maximizing Q ($Q\pi$) and P ($P\pi$), found by the MR = MC rule.
✔ **The revenue-maximizer has a lower P and a higher Q than the profit-maximizer.**

How the monopolist maximizes revenue

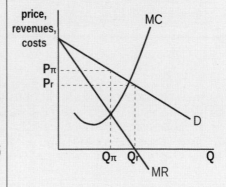

Short-run and long-run equilibrium in monopoly

Because of **high barriers to entry**, new firms cannot enter the market even if the monopolist is earning abnormal profits (positive economic profits). Therefore it continues to earn abnormal profits in the long run. **The short-run and long-run equilibrium of the profit-making monopolist is the same.** If the monopolist is making a loss (negative economic profit) in the short-run, it may choose to shut down in the long run, or it may continue to operate if it is subsidized by the government (in the event that it is a natural monopoly; see below).

Natural monopoly

natural monopoly = a monopoly with economies of scale so large that when it produces output that satisfies the demand of an entire market, it is still experiencing economies of scale (falling average costs); it is therefore not in society's interest to break it up, because two or more firms producing the same level of output would do so at higher average costs

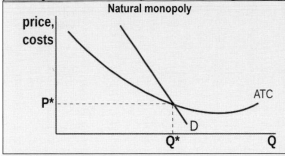 **Natural monopoly**	The demand curve of the natural monopolist intersects its ATC curve at a point where average costs are still falling (it is still experiencing economies of scale). The reasoning is that if the firm is earning at least normal profit, where P = ATC, it cannot produce any Q greater than Q*, because if it did, P* (given by the D curve) would be lower than ATC, and the firm would be making a loss. Therefore it must produce a Q less than Q*, but then it is experiencing economies of scale. If this firm were split up into two or more firms, each one would have substantially higher average costs. Therefore it is not in society's interests to split it up. Natural monopolies usually have high capital costs, and include mainly public utilities, such as water, electricity and natural gas companies.

Price and output in monopoly compared with perfect competition

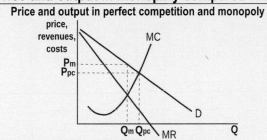 Price and output in perfect competition and monopoly	The firm in perfect competition has output Qpc and price Ppc, determined by the intersection of demand and the MC curve (which in perfect competition is the S curve). The monopolist has its output determined by MR = MC, which is Qm, sold at price Pm. ✔ Therefore the monopolist has **a higher price and a lower quantity produced** than the perfectly competitive firm. ✔ This result makes monopoly undesirable from consumers' point of view.

Efficiency in monopoly

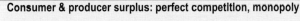

Consumer & producer surplus: perfect competition, monopoly	Productive & allocative efficiency: perfect competition, monopoly
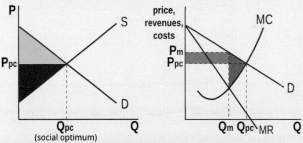	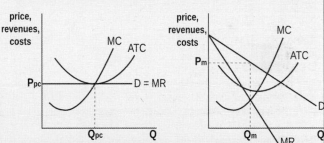

The higher price and lower quantity produced by the monopolist have effects on consumer and producer surplus: • Lower Q at Qm ⇒ resource misallocation results, due to lower production than the social optimum level (Qpc), leading to **welfare loss** (brown area) and allocative inefficiency; • Higher P at Pm ⇒ consumer surplus decreases by the amount of the green area, taken by producer surplus; the monopolist gains at the expense of consumers.	The profit-maximzing monopolist cannot achieve productive and allocative efficiency: it is productively and allocatively **inefficient**: • Productive inefficiency: at the point of production, Qm, **ATC is not minimum**; • Allocative inefficiency: at the point of production, Qm, **P > MC**; this shows that the value consumers attach to the last unit of the good (= P) is greater than what it costs to produce it (= MC).

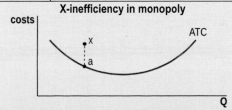 X-inefficiency in monopoly	The monopolist faces an additional type of inefficiency arising from its lack of competitors, making it less careful to keep costs as low as possible. **X-inefficiency** means that the monopolist's ATC may be higher than necessary; it may produce at a point such as X, rather than at point a, which is on its ATC curve. X-inefficiency may arise from poor management, inefficient workers, and a lack of concern about keeping costs low, all of which are due to lack of competition.

Positive characteristics of monopoly

Research and development Due to its abnormal profits in the long run, the monopolist has funds to carry out R&D leading to new products and technologies; benefitting consumers and society.	**Possible lower prices due to technological innovations** The development and use of new technologies may lead to lower costs and hence to lower prices enjoyed by consumers.
Economics of scale Due to their large size, monopolistic firms are in a position to achieve large economies of scale, involving lower average costs in the long run, leading to lower prices for consumers.	**Natural monopolies** In the event that a firm is a natural monopoly, it can achieve economies of scale so large and average costs so low that it is in society's interest to maintain it as a monopoly.

Evaluating policies to regulate monopoly power

monopoly power = the ability to influence price due to a downward sloping demand curve, leading to resource misallocation and welfare loss; **both monopolies and oligopolies exercise a considerable amount of monopoly power**	The inefficiencies of monopoly and oligopoly lead to government efforts to **control and limit the degree of monopoly power**, aiming to bring prices and quantities more in line with competitive markets, and to limit resource misallocation and welfare loss.

Free, unregulated monopolies are as a rule illegal; monopolies are allowed to exist mainly if they are **natural monopolies**, in which case they are regulated by the government; this applies to both publicly and privately owned monopolies.

Legislation to limit monopoly power

Legislation promoting competition Most countries have laws that: • do not permit formation of monopolies (except natural monopolies) • do not permit **collusion** (agreements to fix prices and share output) among oligopolistic firms; see p 36) • regulate mergers (agreements between firms to join together) imposing limits on the size of the merged firm, to avoid excessive monopoly power	☑ Legislation is essential since greater competition is in the interests of consumers and society, leading to greater quantities produced and lower prices, while monopoly power leads to allocative inefficiency and welfare loss. ☒ Vague laws allow for different interpretations of anti-competitive behavior. ☒ There are differences between countries and changes over time on how much monopoly power is too much, and on how large mergers should be, depending on political views. ☒ There are different degrees of enforcement of laws. ☒ There are major difficulties in finding evidence of collusion in oligopoly.
Nationalization = transfer of firm ownership from the private to the public or government sector ☑ Government ownership allows the government to regulate natural monopolies forcing them to lower prices and increase quantities produced in the interests of consumers, reducing allocative inefficiency and welfare loss. ☒ Government ownership often leads to inefficiencies and higher than necessary costs of production, as governments are not driven by the goal to maximize profits.	**Trade liberalization** = the removal of trade restrictions (tariffs, quotas, see p 64) so that imports can enter freely into a country. ☑ Increased imports into a country increase competition faced by domestic firms with foreign producers; domestic firms with a substantial degree of monopoly power are forced to lower prices thus facing reduced monopoly power. ☒ Inefficient domestic firms may go out of business, with a corresponding increase in unemployment.

Regulation of natural monopoly

Average cost pricing is a method used by governments to force natural monopolies to produce where **P = ATC**, given by the intersection of D with ATC, resulting in quantity Qacp and price Pacp, where the firm earns normal profit, since P = ATC. ☑ The regulated monopolist produces a larger Q and sells it at a lower P than the unregulated monopolist who makes abnormal profit (P > ATC). ☑ Since P = ATC, the monopolist earns normal profit, and so does not make any loss (that would require subsidies by the government). ☑ Since P is lower and Q is higher, consumer surplus increases. ☒ Productive efficiency is not achieved (production is not at minimum ATC). ☒ Allocative efficiency is not achieved (P > MC), so there is welfare loss. ☒ Since the firm is guaranteed a price P = ATC, it has no incentive to keep its costs as low as possible.	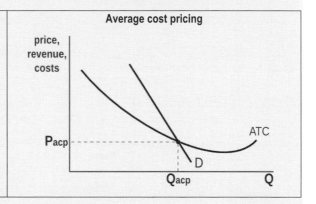

Quantitative topics in perfect competition and monopoly

The following information shows the profit-maximizing or loss-minimizing equilibrium of three firms:	(a) Firm X has ATC = AVC + AFC = 7 + 2 = $9. Since P = $12, P > ATC, therefore **Firm X makes abnormal profit**. Firm Y has ATC = AVC + AFC = 17 + 4 = $21. Since P = $20, P < ATC, therefore **Firm Y makes a loss**. Firm Z has ATC = AVC + AFC = 20 + 7 = $27. Since P = $27, P = ATC, therefore **Firm Z makes normal profit**. (b) Firm A has profit per unit = P – ATC = 12 = 9 = $3. Profit per unit x units of output = 3 x 170 **$510 = abnormal profit**. Firm B has loss per unit = ATC - P = 21 – 20 = $1. Loss per unit x units of output = 1 x 350 = **$350 = loss**. Firm C has **zero abnormal profit or loss**. (c) Firm **Y should not shut down** because P > AVC (20 > 17). It is covering its variable costs plus a portion of fixed costs, so loss < fixed costs. If it shuts down, loss will equal its fixed costs.

	Q (units)	P ($)	AVC ($)	AFC ($)
Firm X	170	12	7	2
Firm Y	350	20	17	4
Firm Z	420	27	20	7

(a) Explain which firm is making abnormal profit, normal profit, or loss.
(b) For each firm, calculate its total amount of profit or loss.
(c) Explain whether or not the loss-making firm should shut down.

Using the information below, (a) calculate the firm's break-even price and shut-down price; (b) find the corresponding level of output of each.	You must calculate TC, ATC and AVC.	Using the data below, calculate (a) profit-maximizing P and Q, and (b) revenue-maximizing P and Q:	(a) Profit-maximizing Q is where MC = MR = $4, so it is 3 units, at P = $6. (b) Revenue-maximizing Q is where MR = 0, so it is 5 units, at P = $4.

Q (units)	TFC ($)	TVC ($)
5	5	17
6	5	20
7	5	24
8	5	29

Q (units)	TC ($)	ATC ($)	AVC ($)
5	22	4.40	3.40
6	25	4.17	3.33
7	29	4.14	3.43
8	34	4.25	3.62

(a) Break-even P = $4.14 = min ATC;
Shut-down P = $3.33 = min AVC
(b) The firm breaks even at Q = 7 units; it shuts down at Q = 6 units

Q units	P ($)	MR ($)	MC ($)
1	8	8	4
2	7	6	3
3	6	4	4
4	5	2	5
5	4	0	6
6	3	-2	7

✔ The firm that maximizes revenue has a lower P and higher Q than the firm that maximizes profit.

1.5.6 Monopolistic competition

Assumptions of the model

There is a **large number of firms**, each of which acts independently of the others.	There is **freedom of entry and exit** in the industry; there are no (or low) barriers to entry.
There is **product differentiation** = each firm tries to make its product different from others; products can be differentiated by appearance, taste, color, size, quality, packaging, branding, services (such as warranties), location (easy access by consumers); it forms the basis of **non-price competition**	Ex restaurants, hairdressers, drycleaners, furniture, supermarkets, food producers, shoes, clothing

Product differentiation, non-price competition and the demand curve

Product differentiation is crucially important, used by firms to create monopoly power. The more consumers can be convinced of a product's superiority over its substitutes produced by rival firms, the greater the monopoly power of a firm.	✔ The firm in monopolistic competition therefore faces **a downward sloping demand curve**, where price and quantity demanded are inversely related.

price competition = competition between firms to attract customers away from the products of other firms by lowering the price of the product	**non-price competition** = competition between firms to attract customers on the basis of factors other than price, through **product differentiation**	✔ Monopolistically competitive firms use both price and non-price competition. **The more successful the non-price-competition, the greater the monopoly power**, and the lower the reliance on price competition.

Profit maximization (and loss minimization) in the short run

Profit maximization and loss minimization in monopolistic competition are **the same as in monopoly**. The reason is that each firm behaves like a monopoly for its own particular product, due to product differentiation. ✔ The profit-maximizing level of output and price are Qπ and Pπ. Total profit is shown by the green area. ✔ The loss-minimizing level of output and price are Qloss and Ploss. Total loss is shown by the red area.	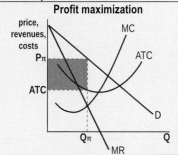 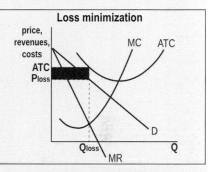

Normal profit in the long run

Due to free entry and exit, **firms in the long run earn normal profit**.

✔ New firms are attracted into industries earning abnormal profit (positive economic profit), and capture part of the market share of existing firms. Therefore the D curve facing each existing firm shifts left until it is tangent to the ATC curve, so P = ATC.

✔ Some firms exit loss-making industries, causing the market share of remaining firms to increase; the D curve facing each firm shifts right until it is tangent to the ATC curve, so P = ATC.

Efficiency in monopolistic competition

In long run equilibrium, firms in monopolistic competition:

✔ do not achieve productive efficiency, since the profit-maximizing output, Qe is not at minimum ATC;

✔ do not achieve allocative efficiency, since at the profit-maximizing output, Qe, P > MC, indicating that too little of the good is being produced to what consumers want.

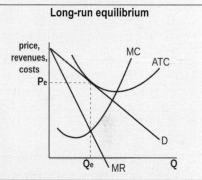

Criticisms of the model

• The diagrams above suggest that profit maximization involves only P and Q decisions by the firm, whereas in fact an important part of firm activity involves decisions on product differentiation.	• Product differentiation and the presence of what are in effect many monopolies does not allow analysis at the industry level, as it is not possible to add up demand curves.
• In reality, there may be more barriers to entry than the model assumes.	• Product differentiation presupposes research and development (R&D), but the lack of abnormal profits in the long run suggests that this is not possible. Yet firms in monopolistic competition do carry out some R&D.

1.5.7 Oligopoly

Assumptions of the model

There is a **small number of large firms**, each of which is aware of the presence of the others.	Firms sell either a **homogeneous** product (ex oil) or **differentiated** product (ex cars).
There are high **barriers to entry**, making it difficult for new firms to enter the industry.	There is **interdependence among the firms**, due to their small number; the actions of each one affect all of the others.

Interdependence and the dilemma to compete or to collude

The interdependence of firms in oligopoly makes them have **strategic behavior**, so that each firm tries to predict the actions of rival firms, and to base its own actions on how it expects its rivals to behave (like in a game of chess). Their strategic behavior leads them to conflicting incentives:

The incentive to compete Firms face the incentive to compete with each other for the purpose of capturing part of their rival firms' market share.	**The incentive to collude** = make an agreement to fix prices and share the market between themselves so as to limit competition between them.

Game theory: strategic interdependence and the incentives to compete or to collude

game theory = a mathematical technique used to analyze the behavior of interdependent decision-makers who use strategic behavior; one such game is based on the **prisoner's dilemma** = a game showing how two rational decision-makers who try to make themselves as well off as possible by using strategic behavior end up becoming worse off.

Game theory is very useful to demonstrate important features of the behavior of oligopolistic firms. Suppose there are two firms, A and B, and they each have two pricing strategies, "high price" and "low price". There are four possible outcomes.
- The firms begin in outcome 4, where due to price competition, they both use the low price strategy and earn low profits of $30 million each.
- They realize that if they **agree to collude** and fix price at a higher level, they can be at outcome 1 where they both make higher profits of $50 million each.
- While colluding, they face a dilemma. Each one figures that if it breaks the agreement, and lowers price, it will make the higher profit of $70 million while the rival will make $20 million (outcomes 2 and 3). Each one also thinks that if it doesn't lower its price, the rival will, and will beat it to the higher profits. Therefore at least one of them will cut its price.
- The high price firm ending up with $20 million after its rival cuts the price realizes that it will be better off if it also cuts its price, as it will then make $30 million.
- Therefore they both break the agreement, and end up in box 4 again, where they are worse off relative to outcome 1, earning lower profits of $30 million each.

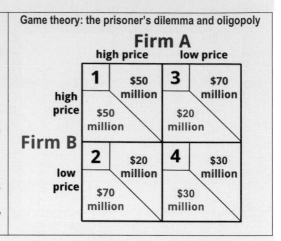

Game theory: the prisoner's dilemma and oligopoly

Key points demonstrated by the prisoner's dilemma game:

- The firms show **strategic behavior**, as each bases its actions on what it guesses the other will do.
- The firms show **strategic interdependence** = as each one tries to guess what the other will do, the actions of one affect outcomes not only for itself but also for the other.
- The firms face **conflicting incentives**, which are the incentive to compete (price competition) and the incentive to collude by fixing the price.

- **Both become worse off** as a result of price competition, or cutting prices in an effort to capture part of the rival's market share.
- Therefore **price competition is strongly avoided**, as it may lead to a **price war** = a situation where firms retaliate against each other by lowering prices to the point that they may end up making losses.

The concentration ratio

Concentration ratio = a measure used to determine the degree of competition in an industry, and whether firms have too much **monopoly power**; it measures the percentage of output produced by the largest firms in the industry. Ex A five-firm concentration ratio of 45% means that the largest five firms produce 45% of industry output; a seven-firm ratio of 80% means that the top seven firms are responsible for 80% of output. The **higher the concentration ratio, the lower the degree of competition in the industry and the higher the degree of monopoly power**. An industry is held to be oligopolistic if the four largest firms are responsible for 40% of output. The concentration ratio suffers from some limitations: it cannot account for: the relative sizes of the largest firms; possible competition from imports; the degree of competition of the industry in global markets.

Collusive oligopoly

Formal collusion and cartels

formal collusion = collusion between firms leading to the formation of a cartel
cartel = an agreement between firms with the objective to maximize profits by behaving **as if they were a monopoly** and restricting competition between them, usually by fixing prices at a higher level and limiting output; cartels are formed by collusive oligopolies. The profit-maximizing output is split between the cartel members (possibly by use of historical market shares, or some other rule).
✔ The monopoly diagram shows profit-maximization by a cartel.
✔ Cartels are illegal in most countries, because their members behave like a monopoly, with significant **monopoly power** leading to higher prices and lower output than what arises in more competitive markets, and substantial welfare loss.

Ex Organization of Petroleum Exporting Countries (OPEC), composed of thirteen oil-producing countries that restrict oil output leading to a higher oil price.

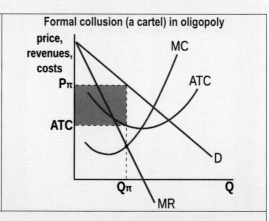

Formal collusion (a cartel) in oligopoly

Why cartels are difficult to maintain

- Cartel members face the incentive to cheat on the cartel by secretly lowering their price, this way capturing rivals' market share.
- Cheating by one or more firms may lead to a price war involving retaliatory price cuts, making all the firms worse off and leading to cartel break-down.
- Differing costs of production among cartel members may lead to disagreements as higher-cost firms want to fix a higher price and vice versa.

- It is important to have a dominant firm in the cartel, that takes on a leadership role, making it easier to resolve differences and arrive at agreements; lack of a dominant firm can lead to cartel break-down.
- The larger the number of firms in an industry that are joining the cartel, the more difficult it is to reach an agreement, and the easier for the agreement to break down.
- During recessions, with falling sales and profits, firms have a greater incentive to cheat by lowering prices.

Tacit collusion

tacit collusion = cooperation between firms in oligopoly to restrict competition and fix prices **without a formal agreement**

price leadership = a form of tacit collusion where a dominant firm in the industry sets a price, and also initiates price changes; the remaining firms accept the leader's price, becoming effectively price-takers	**limit pricing** = a form of tacit collusion where firms agree informally to set a price that is lower than the profit-maximizing price, so as to discourage new firms from entering into the industry

Non-collusive oligopoly

The kinked demand curve model	The kinked demand curve
Oligopolistic firms often do not collude, yet there is still price stability (price rigidities) in oligopolistic markets. The kinked demand curve shows how this can happen. Suppose there are two firms, Y and Z, producing output Q* and selling it at price P*. • Y asks, if I raise my price above P* what will Z do? Most likely Z will not raise its price, because by maintaining a lower price than mine, it will be able to capture a large part of my market share $\Rightarrow$ my D appears elastic when P > P*, because as my P⇑, Q⇓ proportionately more $\Rightarrow$ my TR⇓. **Therefore I should not raise my price above P*.** • Y asks, if I lower my price below P*, what will Z do? Most likely Z will lower its price too, to avoid losing market share to me $\Rightarrow$ my D is inelastic when P < P*, because as my P⇓, Q⇑ proportionately less $\Rightarrow$ my TR⇓. **Therefore I should not lower my price below P*.** • Z asks the same questions as Y and tries to guess Y's responses. Z's reasoning is the same as Y's. **Therefore Z also does not raise or lower its price.** ✔ As both (or all) firms in the industry reason this way, **price and quantity remain at P*, Q*** ✔ The firms profit-maximize by the rule MR = MC. The broken part of MR (due to the kink in D) allows firms with different costs (MCs) to profit-maximize at the same Q and P.	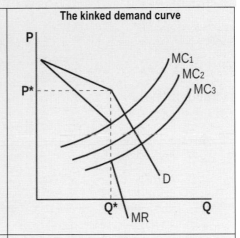

Insights of the model	Limitations of the model
☑ The model explains why **there is price stability** (price rigidities) in oligopoly even though the firms do not collude. ☑ The model shows that firms **use strategic behavior**, basing their actions on guess about what their rivals will do. ☑ The model shows that the firms avoid lowering prices to gain market share, i.e. **they avoid price competition**, as this can lead to lower revenues and profits, as well as to price wars.	☒ The model cannot explain how the firms got to the point of the kink (bend) in the D curve, where they produce output Q* at price P*. ☒ The model does not hold in periods of inflation (a rising overall price level), when firms increase their prices due to higher costs and/or increasing demand.

The importance of non-price competition in oligopoly	
• Fear of price wars leads oligopolistic firms to compete with each other on the basis of non-price factors. • Important non-price factors are new products and product differentiation, advertising and branding.	• Oligopolistic firms earn abnormal (positive economic) profits, offering them the resources for research and development, advertising and branding. • Product differentiation, advertising and branding lead to greater monopoly power and ability to influence price, and greater abnormal profits.

Comparing oligopoly with monopoly

Similarities Oligopoly is similar to monopoly because of:	Differences Oligopoly differs from monopoly because:
• high barriers to entry • significant monopoly power • abnormal profits in the long run • allocative and productive inefficiency • higher prices and lower output than competitive firms • possible X-inefficiency due to lack of price competition in oligopoly • need for government policies ensuring no abuse of monopoly power • large economies of scale • ability to carry out R&D, leading to new products and technologies	• it consists of several firms rather than one (or single dominant) • firms use strategic behavior • firms strive for major product differentiation (if products are not homogeneous) • firms face strong non-price competition • firms have high advertising and branding costs • firms may behave collusively (like a monopoly), and yet avoid detection because they are not a single firm, thus escaping laws protecting consumers against abuse of monopoly power

1.5.8 Price discrimination

price discrimination = selling a product at different prices to different consumer groups, where the price differences are not due to difference in costs of production	Ex hotels offer lower prices for winter and mid-week stays; airlines increase their prices as the date of travel approaches; hairdressers may offer higher prices for women than men; cinemas may offer lower prices for children and older people

Conditions that must be satisfied for price discrimination to take place

The firm must have some monopoly power (ability to influence price); a perfectly competitive firm, being a price taker, cannot practice price discrimination.	The firm must be able to separate consumer groups so that there is no possibility of resale (buying at the low price and re-selling at the high price). Separation can be by time, age, gender, geographical location.
Different consumer groups must have different price elasticities of demand for the product: low PED $\Rightarrow$ higher price; high PED $\Rightarrow$ lower price.	

Profit maximization in third-degree price discrimination

| Of two consumer groups, the first has a lower PED than the second. The two MR curves (MR$_1$ and MR$_2$) are added together to give total MR, which the firm equates with its MC to maximize profit. This gives Q*, which the firm divides between the two groups by equating MC=MR=MR$_1$=MR$_2$, giving outputs Q$_1$ and Q$_2$, and prices P$_1$ and P$_2$ (given by the D curve).
✔ Group 1, with the **lower PED, pays a higher P**; Group 2, with the **higher PED pays a lower P**.
✔ **Price discrimination results in higher revenues and profits for firms.** | 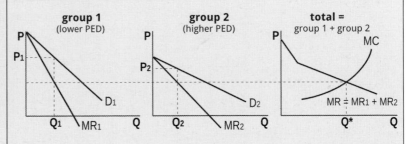 |

Comparison of market structures

Market structures are shown in order of increasing market power.

	Perfect competition	Monopolistic competition	Oligopoly	Monopoly
Assumptions of the model	• many small firms • homogeneous product • no barriers to entry • perfect information • perfect resource mobility	• many firms, varying sizes • differentiated product • no or low barriers to entry	• few large firms • homogeneous or differentiated product • high barriers to entry • firm interdependence • strategic behavior	• single or dominate firm • produces a good with no close substitutes • high barriers to entry
Characteristics				
Number of firms	very many	many	few	single, or one dominant
Size of firms	small	small to medium	large	large
Barriers to entry	none	none, or low	high	high
Type of product	homogeneous	differentiated	homogenous (ex oil) or differentiated (ex cars)	no close substitutes
Product variety	none	high	high (if differentiated)	limited
Degree of monopoly power and demand curve	no power; face horizontal demand curve (are price takers)	some power; face downward sloping demand curve (are price makers)	significant power: face downward sloping demand curve (are price makers); monopoly and collusive oligopoly have the highest degree of power due to lack of competition	
Degree of independent action	firms act independently due to their large number		are interdependent due to their small number, leading to strategic behavior and/or collusion	firm acts independently due to being a single or dominant seller
Type of competition faced	perfect, due to homogeneous products (no price or non-price competition)	both non-price and price competition, but non-price competition is preferred	non-price competition is greatly preferred; price competition is strongly avoided due to fear of price wars and reduced profits	none or almost none, since it is sole or dominant firm in the market
Short-run versus long-run equilibrium	they differ, due to no barriers to entry in the long run, allowing free entry and exit		they are the same, due to high barriers to entry	
Long run profits	normal	normal	abnormal	abnormal
Level of prices and output in the long run	lower P and higher Q than all other market structures, due to productive and allocative efficiency, and lack of abnormal profits in the long run	higher P and lower Q compared with perfect competition, due to lack of productive efficiency; but lower P and higher Q than monopoly and oligopoly due to lack of abnormal profits in the long run	higher P and lower Q compared with perfect competition and monopolistic competition due to productive and allocative inefficiency, and abnormal profits in the long run; more so in the case of collusion	higher P and lower Q compared with perfect competition and monopolistic competition due to productive and allocative inefficiency, and abnormal profits in the long run
Productive and allocative efficiency in the long run	both	neither is achieved in all three market structures; monopoly (and collusive oligopoly which behaves like a monopoly) may be the least efficient of all market structures due to lack of competition and highest degree of monopoly power		
Economies of scale	none, due to small size	possibly some, but if so limited, due to small size	large, due to size; may lead to lower prices due to lower average costs	
Ability to do research and development	very limited, since earn only normal profits in the long run, and face no incentive due to product homogeneity	some, necessitated by the need to differentiate products, but limited due to normal profits in the long run	high, due to ability to earn abnormal profits in the long run, and incentive to innovate in order to maintain/increase monopoly power	high, due to ability to earn abnormal profits in the long run, but less innovative than oligopoly as monopoly position is secure due to high entry barriers

2.1 THE LEVEL OF OVERALL ECONOMIC ACTIVITY

The circular flow of income model

The **circular flow of income model** provides an overview of important relationships in the macroeconomy.

	Factors of production	Payment by firms = consumer income
The circular flow of income in a closed economy (= no foreign trade) with no government or financial markets is shown by the **brown** lines below. Consumers, who sell factors of production to firms, receive **income** from firms (**upper brown line**), and spend all this income to buy goods and services; this spending is **consumer expenditure**, and is equal to the quantity of each good and service bought times its respective price, known as the **value of output** (**lower brown line**). Firms buy the factors of production from consumers and use them to produce goods and services. Therefore income flow = expenditure flow = value of output flow	land labor capital entrepreneurship	rent wages interest profit

Circular flow of income model

consumer income

factors of production

CONSUMERS — **FIRMS**

goods and services

consumer expenditure = value of output

Leakages → saving → taxes → import spending

investment spending — government spending — export spending — Injections

The circular flow of income in an open economy (= with foreign trade) with **government and financial markets** includes **leakages** (**red**) and **injections** (**green**). Though paired together, leakages are usually not equal to injections:	**leakage** = money that leaves the circular flow	**Injection** = money that enters the circular flow
✔ If the **sum of injections > the sum of leakages** ⟹ circular flow grows bigger, production of goods and services ⇑, income ⇑, the economy grows, unemployment ⇓ ✔ If the **sum of injections < the sum of leakages** ⟹ circular flow shrinks, production of goods and services ⇓, income ⇓, the economy is in recession, unemployment ⇑	**Leakages are paired with injections:**	
	leakges: saving (S) taxes (T) import spending (M)	**injections:** investment spending (I) government spending (G) export spending (X)

Distinguishing between GDP and GNI (GNP)

GDP = the total value of all final goods and services (output) produced within the boundaries of a country, in a year, regardless of who owns the factors of production	GNI (GNP) = the total income received by the residents of a country in a year, regardless where the factors of production owned by the residents are located
GDP (the value of output) is likely to differ from **GNI** (income received by the residents of a country) because income of factors of production usually flows across international boundaries. Therefore income received may be greater or less than the value of output produced:	

GNI = GDP + factor income received from abroad – factor income sent abroad   =   GDP + net factor income from abroad

Factor income received from abroad is likely to include	Factor income sent abroad is likely to include
• income received by domestic residents sent to them by relatives working abroad (known as **remittances**) • profits of multinational corporations (also a form of income) earned abroad and sent home (known as **profit repatriation**)	• wages of foreign workers working domestically sent to their relatives back home (**remittances**) • profits of foreign multinational corporations operating domestically sent back to their home country (**profit repatriation**)

✔   GDP is a better measure of the value of output produced by a country than GNI (GNP).
✔   GNI (GNP) is a better measure of the amount of income earned by the residents of a country.

Distinguishing between nominal and real values

Nominal GDP/GNI are measures of output and income in terms of **current prices** (prices prevailing at any given moment).

Real GDP/GNI are measures of output and income in terms of **constant prices** that prevail in one particular year; therefore real values eliminate the influence of price level changes over time.
✔   **Real values must always be used to make comparisons over time**, in order to get a more accurate picture of changes in output and income without the influence of price changes.

Distinguishing between total and per capita values

$$\text{per capita GDP} = \frac{\text{total GDP}}{\text{population}} \qquad \text{per capita GNI} = \frac{\text{total GNI}}{\text{population}}$$

✔ **Total GDP and GNI** provide an indication of the size of an economy.
✔ **Per capita GDP** provides an indication of the amount of output corresponding to each person in the population on average.
✔ **Per capita GNI** provides an indication of how much income is received by each person in the population on average and **is therefore a better indicator of standards of living.**

The three ways to measure economic activity!

Economic activity is measured by use of GDP and GNI (GNP) figures. These measures are important for:

- understanding how an economy's output and income change (grow or shrink) over time
- making comparisons with other economies/countries, and
- formulating policies to achieve important economic objectives (ex low unemployment, low and stable rate of inflation)

You can understand the ways to measure GDP if you remember that **income flow = expenditure flow = value of output flow**.
All three approaches lead to the same results after adjustments for statistical errors.

Measuring GDP by the expenditure approach:	Measuring GDP by the income approach:	Measuring GDP by the output approach

Adds up total spending to buy all final goods and services within a year. There are four components of spending:
 	
Consumption spending (C) All spending by consumers to buy goods and services
Investment spending (I) All spending by firms to buy capital goods plus all private construction
Government spending (G) All spending by the government, including labor costs and infrastructure (roads, airports, ports, etc.)
Net exports (X-M) = exports (X) – imports (M) All spending by foreigners to buy exports minus all spending by domestic consumers to buy imports
 	
✔ **C + I + G + X-M = GDP, where GDP is a measure of economic activity.**
 	
✔ This approach allows comparisons of the relative contribution of C, I, G, and X-M to GDP.
	Adds up all income earned by the four factors of production in the course of producing total output within a year:
	Rent earned by **land**
	Wages earned by **labor**
	Interest earned by **capital**
	Profit earned by **entrepreneurship**
	
	✔ **Rent + wages + interest + profit = national income**
	
	National income is another measure of economic activity, and can be used to calculate GDP after certain adjustments are made.
	
	✔ This approach allows comparisons of the relative income shares of factors of production (ex labor's share) and contributions of these to national income (and hence to GDP).
		Adds up the value of each good and service (PxQ) produced in the economy within a year, thus obtaining the value of all final goods and services, which is equal to GDP.
		
		The value of goods and services is calculated for each sector in the economy, such as:
		- goods in the agricultural sector
		- goods in the manufacturing sector
		- services in the
		   o health sector
		   o education sector
		   o finance sector, etc.
		
		✔ This approach allows comparisons of the relative contribution of each sector to GDP.

Evaluating the use of national income statistics

National income statistics are used to calculate GDP, GNI/ GNP (and national income), but are not always accurate as a basis for making comparisons over time and between countries, and for arriving at conclusions about standards of living in different countries because:

GDP (or GNI) may underestimate standards of living because they	GDP (or GNI) may overestimate standards of living because they	GDP (or GNI) may over - or underestimate standards of living because they
☒ do not include output sold in the underground (informal) economy (ex unreported income of a plumber) ☒ do not include output that is not sold in markets (ex food grown for own consumption) ☒ do not take into account improvements in quality of goods and services (ex improved computers) ☒ do not take into account standard of living factors (ex levels of education, health, life expectancy)	☒ do not take into account the value of negative externalities that reduce standards of living (ex pollution) ☒ do not take into account the destruction of natural resources (ex forests, wildlife, soil quality)	☒ disregard what output consists of (ex high military goods output and low merit goods output, or the reverse) ☒ disregard the distribution of income (ex high income inequality, or low income inequality) ☒ disregard differing price levels in different countries (ex $100 of output translates into more output in a low price country than in a high price country)

Some of these deficiencies are partly corrected through the following :

☑ **The Human Development Index (HDI)** , which measures standard s of living in three dimensions: per capita income, health and educational attainment (see p 80)
☑ The use of **purchasing power parity (PPP) exchange rates**, which correct for differing price levels in different countries (see p 79)
☑ The use of **green GDP** measures, which take into account environmental destruction (see below)

The meaning and significance of green GDP

Green GDP is a measure of GDP that takes into account environmental destruction arising from production and consumption activities . Since GDP does not consider environmental destruction, **green GDP < GDP** . In general,

green GDP = GDP – value of environmental destruction

Green GDP is significant because (i) it corrects the serious deficiency of conventionally measured GDP which neglects the val ue of environmental destruction **resulting from production methods that destroy natural resources and have major negative (environme ntal) externalities**, and (ii) raises awareness of policy makers and the public of the importance of **clean technologies** that minimize environmental damage and may even increase the quantity and quality of natural resources (natural capital).

The business cycle

business cycle = short-term fluctuations (increases and decreases) in real GDP over time, consisting of four phases: **peak**, **contraction**, **trough**, and **expansion**	potential output = the level of real GDP produced when the economy is on its long-term growth trend, where cyclical unemployment = 0 and unemployment = the natural rate (NRU); also known as **full employment output**

Whereas real GDP in most economies typically tends to increase over long periods of time, it fluctuates a lot over short periods. A distinction can therefore be made between:

short-term fluctuations, involving a cyclical pattern of increases and decreases in real GDP, shown by the **green** line in the figure	long-term growth trend (= potential output) which irons out the cyclical fluctuations, shown by the **brown** line in the figure

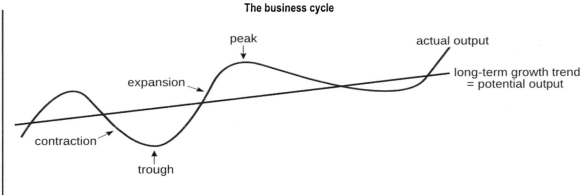

The business cycle

Short-term fluctuations, shown in the business cycle diagram above, typically consist of four phases:				
peak	**contraction**		**trough**	**expansion**
a temporary maximum of real GDP	real GDP ⇓ (negative growth), unemployment ⇑ (cyclical; see p 48), rate of inflation ⇓ (disinflation or even deflation; see p 50); if the contraction lasts two or more quarters it is known as **recession**		a temporary minimum of real GDP	real GDP ⇑, unemployment (cyclical) ⇓, rate of inflation ⇑

The **long-term growth trend** (in the diagram above) is the level of real GDP known as **potential output** or **full employment output** (p 44).

The business cycle and policy	✔ **Demand-side policies** (fiscal and monetary, see p 58-59) aim primarily at reducing the short-term fluctuations of the business cycle. Contractionary policies try to weaken the expansion (inflation) and expansionary policies try to reduce the size of the contraction (cyclical unemployment).
	✔ **Supply-side policies** (see p 61) aim at increasing the slope (steepness) of the long-term growth trend, by increasing the rate of economic growth, and hence the level of potential output.

Distinguishing between a decrease in GDP and a decrease in GDP growth

Decrease in GDP = GDP falls, for ex, from $1.5 billion in one year to $1.3 billion in the next year (= **negative growth**).	**Decrease in GDP growth** = the rate of growth of GDP falls, for ex, from 3% in one year to 2.7 % in the next; note there is positive growth in both years, meaning that in both years GDP increases, but in the second year it increases at a lower rate.

HL topics on calculating measures of economic activity

The following figures are taken from Merryland's national income accounts.

	2005 ($ billion)
Imports	3.50
Income from abroad	2.53
Government spending	7.75
Exports	2.87
Investment spending	7.95
Income sent abroad	3.72
Consumption spending	20.81
Net income from abroad	-1.19
Price deflator (GDP deflator) (2000=100)	107.25

Calculations based on the information in Merryland's national income accounts:

Calculating nominal GDP using the expenditure approach:
Nominal GDP = C + I + G + X – M = 20.81 + 7.95 + 7.75 + 2.87 – 3.50 = **$35.88 billion**

Calculating GNI:
GNI = GDP (nominal) + income from abroad – income sent abroad
= 35.88 + 2.53 – 3.72 = **$34.69 billion**
Alternatively:
GNI = GDP (nominal) + net income from abroad = 35.88 + (- 1.19) = **$34.69 billion**

Calculating real GDP using a price deflator:
✔ The last item in the table tells us that the year 2000 is the **base year** (2000=100)
✔ A **price deflator** is any **price index** used to convert nominal into real values
See p 50 for more examples of prices indexes (indices).
✔ The **GDP deflator** is a type of **price deflator** used to calculate real GDP:

$$\text{real GDP} = \frac{\text{nominal GDP}}{\text{price deflator}} \times 100 = \frac{35.88}{107.25} \times 100 = \$33.45 \text{ billion}$$

✔ The same method can be used to convert **nominal income** into **real income** using a price deflator.

2.2 AGGREGATE DEMAND AND AGGREGATE SUPPLY

Aggregate demand (AD)

The difference between micro demand and macro aggregate demand

Micro demand (D) = the quantity of a single product that consumers are willing and able to buy at different **prices**, over a specific time period, ceteris paribus. The negative relationship between price and quantity is due to diminishing marginal benefits (see p 3).	**Macro aggregate demand (AD)** = the amount of real output (goods and services) that **all buyers** in an economy (consumers, firms, government and foreigners) want to buy at different possible **price levels**, in a year, ceteris paribus. The AD curve has a negative slope (s downward sloping), indicating a negative relationship between the price level and real output, or GDP (equal to real income). This is due to very different factors than micro demand (D); these factors are explained below.

The AD curve has a negative slope (there is a negative relationship between the price level and real GDP) because of three factors:

wealth effect (wealth = value of all assets owned, including property, savings, stocks, bonds, etc); If the price level increases ⇒ real value of wealth ⇓ ⇒ people feel poorer ⇒ spending on output ⇓ ⇒ there is an upward movement along the AD curve, from a to b on AD₁ **interest rate effect** If the price level increases ⇒ consumers and firms need more money for their transactions ⇒ demand for money ⇑ ⇒ interest rate ⇑ ⇒ cost of borrowing ⇑ ⇒ consumer and firm spending ⇓ due to lower borrowing ⇒ there is an upward movement along the AD curve, from a to b on AD₁ **international trade effect** If the price level increases ⇒ exports become more expensive to foreigners ⇒ quantity of exports (X) demanded by foreigners ⇓. Also imports (M) become relatively cheaper to domestic residents ⇒ quantity of imports ⇑ ⇒ (X - M) ⇓ ⇒ there is an upward movement along the AD curve, from a to b on AD₁ ✔ In the event that the price level decreases, the opposite of the above processes will occur and there will be a downward movement along the AD curve, from b to a on AD₁	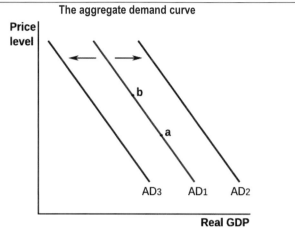 **The aggregate demand curve** An increase in AD causes a shift to the right, from AD₁ to AD₂. A decrease in AD causes a shift to the left, from AD₁ to AD₃.

Determinants of AD (causes of AD shifts)

AD has four components: **consumption spending, investment (firm) spending, government spending, net export spending (value of exports minus value of imports)**. The determinants of AD, which can cause shifts in the AD curve, are grouped under each of the four components.

AD increases, shifting to the right, when

Consumption spending increases. This happens when:	Investment spending increases. This happens when:
• **consumer confidence improves** ⇒ consumers become more optimistic about the future of the economy • **interest rates fall** ⇒ cost of borrowing falls ⇒ consumer borrowing increases (expansionary monetary policy, see p 60) • **wealth increases** (ex stock market or house prices rise) ⇒ consumers feel wealthier • **personal income taxes fall** ⇒ disposable income increases (expansionary fiscal policy, p 58; or market-based supply-side policy, p 62) • **household indebtedness (debt) decreases** ⇒ consumers feel more comfortable about their spending	• **business confidence improves** ⇒ firms become more optimistic about the future of the economy • **interest rates fall** ⇒ cost of borrowing falls ⇒ firm borrowing increases (expansionary monetary policy, see p 60) • **technological improvements occur** ⇒ investment spending increases • **business taxes fall** ⇒ after-tax profits increase (expansionary fiscal policy, p 58; or market-based supply-side policy, p 62) • **corporate indebtedness (debt) decreases** ⇒ firms feel more comfortable about investment spending
Government spending increases. This happens when:	Net export spending (X-M) increases. This happens when:
• **political priorities** of the government change ⇒ spending on various activities increases (ex education, health care, infrastructure, defense, etc) • **economic priorities** of the government change ⇒ the government increases its spending on various activities (expansionary fiscal policy, p 58; or interventionist supply-side policy, p 61)	• **income of trading partners abroad increases** ⇒ demand for a country's exports increases • **a country's exchange rate falls** (depreciation, see p 67) ⇒ exports become cheaper to foreigners and imports become more expensive to domestic residents ⇒ exports increase and imports decrease ⇒ net exports (= X - M) increase • **trade protection abroad decreases** (= fewer restrictions on imports in other countries, see p 64) ⇒ a country's exports increase • **domestic trade protection increases** (= more restrictions on imports from other countries) ⇒ imports fall ⇒ net exports (= X - M) increase

AD decreases, shifting to the left, when

Consumption spending decreases. This happens when:	Investment spending decreases. This happens when:
• **consumer confidence worsens** $\Rightarrow$ consumers become more pessimistic about the future of the economy • **interest rates increase** $\Rightarrow$ cost of borrowing increases $\Rightarrow$ consumer borrowing decreases (contractionary monetary policy, see p 60) • **wealth decreases** (ex stock market or house prices fall) $\Rightarrow$ consumers feel poorer • **personal income taxes increase** $\Rightarrow$ disposable income falls (contractionary fiscal policy, see p 58) • **household indebtedness (debt) increases** $\Rightarrow$ consumers feel less comfortable about spending	• **business confidence worsens** $\Rightarrow$ firms become more pessimistic about the future of the economy • **interest rates increase** $\Rightarrow$ cost of borrowing increases $\Rightarrow$ firm borrowing decreases (contractionary monetary policy, see p 60) • **technology worsens** $\Rightarrow$ investment spending falls (may occur infrequently, perhaps in time of war) • **business taxes increase** $\Rightarrow$ after-tax profits decrease (contractionary fiscal policy, see p 58) • **corporate indebtedness (debt) increases** $\Rightarrow$ firms feel less comfortable about investment spending
Government spending decreases. This happens when:	**Net export spending (X-M) decreases. This happens when:**
• **political priorities** of the government change $\Rightarrow$ spending on various activities decreases (ex education, health care, infrastructure, defense, etc.) • **economic priorities** of the government change $\Rightarrow$ the government decreases its spending on various activities (contractionary fiscal policy, see p 58)	• **income of trading partners abroad decreases** $\Rightarrow$ demand for a country's exports falls • **a country's exchange rate rises** (appreciation, see p 67) $\Rightarrow$ its exports become more expensive to foreigners and imports become cheaper to domestic residents $\Rightarrow$ exports decrease and imports increase $\Rightarrow$ net exports (= X - M) decrease • **trade protection abroad increases** (more restrictions on imports in other countries, see p 64) $\Rightarrow$ a country's exports fall • **domestic trade protection decreases** (= fewer restrictions on imports from other countries) $\Rightarrow$ imports rise $\Rightarrow$ net exports (= X - M) decrease

Aggregate supply (AS)

aggregate supply (AS) = the total amount of real output (goods and services) produced in an economy in a year at different price levels ✔ There are three kinds of AS curves: **short-run aggregate supply (SRAS), long-run aggregate supply (LRAS)** and **Keynesian AS**.	✔ **Short run** in macroeconomics = the period of time when all resource prices (wages and prices of all other factors of production) are constant. ✔ **Long run** in macroeconomics = the period of time when all resource prices (wages and prices of all other factors of production) change to match changes in the price level (resource prices and the price level increase or decrease together).

Short run aggregate supply (SRAS)

In the short run, the AS curve (SRAS) has an upward slope: there is a positive relationship between the price level and real GDP. This is due to **firm profitability**: If the price level increases (with wages and all other factor prices held constant) $\Rightarrow$ firms' profits increase $\Rightarrow$ firms increase the quantity of output they produce $\Rightarrow$ there is an upward movement along the SRAS curve. If the price level falls (with all factor prices constant) $\Rightarrow$ firms' profits fall $\Rightarrow$ firms decrease the quantity of output they produce $\Rightarrow$ there is a downward movement along the SRAS curve.	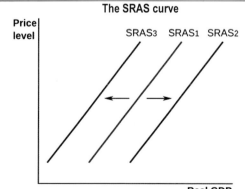 **An increase in SRAS causes a shift to the right: SRAS₁ $\Rightarrow$ SRAS₂** **A decrease in SRAS causes a shift to the left: SRAS₁ $\Rightarrow$ SRAS₃**

Changes in short-run aggregate supply (SRAS curve shifts)

Factors causing SRAS to increase, shifting it to the right:	Factors causing SRAS to decrease, shifting it to the left:
• **fall in resource prices** ex wages or the price of oil fall $\Rightarrow$ costs of production fall • **fall in business taxes** • **increase in subsidies** • **positive supply shock** ex exceptionally good weather $\Rightarrow$ agricultural output increases	• **increase in resource prices** ex wages or the price of oil rise $\Rightarrow$ costs of production increase • **increase in business taxes** • **decrease in subsidies** • **negative supply shock** ex a war $\Rightarrow$ output falls

Equilibrium in the short run and changes in short run equilibrium

In the **AD-AS model**, the intersection of AD and SRAS determine **short-run equilibrium** in the economy, which in turn indicates **equilibrium real output (real GDP)**, shown as Y* and the **equilibrium price level**, pl*.

✔ In macroeconomics, you must always refer to the **price level**, or **average price level**, or **general price level** (not "price").

✔ This equilibrium can change only **if there is a change (shift) in AD or SRAS**, caused by any of the determinants of AD or any of the factors that influence SRAS (see p 42 - 43).

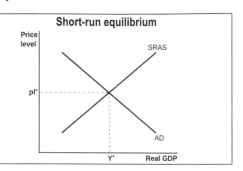

Short-run equilibrium

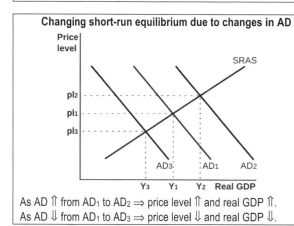

Changing short-run equilibrium due to changes in AD

As AD ⇑ from AD₁ to AD₂ ⇒ price level ⇑ and real GDP ⇑.
As AD ⇓ from AD₁ to AD₃ ⇒ price level ⇓ and real GDP ⇓.

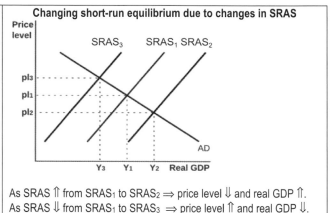

Changing short-run equilibrium due to changes in SRAS

As SRAS ⇑ from SRAS₁ to SRAS₂ ⇒ price level ⇓ and real GDP ⇑.
As SRAS ⇓ from SRAS₁ to SRAS₃ ⇒ price level ⇑ and real GDP ⇓.

Alternative AD-AS models 1: Monetarist/new classical model

This model is based on the assumption that when product and resource markets are free to work competitively according to demand and supply, product prices and resource prices will be flexible in the upward and downward directions, and the economy will be able to move into the **long run**, when resource prices change to match changes in the price level.

Long run aggregate supply (LRAS)

full employment output = **potential output** = output where cyclical unemployment is zero, and unemployment equals the natural rate, occurring when the economy is **at long run equilibrium**

In the long run, the AS curve (LRAS) is vertical at the level of potential output, Yp (= full employment output), because in the long run, resource prices change along with the price level, therefore in **real terms** resource prices remain constant. Thus, as the price level increases or decreases, **firm profitability is constant**, and firms face no incentive to change the quantity of output they produce.

✔ Therefore the quantity of output produced in the long run is independent of the price level.

The LRAS curve and long-run equilibrium

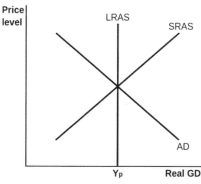

Long-run equilibrium in the monetarist/new classical model

✔ Long-run equilibrium occurs at the level of **potential output**, **Yp**, or full employment output, where **AD and SRAS intersect on the LRAS curve**.

Inflationary and deflationary (recessionary) gaps

An economy's **short-run equilibrium** may differ **from long-run equilibrium**. There are two possibilities: a deflationary gap or an inflationary gap.

| **Deflationary (= recessionary) gap:** short run equilibrium GDP (Ye) < potential GDP (Yp) | A **deflationary gap** occurs when short-run equilibrium GDP (Ye) is less than potential GDP (Yp) **due to insufficient aggregate demand. A deflationary gap can only persist in the short run. In the long run the economy will return to potential output** (= full employment output). To see why, consider the following: |

Suppose the economy is initially at point **x** at long-run equilibrium producing Yp. Due to **a decrease in AD** (AD₁ ⇒ AD₂) it moves to point **y** where the price level has fallen, real GDP is lower at Ye and there is a **deflationary gap**. The economy can remain at **y** only in the short run. In the long run wages and other resource prices will fall to match the fall in the price level ⇒ SRAS increases, i.e. shifts right from SRAS₁ to SRAS₂ where the economy is at point **z**, back at long-run equilibrium again.

✔ In the long run, the only effect of a fall in AD is to cause a fall in the price level, with no effect on real GDP.

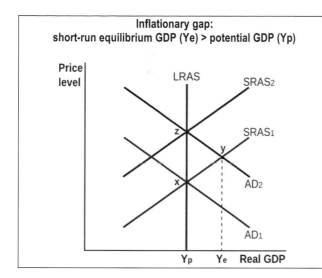

| Inflationary gap:
short-run equilibrium GDP (Ye) > potential GDP (Yp) | An **inflationary gap** occurs when short-run equilibrium GDP (Ye) is greater than potential GDP (Yp) due **to excess aggregate demand. An inflationary gap can only persist in the short run. In the long run the economy will return to potential output** (= full employment output). To see why, consider the following: |

Suppose the economy is initially at point **x** at long-run equilibrium producing output Yp. Due to **an increase in AD** (AD$_1$ $\Rightarrow$ AD$_2$) it moves to point **y** where the price level is higher, real GDP is greater at Ye and there is an **inflationary gap**. The economy can remain at **y** only in the short run. In the long run wages and other resource prices rise to match the increase in the price level $\Rightarrow$ SRAS decreases, i.e. shifts left from SRAS$_1$ to SRAS$_2$, and the economy is at point **z** at long run equilibrium once again.

✔ **In the long run, the only effect of an increase in AD is to cause an increase in the price level, with no effect on real GDP.**

✔ In the monetarist/new-classical model, **fluctuations of output occur only in the short run. In the long run, the economy automatically returns to long-run equilibrium and full employment (potential) output** because of the assumption of full wage-price flexibility. Therefore, long-run equilibrium always occurs at full employment output.

Changes in long-run equilibrium

In the monetarist/new classical model, long-run equilibrium can change:

| **with a constant LRAS and potential output**, leading to changes only in the price level (as shown also above). | **with a changing LRAS**, leading to increasing potential output (economic growth) or decreasing potential output (negative growth) (see p 54 on causes of growth). |

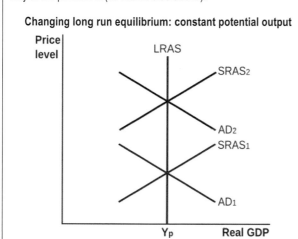

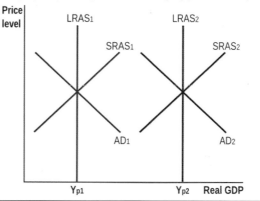

Alternative AD-AS models 2: Keynesian model

This model is based on the assumption that **there is no long run**, because wages (and other resource prices) as well as the price level **do not fall easily**.

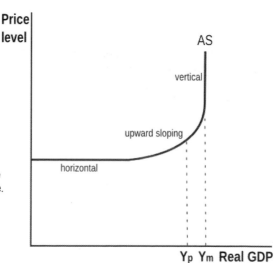

Keynesian AS curve

The three sections of the Keynesian AS curve

(i) The horizontal section occurs because of two factors:
a. wage-price downward inflexibility Wages do not fall easily (they are inflexible downward) because of wage contracts, minimum wages, and unpopularity of wage cuts. The price level also does not fall easily (it is also inflexible downward) because if wages do not fall, a drop in product prices would cut into firms' profits, which firms wish to avoid.
b. spare capacity when the economy is in recession At low levels of output, when the economy is in recession, there is unemployment of labor and other resources, so if firms decide to increase output and demand more resources, there is no upward pressure on wages and the price level, therefore they do not increase.

(ii) The upward sloping section occurs because of r**esource bottlenecks (shortages)** that appear as output increases and approaches full employment or potential output (Yp), causing resource prices to increase. As firms' costs of production rise, firms raise product prices so the price level begins to rise.

(iii) The vertical section occurs because **maximum capacity output** (Ym) is reached, meaning that all resources are employed to their maximum extent, and it is therefore not possible for output to increase further. Any effort to increase output beyond this point results only in increases in the price level.

Equilibrium in the Keynesian model

Equilibrium in this model is given by the intersection of the AD and Keynesian AS curves. There are three possible equilibrium positions.

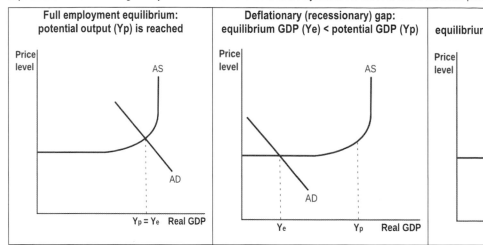

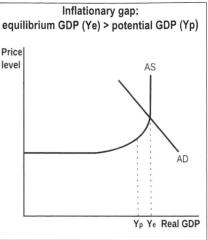

| Full employment equilibrium: potential output (Yp) is reached | Deflationary (recessionary) gap: equilibrium GDP (Ye) < potential GDP (Yp) | Inflationary gap: equilibrium GDP (Ye) > potential GDP (Yp) |

Key conclusions arising from the Keynesian model

✔ Since resource prices and product prices are inflexible downward, the economy cannot move into the long run. This means that **the economy can remain indefinitely stuck in a deflationary (recessionary) gap, caused by insufficient aggregate demand**, and therefore requires expansionary demand-side policies (fiscal and/or monetary) to come out of the recession.	✔ Whereas in the monetarist/new classical model expansionary policies are always inflationary (leading to a higher price level due to the upward sloping SRAS curve and the vertical LRAS curve), in the Keynesian model **expansionary policies do not lead to any increase in the price level when the economy is in recession** (the horizontal part of the curve). Increases in AD become inflationary only as the economy approaches full employment output.

Shifts in aggregate supply over the long term and economic growth

Over the **long term** (a long period of time) the LRAS and the Keynesian AS curves can shift, indicating that **potential output, Yp, changes. Usually these shifts are to the right, indicating** economic growth (= growth in real GDP; see p 54). Factors shifting the curves include:

• **increases in quantity of factors of production**, ex an increase the amounts of capital goods or the amount of labor	• **reductions in the natural rate of unemployment**, ex a fall structural unemployment is similar to an increase in labor quantity
• **improvements in quality of factors of production**, ex an improvement in labor quality due to more education and skills	• **improvements in efficiency**, meaning better use of scarce resources and lower costs of production
• **technological changes** which could involve improvements in the quality of capital goods (such as information technology)	• **institutional changes**, ex reduction in bureaucracy, or reduction in government regulation of the private sector, or encouragement of increased competition, which may increase efficiency (lower costs of production), allowing firms' output to increase.

✔ In the event that the opposite of the above occur, the **AS curves shift to the left, indicating** negative economic growth.

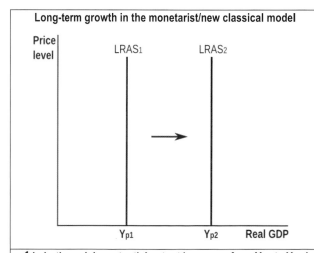

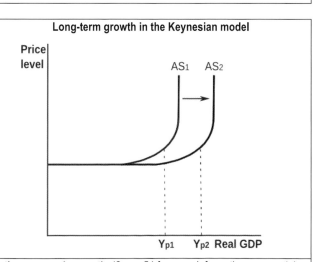

| Long-term growth in the monetarist/new classical model | Long-term growth in the Keynesian model |

✔ In both models, potential output increases from Yp1 to Yp2 indicating economic growth. (See p 54 for more information on growth.)

HL topic The Keynesian multiplier

Keynesian multiplier = a multiplied effect on AD, and hence on real GDP (= real income), due to a change in spending

$$\text{multiplier} = \frac{\text{change in real GDP}}{\text{initial change in spending}} \qquad \Rightarrow \qquad \text{change in real GDP = multiplier x initial change in spending}$$

marginal propensity to consume (MPC) = $\Delta C/\Delta Y$ = fraction of additional income used to consume (buy) domestic products

marginal propensity to save (MPS) = $\Delta S/\Delta Y$ = fraction of additional income (Y) that goes toward saving (S)
marginal propensity to tax (MPT) = $\Delta T/\Delta Y$ = fraction of additional income (Y) paid as taxes (T)
marginal propensity to import (MPM) = $\Delta M/\Delta Y$ = fraction of additional income (Y) spent on imports (M)

> MPS+MPT+MPM determine the size of leakages from the spending flow (see circular flow model, p 39)

✔ MPC + MPS + MPT + MPM = 1   ⇒   1 – MPC = MPS + MPT + MPM

Understanding the multiplier

Because **spending of one individual is the income of another**, any change in spending leads to a chain reaction of income changes and further spending changes, so that the final change in income (= GDP) is greater than the initial change in spending. Ex The government increases spending on school supplies by $100 ⇒ the sellers of school supplies receiving the $100 of **income** spend this depending on their marginal propensities: assuming MPC = 0.75 (and MPS + MPT + MPM = 0.25), 75% of $100 = $75 is spent on **consumption** of goods and services, and the remaining 25% of $100 = $25 leaks out of the spending flow, going toward saving, taxes and buying imports ⇒ the sellers of $75 of goods and services spend this **income** according to the same marginal propensities: since the MPC = 0.75, 75% of $75 = $56.25 is spent on **consumption** of goods and services, and the remaining 25% of $75 = $18.75 goes toward saving, taxes and buying imports ⇒ the same process continues ad infinitum until additional income created reaches zero. The chain reaction of consumption spending that began from an initial change in government spending results in an increase in income (= GDP) **greater than the initial change in spending**.

$$\text{multiplier} = \frac{1}{1-\text{MPC}} \qquad \text{Since 1 – MPC = MPS + MPT + MPM} \qquad \Rightarrow \qquad \text{multiplier} = \frac{1}{\text{MPS}+\text{MPT}+\text{MPM}}$$

✔   The smaller the total of leakages, the bigger the MPC, and the larger the multiplier.

✔   The multiplier works in exactly the same way for **decreases in spending** ⇒ **multiplied decrease in AD and real GDP**.

The multiplier in relation to injections and leakages in the circular flow of income model

Injections into the spending flow initiate a change in spending:

investment spending
government spending
foreigners' spending on exports

income flows through the economy

Leakages from the spending flow affect the MPC and the multiplier ⇒ final change in real GDP > initial change in spending:

saving
taxes
domestic spending on imports

Importance of the multiplier

Since any increase or decrease in spending has a multiplied effect on real GDP, it is important for policy-makers to know the size of the multiplier. Ex The "troika" of lenders to Greece (the IMF, European Central Bank and European Commission) underestimated the size of the multiplier in Greece, with the result that when austerity measures were imposed (decreases in government spending and increases in taxes), the resulting decrease in Greece's real GDP was much greater than expected, leading to a recession that was much more serious than anticipated.

Calculating the effects of injections on real GDP using the multiplier

In Merryland, the MPC = 0.8, and real GDP = $33.45 billion. If investment spending **falls** by $0.75 billion, **calculate the change in real GDP and the final value of real GDP**.

MPC=0.8, therefore multiplier = 1/(1 - 0.8) =5. Fall in real GDP= 5 x 0.75 = **$3.75 billion**. Final value of real GDP= 33.45–3.75=**$29.70 billion**. The **same problem** could be expressed in terms of the MPS + MPT + MPM = 0.2 ⇒ multiplier = 1 / 0.2 = **5**. The rest of the solution is same as above.

The impact of the multiplier using a Keynesian AD-AS diagram

If investment spending increases by $10 billion, and the MPC= 0.75, so that the multiplier is 4, AD will increase by **$40 billion** (= 10 x 4) at every price level.

✔ **The $40 billion increase = an initial increase in AD of $10 billion (equal to the increase in investment spending) plus an additional $30 billion due to the multiplier, so that $10 + $30 = $40 billion**.

✔ The final increase in real GDP depends on **where on the Keynesian AS curve AD shifts**. If AD increases in the horizontal part, the change in real GDP will be the same as the change in AD = $40 billion. But if AD increases in the upward sloping or vertical part of the AS curve, the increase in real GDP will be smaller than the increase in AD.

✔ The full multiplier effect is felt on real GDP only in the horizontal part of the AS curve, where the price level is constant.

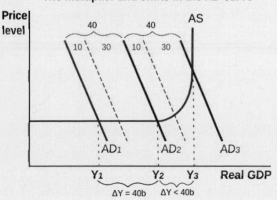
The multiplier and shifts in the AD curve

2.3 MACROECONOMIC OBJECTIVES

2.3.1 MACROECONOMIC OBJECTIVES 1: LOW UNEMPLOYMENT

unemployment = the number of people in the labor force who are actively looking for work but do not have a job
unemployment rate = the number of unemployed people expressed as a percentage of the labor force

$$\text{unemployment rate} = \frac{\text{number of unemployed people}}{\text{labor force}} \times 100$$

The **labor force** consists of the number of people who are employed plus the number who are unemployed.
underemployment = people who are employed, but who (i) work part-time when they would rather work full-time, or (ii) work at a different skill or lower skill level than what they were trained for (ex an engineer working as a waiter)
hidden unemployment = people without a job who are not included in official unemployment figures because they are not actively seeking a job, as well as people who are underemployed yet counted as fully employed in official unemployment figures

Difficulties in measuring unemployment
The unemployment rate is usually an **inaccurate estimate** of "true" unemployment because:

• it does not include **discouraged workers**, or people who would like to work but gave up looking because they became too discouraged (part of hidden unemployment) • it counts all underemployed workers as fully employed workers, even if they are working part-time or they are doing a job that does not utilize their skills (also part of hidden unemployment)	• it does not include people working in the underground (unregistered) economy • it measures unemployment as an average over a country's whole population, whereas the unemployment rate can be very different for different population groups, according to different regions in a country, different ethnic groups, different age groups, and gender

Consequences of unemployment

Economic consequences	Personal and social consequences
☒ **loss of real output** (real GDP) since fewer people are working to produce output (use PPC diagram to illustrate, see p 2, 54) ☒ **loss of government tax revenue** due to loss of income taxes, since the unemployed have no income from work ☒ **higher cost of unemployment benefits** that the government must pay to the unemployed ☒ **loss of income** of the unemployed workers ☒ **increased inequality in the distribution of income and more poverty**, since the unemployed suffer a loss of income	☒ **increased crime rates** ☒ **increased stress levels** leading to poorer health ☒ **increased indebtedness** as people borrow more to make ends meet ☒ **increased homelessness** as increasing poverty could force indebted consumers into bankruptcy and loss of their homes ☒ **more family breakdown** due to the strain of increasing poverty and inability to make ends meet

Overview of types and causes of unemployment

Cyclical unemployment occurring in deflationary gaps, due to insufficient AD	Natural unemployment occurring when the economy produces potential output (= full employment output) at long-run equilibrium, when cyclical unemployment = 0

is equal to
frictional unemployment + structural unemployment + seasonal unemployment

↓
arising from

changes in   changes in   labor market
demand for labor   geographical location   rigidities
skills   of industries

Types and causes of unemployment

Cyclical unemployment (= demand-deficient unemployment), caused by falling AD in the downward (contraction) phase of the business cycle (deflationary gap) is a serious type of unemployment, lasting as long as the economy is in recession (or longer). AD falls ⇒ real output falls from the full employment level (Yfe) ⇒ demand for labor falls ⇒ cyclical unemployment results.

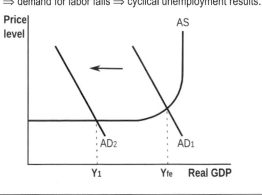

Evaluating policies to deal with unemployment

Need expansionary demand-side policies to shift AD to the right and eliminate the deflationary gap ⇒ real GDP increases to the level of potential output (full employment output) (see p 59, 60 for evaluation of expansionary fiscal and monetary policies).

Expansionary fiscal policy (G⇑, T⇓)
☑ can pull the economy out of a deep recession
☑ G ⇑ impacts directly on the economy
☒ time delays
☒ possible political interference
☒ crowding out

Expansionary monetary policy (interest rate ⇓ ⇒ C⇑, I⇑)
☑ quicker to implement
☑ no political interference
☑ no crowding out
☒ ineffective in deep recession as (i) interest rates cannot fall below 0%; (ii) banks may be unwilling to lend; firms and consumers may be unwilling to borrow

Frictional unemployment is **short-term**, and affects workers who are in between jobs, such as when a worker is fired, or voluntarily leaves a job in search of a better one.	**Need interventionist supply-side measures** (see p 61) to provide information between job seekers and employers through the creation of job centers and employment agencies ☑ reduces the time workers spend unemployed ☒ opportunity costs of government spending ☒ negative effects on the government budget
Seasonal unemployment is also **short-term**, affecting workers with jobs that change according to seasons. Ex workers in the tourist industry lose their job during some winter months.	**Need interventionist supply-side measures** (see p 61) as with frictional unemployment. Information should be provided on job availability during various seasons throughout the year ☑ ☒ Same as frictional unemployment
Structural unemployment has **three main causes** and is serious as it is **long-term**:	
1. Changes in the demand for particular labor skills due to: • **technological change** For example, computer technology led to a drop in the demand for typists, who became structurally unemployed, while increasing the demand for computer specialists. • **changes in the structure of the economy**, involving growth of some industries and decline of others. For example, agriculture in many countries is declining in importance over time, and agricultural workers become structurally unemployed, while other industries (in manufacturing or services) gain in importance. This can be shown in an S and D diagram for the product produced by the declining industry. As D falls, Q supplied falls and workers no longer needed by the declining industry lose jobs. 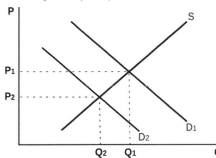	**Need interventionist supply-side measures** (see p 61) consisting of: • training programs for workers seeking new skills • grants and low interest loans to young workers seeking training and re-training • grants to firms that offer on-the-job training • government hiring and training of workers • provision of subsidies to workers to help them relocate • provision of subsidies or tax incentives to firms to encourage them to move to high unemployment regions ☑ effective in reducing unemployment ☒ opportunity costs of government spending ☒ negative effects on the government budget **Market-based supply-side measures** (see p 61) would include: • reducing minimum wages in depressed regions so firms can be attracted by low wage costs • lowering unemployment benefits to make low-paying jobs more attractive to unemployed workers • reducing labor protection in order to make hiring easier (due to lower costs of firing), ex lower compensation payments ☑ might reduce unemployment ☒ increase worker insecurity ☒ lead to more unequal income distribution ☒ lead to greater poverty as workers lose protection ☒ may not always be effective in reducing unemployment
2. Changes in the geographical location of industries and therefore jobs Firms and often entire industries sometimes relocate to other regions in a country or other countries, often in search of lower labor costs or other favorable conditions (such as lower taxes). The workers who are left behind become structurally unemployed.	**Need interventionist supply-side measures** (see p 61) ex subsidies to families to help them relocate to low-unemployment regions, subsidies to firms to induce them move to economically depressed regions ☑ effective in reducing unemployment ☒ opportunity costs of government spending ☒ negative effects on the government budget.
3. Labor market rigidities are factors that do not allow the labor market to work freely according to demand and supply, thus resulting in unemployment (as well as higher labor costs for firms); they include: • **strong labor unions**, which negotiate higher than equilibrium wages, leading to unemployment • **high unemployment benefits**, which may reduce workers' incentive to work • **labor protection laws**, which make it difficult and costly for firms to fire workers, due to long notice periods and high compensation. This makes firms more reluctant to hire new workers, thus causing unemployment • **minimum wage legislation**, leading to an excess supply of labor and hence unemployment (see diagram p 18)	**Need market-based supply-side policies** consisting of **labor market reforms** (see p 62), such as: • reducing the power of labor unions • reducing unemployment benefits • reducing labor protection • reducing or eliminating the minimum wage The above labor market reforms: ☑ may lower unemployment without any negative effect on the government budget ☒ increase worker insecurity ☒ lead to more unequal income distribution ☒ lead to greater poverty as workers lose protection

✔ **Market-based supply-side policies** cannot deal with cyclical unemployment, which is due to insufficient AD. However **interventionist supply-side policies** can help reduce cyclical unemployment because they have demand-side effects leading to increases in AD (p 61).	✔ **Demand-side policies** cannot generally deal with natural unemployment (frictional/seasonal/structural). An important exception is **expansionary fiscal policy involving government spending on targeted sectors** (new technology development, infrastructure, education, health care) which are the same as certain interventionist supply-side policies and can help reduce structural unemployment (p 61).

2.3.2 MACROECONIC OBJECTIVES 2: LOW AND STABLE RATE OF INFLATION

inflation = a sustained increase in the general price level	**deflation** = a sustained decrease in the general price level
disinflation = a fall in the rate of inflation (for example, 7% in 2010 followed by 5% in 2011)	

How inflation and deflation are measured

consumer price index (CPI) = a measure of the cost of living of the typical household and how this changes over time; the CPI compares the cost of buying a **fixed basket of goods and services** from one year to the next. By calculating the value of the same basket from year to year, the CPI offers an estimate of how prices change on average from year to year.

Why the CPI is inaccurate as a measure of inflation and deflation

The CPI is based on a fixed basket of goods and services valued at specific prices, therefore

☒ different income groups consume different combinations of goods and services than those included in the basket ☒ consumers change their consumption patterns over time, depending on changes in relative prices, changes in tastes and preferences, and the introduction of new products	☒ the quality of products may improve over time, but the CPI cannot account for this ☒ there may be regional variations in prices, which the CPI cannot account for ☒ consumers make increasing use of discount stores and sales, which the CPI cannot account for

✔The basket of goods and services is revised periodically (roughly every ten years), but even so it is not possible to fully resolve these problems.

Other ways to measure price level changes

The core (underlying) rate of inflation Some product groups, particularly food and energy (oil) have prices that are highly volatile (fluctuate a lot over short periods), and may be misleading about the inflation trend when included in the CPI. In order to get a more accurate picture of where inflation is headed, economists compute the **core** or **underlying rate of inflation**, which excludes these product groups.	**The producer price index** The **producer price index** (PPI) measures changes in the average prices of factors of production, and therefore measures price level changes from the perspective of producers rather than consumers. Since the PPI measures price level changes at early stages in production, it is useful in predicting changes in future inflation (measured by the CPI).

The GDP deflator (HL topic; see p 41) The GDP deflator is another type of price index that is used to convert nominal GDP into real GDP. It is a measure of the average level of prices of all goods produced in an economy (i.e. all goods included in GDP). ✔ The GDP deflator and CPI differ from each other in that • the GDP deflator consists of prices of all goods and services produced domestically, including some that are not purchased by domestic consumers, namely all capital goods, goods purchased by the government, and exports • the CPI excludes prices of goods and services not purchased by consumers, but includes prices of imported consumer goods. ✔ The GDP deflator and CPI have different uses • The GDP deflator is used to convert nominal GDP into real GDP • The CPI is used to calculate changes in the cost of living of consumers.

Consequences of a high inflation rate

A low and stable rate of inflation **is not a problem for the economy**, because economic activities can be carried out smoothly and the possible negative effects of inflation are very limited. However a high rate of inflation leads to **several problems**:

☒ **Redistribution effects** of inflation result in losers and winners: • **Losses** occur for holders of cash, for savers, for lenders, and for people receiving fixed incomes or wages, because the real value (purchasing power) of their money falls. • **Gains** occur for borrowers, and for payers of fixed incomes or wages, because the real value (purchasing power) of their payments falls • Some of the losses and gains may be avoided through (a) payment of interest to savers and lenders that is at least as high as the rate of inflation, or (b) increases in incomes or wages that are at least as high as the rate of inflation. ☒ There may result **increased inequality in income distribution**, as the wealthy who are in a better position to purchase assets with rising prices (ex real estate, gold) gain relative to lower income groups who are less able to make such purchases. ☒ High inflation leads to **efficiency losses**; the price mechanism is unable to fulfill its signaling and incentive functions effectively because prices rise rapidly and the price increases are not in the same proportion for all goods and services.	☒ **Uncertainty** The inability to predict future prices and price level changes causes uncertainty among firms which cannot accurately predict future revenues and costs of production, and may therefore have a negative effect on investment, and therefore economic growth. ☒ **Less saving** Since savers face a loss on their savings (if they do not receive a high enough rate of interest), the incentive to save is reduced. ☒ **Menu costs** High rates of inflation mean that firms must continuously print or publish new menus, catalogues, price lists, price labels, and price advertizments, which increase their costs of production. ☒ **Damage to export competitiveness** High inflation means that a country's exports become more expensive to foreigners, and therefore are likely to fall, while imports become more attractive as they are cheaper relative to domestic goods. As net exports (X-M) fall, AD decreases, putting a downward pressure on real GDP. In addition, a trade deficit may be created (or increase), putting a downward pressure on the value of the currency (see p 72).

Types and causes of inflation

There are two main types and causes of inflation: **demand-pull inflation** and **cost-push inflation**.

Demand-pull inflation is caused by an increase in AD, hence a rightward shift in the AD curve from AD₁ to AD₂. This may result from a change in any of the components of AD, which are C, I, G, and X-M (see p 42 - 43).	**Cost-push inflation** is caused by a decrease in SRAS, hence a leftward shift in the SRAS curve from SRAS₁ to SRAS₂, resulting from increases in costs of production or supply shocks (see p 43).
✔ In the monetarist/new classical model, an increase in AD always results in an **increase in the price level, as well as in real GDP.**	
(Note: In this model **in the long run**, an increase in AD causes an increase only in the price level, as real GDP remains constant at potential output; see p 45.)	✔ **Cost-push inflation is usually more serious than demand-pull inflation**, because it leads to a fall in real GDP at the same time that the price level is increasing. This is also known as **stagflation** (= stagnation + inflation).
✔ **In the Keynesian model, as long as the economy is in recession (on the horizontal part of the AS curve) an increase in AD causes an increase in real GDP with no increase in the price level.** The price level begins to increase only as the economy approaches full employment output (potential output), Yp. If AD continues to increase beyond Yp, the price level rises very rapidly while real GDP responds less and less as maximum capacity output (Y₃) is approached.	Notice that the Keynesian model is not appropriate to illustrate cost-push inflation.

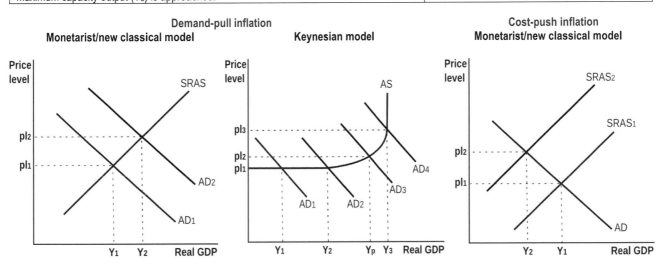

✔ While the two types of inflation are theoretically distinct, in practice it may be difficult to distinguish which is which.

Evaluating policies to deal with inflation

Demand-pull inflation	Cost-push inflation
Need **contractionary demand-side policies** to shift AD to the left: **Contractionary fiscal policy: G ⇓, T⇑** (see p 58-59) ☑ can be effective in addressing high and rising inflation ☑ G ⇓ impacts directly on the economy, since G is a component of AD (= C + I + G + X-M) ☒ time delays ☒ possible political interference, politically unpopular **Contractionary monetary policy: interest rate⇑ ⇒ C⇓, I⇓** (see p 60) ☑ quicker to implement ☑ no political interference ☒ higher interest rates may affect AD after long time lags	Cost-push inflation is far more difficult to address because there is no single or obvious policy that is appropriate. ☒ **Contractionary demand-side policies** are often used, however while they can lower inflation **they make the recession deeper.** ☑ **Supply-side policies** are more appropriate but face the disadvantage of **time lags.** The appropriate policy depends on the **cause** of increased costs. ✔ If cost-push is due to rising wages, policy should aim at **stopping the wage increases (labor market reforms**, see p 62) ✔ If cost-push is due to rising profits caused by excessive monopoly power, policies should try to **decrease the monopoly power of firms** (competition policies, see p 61). ✔ If cost-push is due to a depreciating currency (which causes import prices to rise for domestic buyers), policies should try to **reduce dependence on imports (trade protection**, see p 64). ✔ If cost-push is due to increasing oil prices, policies should try to **reduce oil dependence** (ex incentives to produce alternative energy sources).

Supply-side policies (see p 61-62) that increase LRAS from LRAS₁ to LRAS₂ (hence potential output from Yp₁ to Yp₂) can be used to deal with **both demand-pull and cost-push inflation.** Such policies:

☑ lower inflationary pressures: price level can fall both with a constant AD and with increasing AD (see diagrams)
☑ achieve economic growth
☒ need a long time to take effect
☒ have ambiguous effects on unemployment (see p 62)
☒ may increase income inequalities and poverty (see p 62)

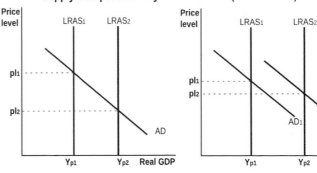

Supply-side policies may lower inflation (even if AD ⇑)

Consequences of deflation

Deflation occurs infrequently because of such factors as infrequently falling wages, thus making it difficult for firms to lower prices, oligopolistic firms' fear of price wars, and the general avoidance of firms to lower prices as this cuts into their profits.

When deflation occurs, it can have **serious consequences**:

☒ **Cyclical unemployment and a deflationary spiral** As the price level falls, consumers and firms avoid spending as they wait for prices to fall further. Therefore a deflationary spiral may set in: price level falls ⇒ spending is postponed ⇒ AD falls ⇒ price level falls further ⇒ spending is again postponed ⇒ AD falls further … This process results in a deepening recession and **high cyclical unemployment**.	Deflation causes the **real value of debt to increase**, resulting in: ☒ **Falling AD** as consumers and firms are less willing to borrow ☒ **Bankruptcies and banking/financial crisis** as borrowers are less able to repay their loans, therefore leading to more bankruptcies. If bankruptcies are widespread, banks suffer losses on their loans, increasing the risk of a banking or financial crisis. ☒ **Other consequences** Deflation gives rise to **redistribution effects** (though these are the exact opposite to those of inflation), as well as **uncertaint**y and **menu costs**; see p 50.

☑ In contrast to inflation, deflation results in an **improvement in export competitiveness**, since lower export prices mean that a country's exports become more attractive to foreigners ⇒ AD⇑ ⇒ real GDP⇑.

Types and causes of deflation

Deflation may be caused by a **fall in AD** ("bad" deflation because real GDP falls) or by **an increase in SRAS** ("good" deflation because real GDP increases). However, no deflation is ever really "good" because regardless of the cause, the risk of a deflationary spiral and banking crisis make it potentially dangerous.

Policies for deflation

Because of the dangers of deflation, economic policy aims at achieving a low and stable rate of inflation (about 2-3%) and not 0% inflation, as this is considered to be dangerously close to deflation. Deflation requires **expansionary demand-side policies** (fiscal and monetary).

HL topics on unemployment and inflation

Calculating the unemployment rate

In the 1st quarter of 2013, Greece's population was 10.77 million, of which 49% were in the labor force, and 1.45 million were looking for a job but unable to find one. **Calculate the unemployment rate.**

Step 1 Find the number of people in the labor force: 10.77 x 0.49 = **5.28 million**
Step 2 Calculate the unemployment rate = number of unemployed people/labor force x 100 = 1.45/5.28 x 100 = **27.46%**

Constructing a consumer price index

The people of Merryland consume three goods: pizzas, hotdogs and books. The second column below shows the quantities of each good consumed by the typical family each year (these are the "weights" of the goods in the basket). The next 4 columns show the price of each good in 2001, 2002, 2003 and 2004.

	Q	P in 2001	P in 2002	P in 2003	P in 2004		Value of basket in each year			
							2001	2002	2003	2004
pizzas	55	$10	$12	$11	$10		$550	$660	$605	$550
hotdogs	78	$3	$4	$5	$5		$234	$312	$390	$390
books	42	$15	$17	$18	$16		$630	$714	$756	$672
							$1414	$1686	$1751	$1612

(a) Find the value of the basket in each of the four years. For each year, multiply Q of each good by its P, and sum up:
    For 2001   55x10 + 78x3 + 42x15 = 550 + 234 + 630 = **$1414**.
The last four columns above show the results for all four years.

(b) Assuming the base year is 2001, construct a price index (PI) for the 4 years.

In general, PI for year X = $\dfrac{\text{value of basket in year X}}{\text{value of basket in base year}}$ x 100.   Therefore:

Year	2001	2002	2003	2004
CPI	100.00	119.24	123.83	114.00

Calculating the rate of inflation

Calculate Merryland's rate of inflation in 2002, 2003 and 2004

(a) using the value of the basket you calculated above:	**(b) using the CPI you constructed above:**
rate of inflation in 2002 = [(1686-1414)/1414] x 100 = **19.24 %** Using the same method: rate of inflation in 2003: **3.85 %** rate of inflation in 2004: **-7.94%**.	2002: [(119.24-100)/100] x 100 = **19.24 %*** 2003: [(123.83-119.24)/119.24] x 100 = **3.85 %** 2004: [(114.00-123.83)/123.83] x 100 = **-7.94%** * Note that this is simply equal to 119.24 -100.00; it is not necessary to perform the calculation when calculating the inflation rate relative to the base year.

✔ Notice that the results for (a) and (b) are identical.

Distinguishing between inflation, deflation and disinflation

✔ Notice that **inflation** occurred in 2002 and 2003, **disinflation** occurred in 2003, and **deflation** occurred in 2004.

Relationships between inflation and unemployment: The Phillips curve
Understanding the short-run Phillips curve (SRPC) through the short-run AD-AS model

The short-run Phillips curve (SRPC) shows an inverse relationship between inflation and unemployment, indicating a trade-off between the two: the higher the inflation rate, the lower the unemployment rate, and vice versa. Until the early 1970s, policy-makers used demand-side policies to bring the economy to a point on the SRPC where they wanted to be.

✔The SRPC presupposes a fixed SRAS curve, and so all movements along the SRPC care caused by changes in AD.

Demand-side policies and the short-run AD-AS model
Expansionary demand-side policies: AD ⇑ from AD_1 to AD_2 ⇒ real output ⇑ ⇒ **unemployment** ⇓, **price level** ⇑ ⇒ **movement up the SRPC** (ex from point **a** to point **b**).
Contractionary demand-side policies: AD ⇓ from AD_1 to AD_3 ⇒ real output ⇓ ⇒ **unemployment** ⇑, **price level** ⇓ ⇒ **movement down the SRPC** (ex from point **b** to point **a**).

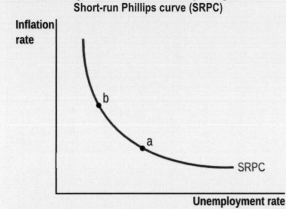

Short-run Phillips curve (SRPC)

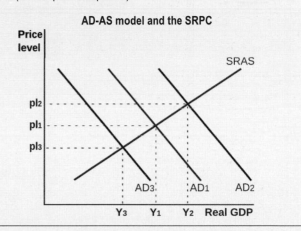

AD-AS model and the SRPC

Cost-push inflation (stagflation) and outward shifts of the SRPC

The oil price shocks of the early 1970s led **SRAS to decrease (shift left)**, causing **cost-push inflation** (see p 51), which came to be known as **stagflation** (= short for "stagnation" and "inflation", referring to recession and inflation that occur together). With cost-push inflation, **the price level increased and unemployment also increased** (as real GDP fell). **Higher inflation and higher unemployment appear as an outward-shifting SRPC (a ⇒ b).**

✔ When SRAS ⇓, the SRPC shifts outward and to the right. (Similarly, if SRAS ⇑, the SRPC shifts inward and to the left.)

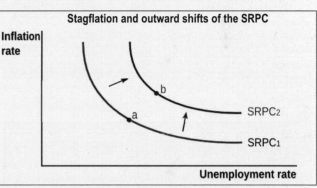

Stagflation and outward shifts of the SRPC

The long-run Phillips curve (LRPC)
In the late 1970s, Milton Friedman argued that in the long run (when wages and all other factor prices change to match changes in the price level) there is no trade-off between inflation and unemployment. **The long-run Phillips curve (LRPC) is vertical at the natural rate of unemployment (NRU), indicating that in the long run, the level of unemployment is independent of the price level and the rate of inflation.**

The vertical LRPC in terms of the long-run AD-AS model
In the diagrams below, the vertical LRPC at the NRU corresponds to the vertical LRAS curve at potential output (Yp), where unemployment = NRU.
Suppose the economy is in long-run equilibrium, at x on the LRPC and LRAS curves, and AD ⇑ from AD_1 to AD_2. **In the short run**, with wages (and other factor prices) fixed, there is an **inflationary** gap in the AD-AS model at point **y**, while the economy moves up $SRPC_1$ to point **y** where inflation ⇑ and unemployment ⇓ (unemployment < NRU). **In the long run**, wages ⇑ to meet the increase in the price level ⇒ $SRAS_1$ decreases to $SRAS_2$ moving the economy to point z ⇒ $SRPC_1$ shifts to $SRPC_2$ (as shown above with cost-push inflation) ⇒ the economy returns to LRPC and LRAS at point z.

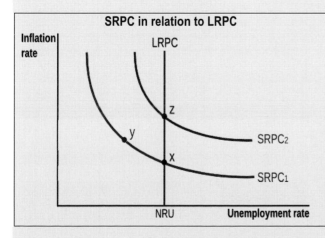

SRPC in relation to LRPC

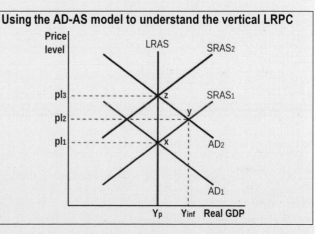

Using the AD-AS model to understand the vertical LRPC

✔ **In the long run, there is no trade-off between inflation and unemployment.** Therefore according to this model, the use of demand-side policies to lower unemployment to levels below the NRU will only cause inflation, shown by a movement up the LRPC curve from point x to z.

2.3.3 MACROECONOMIC OBJECTIVES 3: ECONOMIC GROWTH

economic growth = growth in real GDP over a period of time, usually expressed as a percentage change in real GDP; it is often calculated in **per capita** terms (per person in the population)

Using diagrams to illustrate economic growth

The production possibilities curve (PPC) model (see p 2)		The LRAS curve* (see p 46)
Increase in actual output	Increase in production possibilities	Increase in potential output

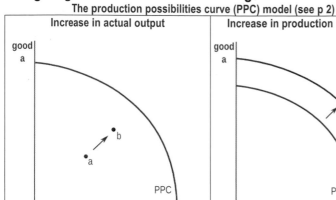

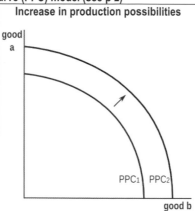

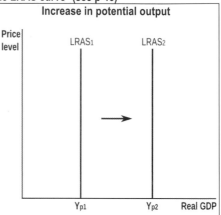

| The economy moves from **a** inside the PPC to **b** closer to the PPC, indicating greater **actual output** produced, due to:
• lower unemployment
• greater productive efficiency (producing at a lower cost, i.e. with fewer resources)
(see p 2 for more details) | The economy's PPC shifts outward, indicating an increase in **production possibilities**, due to:
• larger quantity of resources
• better quality of resources
• improved technology | The economy's LRAS curve shifts outward, indicating an increase in **potential output** (Yp), or full employment output, due to:
• larger quantity of resources
• better quality of resources
• improved technology
• the remaining factors listed on p 46
* The Keynesian AS curve can also be used. |

The importance of investment in three types of capital for economic growth

Investment in physical capital (= a produced factor of production, including machines, factories, tools, roads, telecommunications, etc.) results in a **larger quantity of capital goods**, as well as in **improved quality of capital goods** if these embody (include) technological improvements (ex more or better machines, roads, telecommunications)	**Investment in human capital** (= the skills, knowledge, education and good health that are acquired by people and make them more productive) results in an **improved quality of the labor force**, due to greater education, skills, knowledge and health (ex building more schools and hospitals)	**Investment in natural capital** (= another term for "land" plus all natural resources such as biodiversity, soil quality, the ozone layer, etc) results in a **greater quantity of natural resources** (renewable) and **improved quality of natural resources** (ex planting more forests, improving soil quality)

The importance of productivity for economic growth

productivity of labor (= output per worker) increases as a result of investments in physical, human and natural capital, because these investments allow each worker to produce more output per hour of work. **This greater output makes economic growth possible**.

The consequences of economic growth often depend on policies pursued by the government

☑ **Improved standards of living** for the population may result from more output produced, especially if this involves merit goods production (education, health care, infrastructure)	☒ **Standards of living may not improve** if output increases involve military goods, or if the needs of the poor (education, health care, infrastructure) are neglected, or if income distribution is highly unequal
☑ **Lower unemployment** may result from new job creation that often accompanies increased output produced	☒ **Unemployment may increase** due to technological change and especially use of **inappropriate technologies** (see p 81)
☑ **Lower inflation** may result from increases in potential output (rightward shift of the LRAS curve; see p 51)	☒ **Higher inflation** may result if growth is linked with AD⇑ (demand-pull), or rising input costs ⇒ SRAS⇓ (cost-push) (see p 51)
☑ **Income distribution may improve**, based on policies that redistribute income (ex human capital creation, transfer payments to protect vulnerable groups, progressive taxes, etc see p 56)	☒ **Income distribution may worsen** if it is based on market-oriented supply side policies (see p 61), or on the growth of industries that don't employ much labor
☑ **A smaller trade deficit in the current account** (see p 71) may result if growth is based on growth of exports	☒ **A larger trade deficit in the current account** (see p 71) may result if growth is based on increased domestic AD, leading to more imports
☑ **Sustainable resource use** could result from growth based on the use of pollution-free technologies and production methods (currently more the exception than the rule)	☒ **Unsustainable resource use** very often results from growth based on use of highly polluting technologies and production methods as well as consumption (ex cars) with numerous negative environmental externalities

HL topic Calculating the rate of economic growth

Merryland's real GDP grew from $34.75 billion in 2005 to $35.31 billion in 2006. Its population grew from 2.11 million to 2.17 million over the same period. Calculate growth in (a) real GDP; (b) real GDP per capita. (c) Explain why one growth rate is positive and the other is negative.
(a) [(35.31 − 34.75) / 34.75] x 100 = **1.61 %**
(b) 2005 real GDP per capita = 34.75 billion / 2.11 million = **$16,469.19**; 2006 real GDP per capita = $35.31 billion / 2.17 million = **$16,271.89**; growth in real GDP per capita = [(16,271.89 − 16,469.19) / 16,469.19] x 100 = **-1.20 %**.
(c) The population grew faster than real GDP, causing growth in real GDP per capita to be negative even though growth in real GDP was positive.

2.3.4 MACROECONOMIC OBJECTIVES 4: EQUITY IN THE DISTRIBUTION OF INCOME

Difference between equality and equity in income distribution

equality = everyone receives an **equal amount of income**
equity = everyone gets a **fair amount of income**, where **fairness** may be interpreted in different ways (ex income according to the amount of work done, or according to abilities, or according to needs, or according to the principle of equality)
✔ **When economists refer to equity in income distribution, they usually mean equality in income distribution.**

Why the market system does not result in an equitable (equal) distribution of income

In a market system, the amount of income received is in accordance with ownership and sale of factors of production (see the **circular flow of income model**, p 39). But ownership is highly unequal: some people have more factors of production to sell than others (ex land or capital in addition to labor), while still others may have none to sell (ex the old, the very young, the sick, the unemployed). Therefore the market system distributes income unequally.

How income inequality is measured: three indicators of income inequality (or equality):

(i) Income shares of percentages of the population
The population may be divided into ten equal parts, each being 10% of the population (= **deciles**), or into five equal parts, each being 20% of the population (= **quintiles**). Data are presented on the percentage of total income in the economy received by each part. Example:

Deciles	Poorest 10%	2nd 10%	3rd 10%	4th 10%	5th 10%	6th 10%	7th 10%	8th 10%	9th 10%	Richest 10%	Total
% of income	2.3 %	3.3%	4.6%	5.4%	7.3%	9.9%	12.7%	14.7 %	18.3%	21.5%	100.0%

The same income distribution is given below as quintiles:

Quintiles	Poorest 20%	2nd 20%	3rd 20%	4th 20%	Richest 20%	Total
% of income	5.6% (=2.3+3.3)	10.0%	17.2%	27.4%	39.8 %	100.0%

(ii) Lorenz curve
This is a visual representation of income shares received by percentages of the population. The **blue** line in the diagram is the line of **perfect income equality** = each decile receives 10% of total income or each quintile receives 20%. The **green line** is a Lorenz curve, based on the quintile data above. ("Cumulative" means that each point is the sum of all previous income shares; ex point **b** shows that 15.6% of income (= 5.6% + 10.0%) is received by 40% of the population (the two poorest quintiles). The **brown** line is another Lorenz curve of an economy with **greater inequality** in income distribution.

✔ **The further away a Lorenz curve is from the line of perfect equality, the more unequal the distribution of income**.

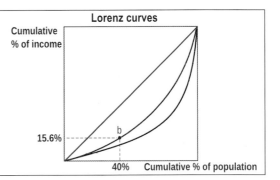
Lorenz curves

(iii) The Gini coefficient
This is a numerical representation of the Lorenz curve.

$$\text{Gini coefficient} = \frac{Y}{Y+Z}$$ (see diagram), and varies from 0 to 1.

If the Gini coefficient = 0, there is perfect income equality.
If the Gini coefficient = 1, there is maximum possible income inequality.

✔ **The lower the Gini coefficient, the greater the income equality**.

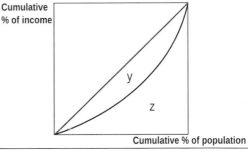
Lorenz curve and Gini coefficient

Poverty: absolute versus relative poverty

poverty = the inability of a consumer or family to satisfy basic physical needs (ex, food, clothing, shelter, etc.) due to low income
absolute poverty = a measure of the number of people in a population with an income level below a predefined "poverty line" that is the minimum income necessary to satisfy basic physical needs

relative poverty = a measure of the number of people in a population with an income level below a predefined level that changes over time, and is defined as a percentage of society's median income; poverty is "relative" to other people's incomes; reflects the idea that people should be able to afford a lifestyle typical of their society

Causes of poverty

- **very low incomes** do not allow people to satisfy their basic physical needs
- **unemployment** deprives people of income and throws people into poverty, even if they receive unemployment benefits, as these are often quite low
- **lack of human capital** means people lack skills, knowledge and education or good health ⇒ they have low productivity ⇒ low incomes
- **discrimination** on the basis of race, gender, age, etc in the job market ⇒ unemployment or lower wages for the same work
- **limited social services (merit goods, ex education, health care, infrastructure)** contribute to poverty as people on low incomes are heavily dependent on merit goods provided/subsidized by the government
- **poverty** can contribute to poverty through the poverty cycle/trap (see p 78)

Consequences of poverty

- ☒ **low living standards**, which may include poor nutrition, high levels of alcoholism, stress ⇒ low productivity ⇒ low income levels
- ☒ **lack of access to health care and education** ⇒ low human capital ⇒ low earning potential
- ☒ **higher mortality levels** (= early deaths)
- ☒ **social problems** such as alcoholism, higher crime rates, which lower the quality of life and burden the government budget with extra expenditures

Distinguishing between direct and indirect taxes

direct taxes = taxes on income and wealth, paid directly to the government (ex personal income taxes, corporate income taxes, wealth taxes)	indirect taxes = taxes on spending to buy goods and services, paid indirectly to the government through the sellers (ex sales taxes, value added taxes (VAT), tariffs)

Progressive, proportional and regressive taxes

progressive taxes = the percentage of income paid as tax (average tax rate) increases as income increases	proportional taxes = the percentage of income paid as tax (average tax rate) remains constant as income increases	regressive taxes = the percentage of income paid as tax (average tax rate) decreases as income increases

Income	Progressive taxes		Proportional taxes		Regressive taxes	
	average tax rate	tax paid	average tax rate	Tax paid	average tax rate	tax paid
$ 1000	10%	$ 100	10%	$ 100	10%	$ 100
$ 2000	15%	$ 300	10%	$ 200	7%	$ 140
$ 3000	20%	$ 600	10%	$ 300	5%	$ 150

✔ Personal income taxes are **usually progressive**, and **sometimes proportional**.

✔ Indirect taxes are **always regressive** (ex a tax of $10 paid to buy a good is a larger fraction of a low income than of a high income).

Methods to promote equity (equality) In Income distribution

Positive and negative effects on efficiency in resource allocation

These methods can be highly successful in redistributing income, but have both positive and negative effects on **efficiency in resource allocation**.

Progressive taxes are an important method used to make income distribution more equal. The more progressive a tax system is (i.e. the more rapidly the average tax rate increases as income increases), the greater the income redistribution achieved: increasingly larger proportions (fractions) of income are taxed away as incomes rise, thus decreasing the income differences between rich and poor. The resulting tax revenues can be used to provide merit goods and transfer payments (see below).	☑ More equal income distribution raises low incomes and so helps poor people acquire human capital ⟹ they become more employable ⟹ unemployment ⇓ and output ⇑ (greater economic growth) ⟹ use of resources improves ☑ More equal income distribution allows people to escape the poverty cycle/trap (see p 78) ⟹ use of resources improves ☑ Progressive income taxes act as **automatic stabilizers**, reducing the size of business cycle fluctuations (see p 59) ⟹ unemployment ⇓ or inflation ⇓ ⟹ use of resources improves ☒ High tax rates may reduce the incentive to work ⟹ unemployment ⇑ ⟹ use of resources worsens
Governments use tax revenues to provide merit goods directly or to subsidize these, including education, health care, and infrastructure (clean water, sanitation, sewerage, etc), making them available to people on low incomes who would otherwise be unable to have access to them.	☑ Merit goods have **positive consumption externalities** (see p 19), involving underallocation of resources (allocative inefficiency); this is at least partly corrected when government provision and/or subsidies of merit goods increase ⟹ allocative efficiency improves ☒ Opportunity costs of government spending ☒ Negative effects on the government's budget
Governments use tax revenues to provide transfer payments (= transfers of income from taxpayers to vulnerable groups, who are people in need), including unemployment benefits, child allowances, pensions, housing benefits, student grants.	☑ Unemployment benefits act as **automatic stabilizers**, reducing the size of business cycle fluctuations (see p 59) ⟹ unemployment ⇓ or inflation ⇓ ⟹ use of resources improves ☒ Some (ex unemployment benefits, child subsidies received by parents) may reduce the incentive to work ⟹ unemployment ⇑ ☒ Opportunity costs of government spending ☒ Negative effects on the government's budget
Governments use price controls, ex price floors to support incomes of farmers and low-skilled workers (minimum wages), and price ceilings to make food, rents more affordable	☒ Minimum wages may lead to unemployment ☒ Price controls in general lead to allocative inefficiency and welfare (deadweight) losses

HL topic Calculations of marginal and average tax rates

average tax rate (ATR) = tax paid / taxable income x 100	marginal tax rate (MTR) = tax rate applied to income in the highest tax bracket

Merryland's personal income taxes are calculated based on the following:

Income brackets (annual income)	Marginal tax Rate (MTR)
$0 - $15,000	0%
$15,001-$35,000	15%
$35,001-$60,000	25%
$60,001 or more	45%

Individual A has income of $32,700 and Individual B has income of $75,200.
What is (a) the amount of tax paid and (b) the average and marginal tax rates of each one?
Individual A: tax paid = (0 x $15,000) + (0.15 x $17,700) = 0 + $2655 = **$2655**
Average tax rate (ATR) = 2655 / 32,700 x 100 = **8.12%**
Marginal tax rate (MTR) = **15%**
Individual B: tax paid = (0 x $15,000) + (0.15 x $20,000) + (0.25 x $25,000) + (0.45 x $15,200) = 0 + $3,000 + $6,250 + $6,840 = **$16,090**
Average tax rate = 16,090 / 75,200 x 100 = **21.40%**
Marginal tax rate = **45%**

✔ In progressive taxation, MTR > ATR; In proportionate taxation, MTR = ATR; in regressive taxation, MTR < ATR.

Overview of macroeconomic policies

Demand-side policies	Supply-side policies
Main focus: on the demand side of the economy	**Main focus**: on the supply side of the economy
Main objective: to eliminate or reduce short-term economic fluctuations, i.e. recessionary (deflationary) and inflationary gaps, and hence to achieve low unemployment (cyclical) and a low and stable rate of inflation; also known as **short-term demand management**	**Main objective**: to promote long term economic growth and hence increase potential output
Main method used: manipulate (increase or decrease) aggregate demand (AD)	**Main method used**: increase aggregate supply (LRAS or Keynesian AS)

Fiscal policy	Monetary policy	Interventionist supply-side policies	Market-oriented supply-side policies
In a recessionary gap, the government uses expansionary policy: G spending ⇑ or income taxes decrease ⇒ C⇑ or business taxes decrease ⇒ I ⇑ ⇒ **AD** ⇑	**In a recessionary gap, the central bank uses expansionary (easy monetary) policy:** money supply ⇑ ⇒ interest rate ⇓ ⇒ cost of borrowing ⇓ ⇒ C ⇑ and I ⇑ ⇒ **AD** ⇑	**Based on government intervention** in the economy, intended to directly increase the productive capacity of the economy **Main policies:** • investment in human capital • investment in research and development (R&D), leading to the development of new technologies • investment in infrastructure • industrial policies ⇒ **AS ⇑ (LRAS or Keynesian AS), hence potential output ⇑**	**Based on institutional changes in the economy intended to develop free, competitive markets** that increase efficiency in production and in the allocation of resources **Main policies:** • policies to encourage competition • labor market reform policies • incentive-related policies ⇒ **AS ⇑ (LRAS or Keynesian AS) hence potential output ⇑**
In an inflationary gap, the government uses contractionary policy: G spending ⇓ or income taxes increase ⇒ C ⇓ or business taxes increase ⇒ I ⇓ ⇒ **AD** ⇓	**In an inflationary gap, the central bank uses contractionary (tight monetary) policy:** money supply ⇓ ⇒ interest rate ⇑ ⇒ cost of borrowing ⇑ ⇒ C ⇓ and I ⇓ ⇒ **AD** ⇓		

✔ **Some demand-side policies have supply-side effects (i.e. influence LRAS or Keynesian AS and potential output).** Expansionary fiscal policy that includes increased government spending on specific areas such as human capital development, or infrastructure, or R&D, will cause not only AD to increase but also AS (LRAS or Keynesian AS) and potential output, because these are the same as certain types of interventionist supply-side policies. Additional demand-side policies with supply-side effects are cuts in business taxes, which increase investment, hence the quantity of capital goods, causing LRAS or Keynesian AS and potential output to increase.	✔ **Some supply-side policies have demand-side effects (i.e. influence AD).** Interventionist supply-side policies such as government investment in human capital, infrastructure and R&D will cause not only AS (LRAS or Keynesian AS) and potential output to increase, but also AD because they involve increases in government spending (G), which is a component of AD. Further, market-based supply-side policies that cause investment (I) to increase (ex cuts in taxes on profits) will also result in AD increases, since investment is also a component of AD.

DEMAND-SIDE POLICIES

These are policies that manipulate (increase or decrease) aggregate demand (AD), aiming to eliminate or reduce short-term economic fluctuations, or inflationary and deflationary (recessionary) gaps; also known as **demand-management**. There are two types of demand-side policies fiscal policy and **monetary policy**.

2.4 FISCAL POLICY

Fiscal policy Is carried out by the government by **changing taxes** (the main part of **government revenue**) and/or **government expenditures**.

Sources of government revenue	Types of government expenditures
• **direct taxes** (mainly) and **indirect taxes** (see p 56)	• **current expenditures** spending for government's day-to-day operations (wages of government workers, supplies, subsidies)
• **sales of goods and services** provided by the government, such as transportation and postal services, electricity, water	• **capital expenditures** spending on public investments (roads, airports, public hospitals and schools, etc.)
• **sale of government-owned enterprises**, called **privatization** (transfer of ownership from government to private owners)	• **transfer payments** (ex unemployment benefits; see p 56)

The budget outcome

government budget = a plan relating government revenue to government spending, usually for a period of a year	**budget surplus** = government revenues > government spending, over the period of a year
balanced budget = government revenues are equal to government spending, over the period of a year	**budget deficit** = government revenues < government spending, over the period of a year, usually made possible by government borrowing
public debt = government debt = the accumulation of budget deficits minus surpluses over time, or the amount owed by the government	

Fiscal policy and short-term demand management

Of the four components of aggregate demand (AD) (C, I, G, X-M), fiscal policy can:
- directly change **government spending** (G), as the government increases or decreases its own expenditures
- indirectly change **consumption spending** (C) by changing personal income taxes: as taxes ⇑, C⇓, and as taxes ⇓, C⇑
- indirectly change **investment spending** (I) by changing business taxes (= taxes on profits): as taxes ⇑, I⇓, and as taxes ⇓, I⇑

Recessionary/deflationary gap: equilibrium real GDP at Y_1 < potential output Yp (= full employment output) due to insufficient AD. The government uses **expansionary policy** to increase AD_1 to AD_2 by:	**Inflationary gap**: equilibrium real GDP at Y_1 > potential output Yp (= full employment output) due to too much AD. The government uses **contractionary policy** to decrease AD_1 to AD_2 by:
• increasing G, or	• decreasing G, or
• decreasing personal income taxes ⇒ consumption ⇑, or	• increasing personal income taxes ⇒ consumption ⇓, or
• decreasing business taxes ⇒ investment ⇑.	• increasing business taxes ⇒ investment ⇓.
In all cases AD⇑, aiming to close the deflationary gap.	In all cases ⇒ AD⇓, aiming to close the inflationary gap.

Expansionary policy: Monetarist/new classical model	**Contractionary policy: Monetarist/new classical model**
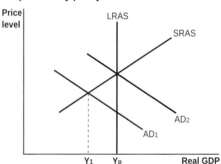	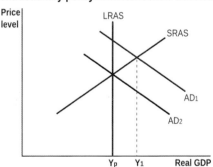
Expansionary policy: Keynesian model	**Contractionary policy: Keynesian model**
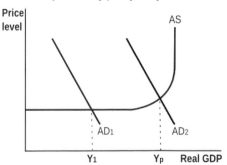	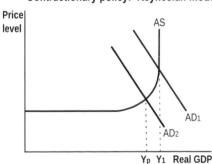
✔ **Expected results using the monetarist/new classical model**: as AD ⇑ ⇒ real GDP ⇑ and the price level ⇑.	✔ **Expected results using the monetarist/new classical model**: as AD ⇓ ⇒ real GDP ⇓ and the price level ⇓.
✔ **Expected results using the Keynesian model**: as AD ⇑ ⇒ real GDP ⇑ but the price level remains constant in the horizontal range of the AS curve, where the economy is in recession, and begins to rise only when potential output (Yp) is approached.	✔ **Expected results using Keynesian model**: as AD ⇓ ⇒ real GDP ⇓ but the price level falls only in the vertical and upward-sloping parts of the AS curve, and remains constant in the horizontal range, where the economy is in recession.

The role of automatic stabilizers

automatic stabilizers = features in the economy that limit the size of economic fluctuations (recessionary and inflationary gaps) **without any government action**, thus stabilizing the economy; the most important are **progressive income taxes** and **unemployment benefits**.

Progressive income taxes	Unemployment benefits
In a recessionary gap, as real GDP and incomes fall, income taxes collected by the government fall proportionately more in a progressive tax system, causing disposable (after-tax) incomes to fall proportionately less, leaving consumers with more income to spend ⇒ AD falls less than it would without progressive taxes.	**In a recessionary gap**, as unemployment increases, government spending on unemployment benefits automatically increases, thus partially compensating for the loss of income and spending of the unemployed ⇒ AD falls less than it would without the unemployment benefits.
In an inflationary gap, as real GDP and incomes increase, income taxes rise proportionately faster in a progressive tax system, causing disposable (after-tax) incomes to rise proportionately less, leaving consumers with less income to spend ⇒ AD increases less than it would without a progressive tax system.	**In an inflationary gap**, as unemployment falls, government spending on unemployment benefits automatically falls, and this partially counteracts (reduces) the increase in incomes and spending of the newly employed ⇒ AD increases less than it would without the unemployment benefits.

Fiscal policy and its impact on potential output and long-term economic growth

Fiscal policy is intended primarily as a short-term demand management tool, but also has effects on long term growth through its **indirect and direct effects on potential output**:

Fiscal policy's indirect effects on potential output
Fiscal policy, by maintaining low rates of inflation (limit inflationary gaps) and low levels of unemployment (limit deflationary/recessionary gaps), can create a favorable economic environment that encourages private investment involving the production of more capital goods, research and development and technological improvements, hence promoting increases in potential output and economic growth.

Fiscal policy's direct effects on potential output		
Government spending on physical capital and research and development (R&D) increases infrastructure (roads, harbors, etc.) and creates new technologies ⇒ increases in quantity and improvements in quality of capital goods ⇒ potential output ⇑	**Government spending on human capital** ex spending on education, training and health care provision increases the quality of the labor force ⇒ potential output ⇑	**Government provision of incentives to invest** ex lower business taxes ⇒ higher after-tax profits ⇒ private investment ⇑ and research and development by firms ⇑ ⇒ potential output ⇑

Evaluating fiscal policy

Strengths of fiscal policy	Weaknesses of fiscal policy
☑ It can target specific sectors of the economy, for example building of schools, hospitals, etc. ☑ Expansionary policy is effective in pulling an economy out of a deep recession (whereas monetary policy may not work; see p 60) ☑ Expansionary policy can affect potential output, leading to economic growth (see above) ☑ Government spending has a direct impact on aggregate demand, in contrast to tax cuts; ex a tax cut to encourage spending may result in higher savings in the event of low consumer confidence	☒ It works with major time lags (delays), involving delays in making decisions, in implementation, and for the effects to be felt ☒ There are political constraints: cuts in taxes and increases in government spending, being popular, may be undertaken for political, not economic reasons; while necessary painful polices may be avoided ☒ Expansionary policy may be inflationary if it lasts too long (AD ⇑) ☒ Expansionary policy may result in larger budget deficits and government debt ☒ It cannot be used incrementally (as interest rates in monetary policy) ☒ **Crowding out** (see below) ☒ Problematic in cost-push inflation (makes recession worse; see p 51)

Crowding out (a possible weakness of fiscal policy)

When a government carries out expansionary fiscal policy, it often needs to borrow in order to pay for increased government expenditures, which causes interest rates to rise. This in turn leads to lower investment and consumption spending due to the higher cost of borrowing, which partly cancels out the expansionary effect of increased government spending on AD: AD_1 ⇑ to AD_2 due to increases in G, and AD_2 ⇓ to AD_3 due to decreases in C and I. Therefore the expansionary effect of increased government spending is reduced.

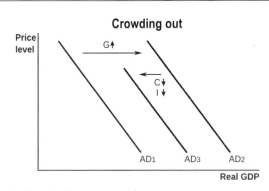

Crowding out

2.5 MONETARY POLICY

Monetary policy Is carried out by the central bank, which determines interest rates by changing the money supply.

The roles of a central bank include being:

• **a banker to the government**: it manages the government's deposits and borrowing, and makes payments for the government • **a banker to commercial banks**: it holds deposits for them and lends to them in the event that they lack sufficient funds	• **a regulator of commercial banks**: it ensures the safety of the commercial banking system • **responsible for determining interest rates**: it conducts monetary policy • **responsible for exchange rate policy**
✔ In many countries, the central bank is independent of the government, in order to ensure that monetary policy is not influenced by political factors (ex expansionary policy that increases real GDP and incomes prior to an election).	

How interest rates are determined

interest = payment for money that has been borrowed, over a certain time period	rate of interest = payment for borrowed money over a certain time period, expressed as a percentage of the borrowed amount; the "price" of money services

The rate of interest is determined in a **money market**, where the supply of money (Sm) is fixed at a level decided upon by the central bank (and is therefore vertical), and the demand for money (Dm) shows the negative relationship between the quantity of money demanded and the rate of interest (r). The equilibrium rate of interest is determined by the intersection of Sm and Dm, and the initial equilibrium interest rate is r_1, given by Dm and Sm_1. If the central bank wishes to **lower the rate of interest**, it increases the supply of money (Sm_1 shifts to Sm_2) and the equilibrium interest rate falls from r_1 to r_2. To **raise the rate of interest** the central bank decreases the supply of money (Sm_1 shifts to Sm_3) and the equilibrium interest rate rises from r_1 to r_3.

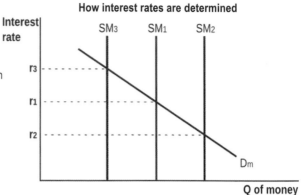

How interest rates are determined

Monetary policy and short-term demand management

Of the four components of aggregate demand (AD) (C, I, G, X-M), monetary policy can influence **consumption spending** (C) and **investment spending** (I) by **changing the money supply and interest rates**. Interest rates determine the cost of borrowing: the higher the interest rate, the higher the cost of borrowing and the lower the amount of consumption and investment spending financed by borrowing. The lower the interest rate, the lower the cost of borrowing and the higher the amount of consumption and investment spending financed by borrowing.

In a **recessionary (deflationary) gap**, there is insufficient AD for the economy to reach potential output Yp (= full employment output).	In an **inflationary gap**, there is too much AD for the economy to be at potential output Yp (= full employment output).
To see the effects of expansionary monetary policy, see the diagrams on p 58 (**they are the same as in the case of expansionary fiscal policy**).	To see the effects of contractionary monetary policy, see the diagrams on p 58 (**they are the same as in the case of contractionary fiscal policy**).
The central bank uses **expansionary (easy monetary) policy** to increase AD from AD_1 to AD_2 aiming to close the recessionary gap by increasing the money supply and lowering the interest rate $\Rightarrow$ consumption spending ⇑ and investment spending ⇑ $\Rightarrow$ AD⇑.	The central bank uses **contractionary (tight monetary) policy** to decrease AD from AD_1 to AD_2 aiming to close the inflationary gap, by decreasing the money supply and increasing the interest rate $\Rightarrow$ consumption spending ⇓ and investment spending ⇓ $\Rightarrow$ AD⇓.
✔ **Expected results using the monetarist/new classical model:** as AD ⇑ $\Rightarrow$ real GDP⇑ and the price level ⇑.	✔ **Expected results using the monetarist/new classical model:** as AD⇓ $\Rightarrow$ real GDP⇓ and the price level ⇓.
✔ **Expected results using the Keynesian model:** as AD ⇑ $\Rightarrow$ real GDP ⇑ but the price level remains constant in the horizontal range of the AS curve, where the economy is in recession, and begins to rise only when potential output (Yp) is approached.	✔ **Expected results using the Keynesian model:** as AD⇓ $\Rightarrow$ real GDP⇓ but the price level falls only in the vertical and upward sloping parts of the AS curve, and remains constant in the horizontal range, where the economy is in recession.

Inflation targeting

In some countries, rather than focus on the goals of low unemployment and low and stable inflation, central banks attempt to achieve a **target rate of inflation** that usually varies between 1.5% and 2.5%, regardless of the rate of unemployment. Based on forecasts of inflation, monetary policy is used to achieve the inflation target: contractionary policy is used if forecasted inflation is higher than the target, and expansionary policy if forecasted inflation is lower than the target.

✔ Whereas inflation targeting usually permits the achievement of a low and stable inflation rate, this may sometimes be achieved **at the cost of high unemployment**, as unemployment is ignored when the central bank makes its policy decisions.

Evaluating monetary policy

Strengths of monetary policy	Weaknesses of monetary policy
☑ There are no political constraints, as the central bank is often independent of the government, and monetary policy does not involve the government budget (government spending and tax revenues)	☒ There are some time lags (delays), though not as serious as in fiscal policy
☑ Interest rates can be adjusted incrementally (in small parts), making it more flexible and suitable to small or frequent changes	☒ It may not be effective in a deep recession because (i) even if the interest rate falls to very low levels, banks may be too fearful to lend and firms/consumers may be too fearful to borrow (due to low confidence); (ii) interest rates cannot fall below zero, even though more expansion may be necessary
☑ Is quicker to implement compared to fiscal policy	
☑ It does not increase budget deficits and debt	☒ May be inflationary if expansionary policy lasts too long (AD increases too much)
☑ There is no crowding out	☒ Problematic in cost-push inflation (makes recession worse; see p 51)

2.6 SUPPLY-SIDE POLICIES

These are policies that aim at increasing aggregate supply (LRAS or Keynesian AS) thus achieving long-term economic growth and hence growth in potential output. There are two types of supply-side policies: **interventionist** and **market-based**.

✔ Before reading this section, you should review the factors that lead to long-term economic growth, shown as rightward shifts in the LRAS or Keynesian AS curves (see p 46, 54).

Interventionist supply-side policies

Interventionist supply-side policies are based on government intervention in the economy intended to directly increase the productive capacity of the economy.

Four main categories of interventionist supply-side policies

Investment in human capital	Investment in infrastructure
Involves government spending on training, re-training and education, and improved access to health care services, leading to a better-trained and healthier workforce, thus increasing the **productivity** of the labor force (see p 54), leading to economic growth and an increase in potential output. At the same time, the increase in government spending results in an increase in AD.	Involves government spending on **infrastructure** = a type of physical capital, ex roads, power supplies, harbors, airports, sanitation, water supplies, which increase **productivity** (p 54) leading to economic growth and an increase in potential output. At the same time, the increase in government spending results in an increase in AD.
Investment in new technology	**Industrial policies**
Involves government spending on research and development (R&D) leading to new technology, which increases the quality of physical capital, thus increasing the **productivity** (p 54) of the labor force (workers working with better capital produce more output). This results in economic growth and an increase in potential output. At the same time, the increase in government spending gives rise to an increase in AD.	Involve government policies intended to promote specific industries. Policies include: tax reductions, tax exemptions, low-interest loans, subsidies and grants for industries that are held to be important to support growth. These policies lead to an increase in investment by firms in these industries resulting in economic growth and an increase in potential output, as well as an increase in AD. Also include support for **infant industries** in developing countries (see p 65).

Evaluating interventionist supply-side policies

Strengths of interventionist supply-side policies	Weaknesses of interventionist supply-side policies
☑ Provide direct support of areas important for growth (human capital, infrastructure, R&D, growth-oriented industries) ☑ Create new jobs and reduce structural unemployment ☑ Put a downward pressure on inflation, due to the increase in productive capacity and LRAS (see p 51) ☑ Result in economic growth and an increase in potential output ☑ Result in improved equity in income distribution if investments in human capital are broadly distributed, increasing job opportunities for all	☒ Need a long time to take effect ☒ Government spending has opportunity costs ☒ Government spending may lead to a budget deficit, increasing the public debt ☒ Government spending may lead to an oversized, and possibly inefficient government sector ☒ The government may make poor choices on what industries to support, leading to inefficiency in the allocation of resources

Market-based supply-side policies

Market-based supply-side policies are based on institutional changes in the economy intended to develop free, competitive markets that increase efficiency in production, improve the allocation of resources and lead to economic growth (increases in potential output).

Three main categories of market-based supply-side policies

1. Policies encouraging competition
Are based on the idea that greater competition increases efficiency in production and improves resource allocation ⇒ potential output increases:

Privatization transfers ownership from the government to private owners. Private ownership of firms ⇒ firms become profit-maximizers (thus wishing to cut costs), bureaucracy decreases, unproductive workers are fired ⇒ efficiency improves ⇒ potential output increases.	**Anti-monopoly regulation** tries to prevent the formation of monopolies (single sellers in a market with high barriers to entry and therefore no competition), or to break up existing monopolies into several firms, on the grounds that monopolies are inefficient, and sell a lower amount of output at a higher price than competitive industries ⇒ efficiency improves ⇒ potential output increases.
Deregulation eliminates or lowers the amount of government regulation of an industry (ex regulation of prices, quantity of output produced, which are used to protect firms from competition), thus exposing firms in the industry to greater competition. Increased competition ⇒ greater efficiency (and quality improvements) ⇒ potential output increases. (Ex airlines, banks and other financial institutions, telecommunications, for which deregulation has meant that new firms can enter previously protected industries).	**Trade liberalization** removes or lowers barriers to trade (tariffs, quotas and others, see p 63), allowing more imports to enter into a country, which increase competition between domestic producers and foreign producers whose goods are entering the domestic market ⇒ efficiency improves ⇒ potential output increases.

2. Labor market reforms

Also known as **increasing labor market flexibility** or **reducing labor market rigidities**, these are intended to increase competition in labor markets, allowing wages to be determined by supply and demand for labor, often lowering labor costs for firms and leading them to hire more labor; these policies may also reduce structural unemployment (remember that one cause of structural unemployment is labor market rigidities; see p 49) ⇒ potential output increases:

Reducing labor union power results in lower wages (because labor unions often negotiate high wage increases with employers) ⇒ labor costs fall ⇒ firms hire more labor, production increases, structural unemployment falls ⇒ potential output increases.	**Abolishing or reducing minimum wages** results in lower wages for unskilled workers ⇒ labor costs fall and structural unemployment falls ⇒ potential output increases.
Reducing unemployment benefits may result in increased employment, as it reduces incomes of unemployed workers, thus causing them to seek employment and take on a job ⇒ structural unemployment falls ⇒ potential output increases.	**Reducing job security** makes it easier and less costly for firms to fire workers (by reducing worker compensation), therefore firms may hire workers more easily ⇒ labor costs fall and structural unemployment falls ⇒ potential output increases.

3. Incentive-related policies

Are policies involving tax cuts, intended to increase incentives of people to work and of firms to invest. As hours worked increase, and as investment increases there is growth in output ⇒ potential output increases:

Cuts in personal income taxes mean that people's after-tax incomes increase, causing them to wish to work more ⇒ hours worked increase, equivalent to an increase in the quantity of labor ⇒ potential output increases.	**Cuts in taxes on capital gains** (= taxes on profits from stocks and bonds) **and on interest income** mean that people have a greater incentive to save (in the form of purchases of stocks and bonds, or as savings deposits in banks) since they will have to pay lower taxes on their savings. Increased savings means that there are more funds available for investment by firms, more capital goods creation and more research and development and new technologies ⇒ potential output increases.
Cuts in business taxes mean that firms' after-tax profits increase, leaving them with more funds to invest in capital goods or to engage in research and development; increases in investment and more technological improvements ⇒ potential output increases.	

Evaluating market-based supply-side policies

Strengths of market-based supply-side policies

☑ improved efficiency in production, meaning lower costs of production ☑ improved allocation of resources, since better use is made of available resources as there is less resource waste (ex labor resources) ☑ creation of new jobs and reduction in structural unemployment ☑ do not increase deficits and debt	☑ improvement in product quality due to increased competition between firms ☑ downward pressure on inflation, due to the increase in LRAS (see p 51) ☑ economic growth, or an increase in potential output

Weaknesses of market-based supply-side policies

☒ Supply-side policies in general need a long time to take effect.

Policies encouraging competition:

Privatization
☒ private firms are likely to sell at higher prices and produce lower quantities compared to the government, which is not in the public interest, hurting especially lower income people (ex water supplies, sanitation, transportation)
☒ increased unemployment may result, as private firms lay off workers due to cost-saving, leading to a worsening distribution of income
☒ there may be negative effects on the environment as private, profit-oriented firms may be less concerned about sustainable resource use and avoidance of negative production externalities in the form of pollution and environmental degradation

Deregulation
☒ increased unemployment may result (due to cost saving), hence a worsening distribution of income
☒ it may not always be in the public interest (ex financial deregulation in the United States led to the global financial crisis in 2008)

Trade liberalization
☒ likely to have short-term losses for some stakeholders, as less efficient firms shut down, resulting in increased unemployment.

Labor market reforms
☒ lower social protection is likely to result, which increases worker insecurity
☒ lower wages and incomes are likely to result, which increase poverty and inequalities in income distribution
☒ in the case of reduction of unemployment benefits, there results a loss of an important **automatic stabilizer** needed to smooth out the fluctuations of the business cycle (see p 59)

Incentive-related policies
☒ income tax cuts may be ineffective, resulting in the desire for more leisure (time away from work) rather than a desire to work more
☒ cuts in business taxes, capital gains taxes and taxes on interest income may worsen the distribution of income, as most of these taxes are paid by high income earners
☒ cuts in taxes may lead to a larger budget deficit and public debt

3.1 INTERNATIONAL TRADE
Free trade
free trade = international trade with no government intervention imposing restrictions of any kind on imports or exports
The benefits of trade
International trade based on **exports** (sales abroad) and **imports** (purchases from abroad) offers numerous advantages to trading countries:

☑ **Greater choice for consumers** Ability to import goods and services from other countries increases the range of these available to consumers.	☑ **More efficient allocation of resources** Free trade (with no trade barriers) leads to a better allocation of resources globally.
☑ **Benefits for producers of economies of scale** (see p 27) The ability of firms to sell to other countries increases the size of their markets and allows them to achieve lower costs as they grow in size.	☑ **Ability to acquire needed resources** Resources that are not available domestically can be imported, thus increasing the range of goods that can be produced domestically.
☑ **Increased competition** As products enter a country from abroad, domestic firms experience greater competition, which forces them to try and lower their costs of production.	☑ **Ability to acquire foreign exchange** Foreign exchange, needed to pay for imports (see p 67) is acquired when a country exports, thus making it easier to continue to trade.
☑ **Greater efficiency in production** Increased competition means that less efficient firms (with higher costs of production) are forced to lower their costs or go out of business.	☑ **Greater flow of ideas and technology** The international exchange of goods and services allows new ideas and technology to spread from country to country.
☑ **Lower prices for consumers** With greater competition among firms and improved efficiency (lower costs), prices paid by consumers fall.	☑ **An "engine for growth"** Due to the above factors, trade leads to greater economic growth.

The World Trade Organization (WTO) functions and objectives

• The WTO is an international organization with the key objective to promote free trade among countries around the world.	• It provides a set of trading rules that all member countries must follow when trading with each other.
• It is a negotiating forum, encouraging talks and trade negotiations between its member countries, usually intended to achieve **trade liberalization** (= removal of trade restrictions between countries).	• It helps to settle disputes between countries, which may arise in the course of their trading, by listening to both sides and then making decisions based on WTO rules.

HL topics Absolute and comparative advantage
The theory of absolute advantage

absolute advantage = a country has an **absolute advantage** in the production of a good if it can produce it with **fewer resources** (= more efficiently) than another country	**Absolute advantage**
theory of absolute advantage = if two or more countries specialize in producing and exporting the goods in which they have an absolute advantage, they will enjoy increased production and consumption of the goods	units of ore — Rockland — Clayland — units of bricks
The PPC diagram shows Rockland with an absolute advantage in production of ore and Clayland in production of bricks. **Rockland should specialize in production and export of ore** and **Clayland in production and export of bricks**. As a result, both countries will enjoy greater production and consumption due to an increase in allocative efficiency.	

The theory of comparative advantage

comparative advantage = a country has a **comparative advantage** in the production of a good if it can produce it at a **lower opportunity cost** than another country

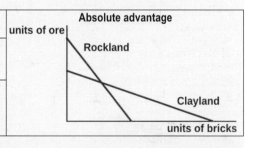

	lumber	wool	Opportunity cost of lumber	of wool
Woodland	12	3	3/12 = 1/4	12/3 = 4
Sheepland	4	2	2/4 = 1/2	4/2 = 2

theory of comparative advantage = if two or more countries specialize in producing and exporting the goods in which they have a **lower opportunity cost** (= greater comparative advantage), they will enjoy increased production and consumption of the goods

Calculating opportunity costs The table shows production possibilities of Woodland and Sheepland producing lumber and wool, plotted as PPCs in the diagram. Although Woodland has an absolute advantage in production of both lumber and wool, the countries can still benefit from trade because they have **different opportunity costs** (different PPC slope). Countries should specialize in production and export of the good with the lower opportunity cost: **Woodland in lumber and Sheepland in wool**. Both will enjoy greater production and consumption due to an increase in allocative efficiency.

Sources of comparative advantage
Countries have different **factor endowments** (= natural resources, factors of production, technology). Ex the United States has large fertile plains appropriate for agriculture. Denmark, Greece, the UK have extensive sea access appropriate for shipping.

Comparative advantage — units of wool — Woodland — Sheepland — units of lumber (axis values 3, 2, 1, 0, 4, 8, 12)

Limitations of the theory of comparative advantage

☒ **Unrealistic assumptions, including** • free trade (no trade protection) • fixed factors of production and technology • full employment • perfect competition • no trade imbalances (X = M all the time) • no transportation costs If these do not hold, the theory may not hold.	☒ **Risk of excessive specialization** If countries specialize too much, they may become vulnerable to events beyond their control, such as a fall in global demand for their exports, or a fall in global price for their exports, which can lead to serious problems (see p 84).
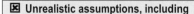	☒ **Inability of developing countries to diversify into manufacturing or services** Many developing countries specialize in **primary commodities** (p 10, 12), but would like to **diversify** into production of manufactured goods and services (p 88). Specialization according to comparative advantage does not allow them to diversify their economies.
	☒ **Arguments in favor of trade protection** There are several arguments that may justify trade protection, in which case the theory may no longer hold (p 65).

Trade protection

Trade protection = government intervention in international trade involving the imposition of **trade barriers** intended to limit the quantity of imports and protect the domestic economy from foreign competition

Tariffs	Quotas	Subsidies
Tariff = a tax on imported goods (indirect)	Quota = a restriction on the quantity of imports	Subsidy = payment by the government to firms to lower costs of production and price

Before the tariff is imposed:
S and D = domestic S and D curves
Sw = world supply curve
Pw = world price = P paid by
   consumers and received by producers
Q_1 = domestic Q supplied
Q_2 = domestic Q dem banded
$Q_2 - Q_1$ = imports
After the tariff is imposed:
S_{w+t} = world supply plus tariff
P_{w+t} = world price plus tariff = P paid by
   consumers and received by producers
Q_3 = domestic Q supplied
Q_4 = domestic Q demanded
$Q_4 - Q_3$ = imports

Before the quota is imposed:
S and D = domestic S and D curves
Sw = world supply curve
Pw = world price = P paid by
   consumers and received by producers
Q_1 = domestic Q supplied
Q_2 = domestic Q demanded
$Q_2 - Q_1$ = imports
After the quota is imposed:
S_q = domestic supply plus quota
P_q = price with quota = P paid by
   consumers and received by producers
Q_3 = domestic Q supplied
Q_4 = domestic Q demanded
$Q_4 - Q_3$ = imports (= quota)

Before the subsidy is granted:
S and D = domestic S and D curves
Sw = world supply curve
Pw = world price = P paid by
   consumers and received by producers
Q_1 = domestic Q supplied
Q_2 = domestic Q demanded
$Q_2 - Q_1$ = imports
After the subsidy is granted:
S_s = domestic supply with subsidy
P_{w+s} = price with subsidy = P received by
   producers (consumers still pay Pw)
Q_3 = domestic Q supplied
Q_2 = domestic Q demanded
$Q_2 - Q_3$ = imports

Effects on stakeholders

Tariffs	Quotas	Subsidies
☑ **Domestic producers gain from all types of protection because:**		
Q produced ⇑ from Q_1 to Q_3 and P received ⇑ from Pw to P_{w+t}	Q produced ⇑ from Q_1 to Q_3 and P received ⇑ from Pw to P_q	Q produced ⇑ from Q_1 to Q_3 and P received ⇑ from Pw to P_{w+s}
☑ **Workers gain from all types of protection because**: domestic employment ⇑ due to increased production		
☒ **Domestic consumers lose**: Q bought ⇓ from Q_2 to Q_4 and P paid ⇑ from Pw to P_{w+t}	☒ **Domestic consumers lose**: Q bought ⇓ from Q_2 to Q_4 and P paid ⇑ from Pw to P_q	**Domestic consumers unaffected**: same Q and same P before and after the subsidy
☑ **Government gains** tariff revenues: the yellow rectangle	**Government unaffected**: no revenues or spending due to the quota	☒ **Government loses**: must pay subsidy equal to the rectangle outlined in bold **brown**
☒ **Domestic society loses**: there is • **inefficiency in production** since higher-cost firms are protected by the higher P • **allocative inefficiency**, shown by welfare loss = **brown triangles** (b+d) (consumer surplus lost due to the tariff = a+b+c+d; producer surplus gained = a; government revenue gained = c; **net loss = b+d**)	☒ **Domestic society loses**: there is • **inefficiency in production** since higher-cost firms are protected by the higher P • **allocative inefficiency**, shown by welfare loss = **brown area** (b+c+d) (consumer surplus lost due to the quota = a+b+c+d; producer surplus gained = a; **net loss = b+c+d**, since quota revenues (= c) are usually taken by exporting countries)	☒ **Domestic society loses**: there is • **inefficiency in production** since higher-cost firms are protected by the higher P • **allocative inefficiency**, shown by welfare loss = **brown triangle** (b) (consumer surplus remains same after the subsidy; producer surplus gained due to the subsidy = a; government spending lost = a+b; **net loss = b**)

Further results of trade protection:

☒ **Higher domestic costs of production due to higher prices of imported inputs**: imported inputs that receive trade protection are sold domestically at higher prices, therefore increasing firms' cost of production

☒ **Loss of export competitiveness**: the higher costs of production (due to the above) make exports less competitive

☒ **Foreign producers lose**: their exports to the protected country fall

☒ **The global economy loses** due to global resource misallocation: some production moves from more efficient producers abroad to less efficient domestic producers

☒ **Risk of retaliation and trade wars**: trade protection can lead other countries to retaliate by imposing their own trade barriers

☒ **Potential for corruption**: trade restrictions may lead to illegal smuggling or payment of bribes (to bypass the trade restrictions)

✔ **Tariffs** are often preferred by governments imposing trade barriers, because they provide tariff revenues.

✔ **Quotas** are often preferred by exporting countries, because their exporters usually get the quota revenues.

✔ **Subsidies** are usually preferred by economists, because there is no welfare loss for consumers who remain unaffected by subsidies.

64

Administrative barriers

Administrative barriers = a variety of obstacles to imports imposed by governments as a form of trade protection, intended to limit the quantity of imports and protect domestic producers from foreign competition. May include complicated bureaucratic procedures and a variety of unnecessary packaging, health, safety, and environmental standards with which imports must comply in order to be admitted into the country. Known as a type of "hidden protection" because it is not always obvious that they are imposed for the purpose of restricting imports.

Arguments in favor of trade protection: an evaluation

☑ **Infant industry argument** An industry that is just beginning to be set up is unable to compete in international markets against well-established firms that have experience and **economies of scale**, and must therefore be protected until they grow and "mature". One of the strongest arguments in favor of trade protection.	☒ It may be difficult to select which particular industries to protect, i.e. which ones have the potential to grow and become efficient producers. Also, protected industries risk not ever becoming very efficient. Further, once the industries grow and mature, it may be difficult to eliminate the protection for political reasons.
☑ **Diversification of developing countries** Many developing countries specialize in production/export of a narrow range of goods, with negative effects on their economies (see p 84). Protection of a variety of industries can help them diversify (see p 88).	☒ The problems are similar to the above: how to choose which industries to protect; how to avoid inefficiency due to dependence of industries on protection; how to remove protection when the industries are well-developed.
☑ **National security** Countries want to be self-sufficient in production of defense goods when threatened, and so often protect industries producing defense-related goods.	☒ The danger is that this can be used as an argument to extend protection to industries that are very indirectly related to production for defense, and may become a type of "hidden protection".
☑ **Health, safety and environmental standards** Such standards are essential for the protection of consumers and the environment.	☒ May be used as an excuse to keep imports out, as in the case of "administrative barriers" (see above), a type of "hidden protection".
☑ **Tariffs as source of government revenue** Many countries, especially developing ones, rely on tariffs as a main source of government revenues.	☒ This occurs due to ineffective tax systems, requiring reform to reduce dependence on tariffs. The continued use of tariffs may delay such needed tax reforms.
☑ **Means of overcoming a trade deficit** A trade deficit arises when the value of exports < the value of imports, which may create **balance of payments** difficulties (see p 71, 73). The use of tariffs and quotas restricts imports and therefore reduces the size of the trade deficit.	☒ Falling imports mean that exports are falling in other countries; this policy may invite retaliation from the affected countries. This should therefore be used only as a short-term emergency measure, and other policies should be used to reduce the trade deficit (see p 73).
☑ **Anti-dumping tariffs** = tariffs imposed by an importing country on goods dumped by another country to raise the price to pre-dumping levels (**dumping** = selling goods (exports) in international markets at a price lower than average cost of production; it is against WTO rules).	☒ It is very difficult to prove that a country is dumping, and can take a very long time to do so. In the meantime, importing countries may take advantage of this long time delay to impose anti-dumping tariffs and gain at the expense of the exporting country.
☑ **Protection of domestic jobs** This is a common argument, and refers to the idea that protection of industries allows domestic production to increase, thus creating additional domestic jobs, while loss of protection allows cheap imports to enter that force domestic firms to shut down thus leading to greater unemployment.	☒ Cheap imports could be due to lower costs of production in other countries, which is an important justification for trade. Therefore trade protection shifts production from low-cost efficient producers to high-cost inefficient ones, and should be avoided as it contributes to global allocative inefficiency and invites retaliation.

HL topic Calculations of the effects of tariffs, quotas and subsidies

Calculations of the effects of tariffs

In the market for potatoes in Merryland, the free trade situation is shown in **green**. Merryland imposes a tariff of M$4 per unit of potatoes, shown in **brown**.

1. Draw the supply curve for potatoes facing Merryland after the tariff.
The supply curve is Sw+t appearing in brown

2. Calculate the change in domestic production due to the tariff.
Before: 20 units produced; after: 50 units produced; production ⇧ by = 30 units

3. Calculate the change in consumption due to the tariff.
Before: 100 units; after: 70 units; consumption ⇩ by 30 units (70 - 100 = - 30)

4. Calculate the change in the quantity of imports (M) due to the tariff.
Before:100-20 = 80 units; after: 70-50 = 20 units. Q of M ⇩ by 60 units (20-80= -60)

5. Calculate the P paid by consumers and received by producers with the tariff. Pw+t = 7 + 4 = M$11

6. Calculate the change in consumer expenditure due to the tariff.
Before: 7 x 100 = M$700; after: 11 x 70 = M$770. Expenditure ⇧ M$70 (= 770-700)

7. Calculate the change in producer revenue due to the tariff.
Before: 7 x 20 = M$140; after: 11 x 50 = M$550. Revenue ⇧ by M$410 (= 550-140)

8. Calculate the effects on the government budget.
Tariff revenue = tariff per unit x Q of M = M$4 x 20 units = M$80

9. Calculate the value of exports lost by exporters of potatoes to Merryland.
Value of X before: 7 x (100 – 20) = 7 x 80 = M$560. Value of X after: 7 x (70 – 50) = M$140. Value of X lost = M$420 (140 - 560 = - 420)

10. Calculate the welfare loss due to the tariff.
Area a = [4 x (50 – 20)] / 2] = (4 x 30) / 2 = M$60; area b = [4 x (100 – 70)] / 2] = (4 x 30) / 2 = M$60. Total welfare loss = area a + area b = 60 + 60 = M$120

11. Calculate the change in consumer surplus (CS).
CS falls by the amount of the dotted red shape since P paid by consumers rises from Pw to Pw+t. Loss of CS = [(Pw+t – Pw) x 70] + area of triangle b = [(11 – 7) x 70] + 60 = 280 + 60 = M$340

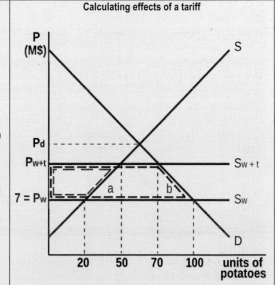

Calculating effects of a tariff

12. Calculate the change in producer surplus (PS).
PS increases by the amount of the dotted blue shape since P received by producers increases from Pw to Pw+t. Gain of PS = [(Pw+t – Pw) x 50] - area of triangle a = [(11 – 7) x 50] - 60 = 200 - 60 = M$140

Calculations of the effects of quotas

In the market for textiles in Merryland, the free trade situation is shown in **green**. Merryland imposes a quota of 2030 units.

1. Does Merryland have a comparative advantage or disadvantage in textiles?
It has a comparative disadvantage since its domestic price, Pd > Pw

2. Draw the new supply curve (Sq) facing Merryland after the quota.
The supply curve, Sq, is shown in **brown**.

3. Calculate the Q of textiles consumers purchase after the quota.
Q purchased by consumers after the quota = domestic production after the quota + quota = 1820 + 2030 = 3850 units, shown in **red**.

4. Calculate the change in the Q of imports (M) due to the quota.
Q of M before: 4700 – 910 = 3790 units; Q of M after: 2030 units (= quota)
Q of M ⇓ by 1760 units (2030 – 3790 = - 1760)

5. Calculate the change in consumer expenditure due to the quota.
Before: 5 x 4700 = M\$23,500; after: 8 x 3850 = M\$30,800.
Consumer expenditure ⇑ by M\$7300 (= 30,800 – 23, 500)

6. Calculate the change in producer revenue due to the quota.
Before: 5 x 910 = M\$4550; after: 8 x 1820 = M\$14,560.
Revenue ⇑ by M\$10,010 (= 14,560 – 4550)

7. Explain the likely effect on the government budget.
Assuming the quota revenues go to foreign exporters (the most common practice) there are no effects on the government budget.

8. Calculate the value of textile exports to Merryland lost by exporters
Value of X before: 5 x (4700 - 910) = 5 x 3790 = M\$18,950
Value of X after: 5 x quota = 5 x 2030 = M\$10,150
Value of X lost = M\$8800 (10,150 – 18,950 = - 8800)

9. If quota revenues are taken by exporters, calculate the total effect of the quota on exporters.
Exporters gain quota revenues = (8-5) x 2030 = 3 x 2030 = M\$6090.
Exporters lose exports = M\$8800 (see question 8 above).
Net loss = M\$2710 (6090 – 8800 = - 2710

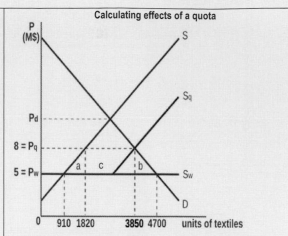
Calculating effects of a quota

10. Calculate the welfare loss due to the quota (assuming quota revenues are taken by foreign exporters).
area a = [3 x (1820 – 910)] / 2 = (3 x 910) / 2 = M\$1365;
area b = [3 x (4700 – 3850)] / 2 = (3 x 850) / 2 = M\$1275;
area c = 3 x (3850 – 1820) = M\$6090
Total welfare loss = a + b +c = 1365 + 1275 + 6090 = M\$8730

✔ **Note on drawing a quota diagram**
Students sometimes have difficulty drawing a quota diagram but it is very easy once you realize that it is similar to a tariff diagram.

Look at the two diagrams at the top of p 64.
1. Draw a tariff diagram.
2. The Sw+t line drawn at Pw+t (in the tariff diagram) becomes a dotted line at Pq (in the quota diagram).
3. In your quota diagram, at the point where the D curve is cut by the Pq line, draw Sq as a line parallel to S. (The horizontal difference between S and Sq is the amount of the quota.)

Your quota diagram is complete.

Calculations of the effects of subsidies

In Merryland's market for apples, the free trade situation is shown in **green**. A subsidy of M\$5 per unit of apples is granted.

1. Does Merryland have a comparative advantage or disadvantage in apples?
It has a comparative disadvantage because its domestic price, Pd > Pw

2. Draw the new supply curve that resulted after the subsidy.
The new supply curve, Ss, is shown in **brown**.

3. Calculate the price received by producers after the subsidy was granted.
The P received by producers is Pw + subsidy/unit = Pw+s = 9 + 5 = M\$14

4. Calculate the change in the quantity of imports (M) due to the subsidy.
Before: 780 –140 = 640 units; after: 780 – 280 = 500 units
Q of M ⇓ by 140 units (500 – 640 = - 140)

5. What is the change in consumer expenditure due to the subsidy?
There is no change, since P paid and Q bought are the same

6. Calculate the change in producer revenue due to the subsidy.
Before: 9 x 140 = M\$1260; after: 14 x 280 = M\$3920
Revenue ⇑ by M\$2660 (= 3920 – 1260)

7. Calculate the effect on the government budget.
Government spending on subsidy = subsidy/unit x Q produced = 5 x 280 = M\$1400 = the area of the rectangle outlined in bold **brown**

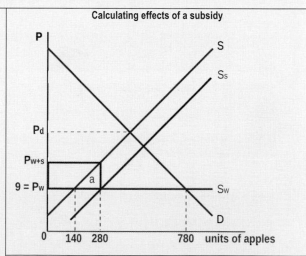
Calculating effects of a subsidy

8. Calculate the value of exports (X) lost by exporters of apples to Merryland.
Value of X before: 9 x (780 – 140) = 9 x 640 = M\$5760
Value of X after: 9 x (780 – 280) = 9 x 500 = M\$4500
Value of X lost = M\$1260 (4500 – 5760 = - 1260)
Alternatively: value of X lost = Pw x fall in M = 9 x (280 - 140)
= 9 x 140 = M\$1260

9. Calculate the welfare loss due to the subsidy.
Welfare loss = area a = [subsidy/unit x (280 –140)] / 2 = (5 x140) / 2 = M\$350

3.2 EXCHANGE RATES

Freely floating exchange rates

exchange rate = the value of one currency expressed in terms of another; can be thought of as the "price" of a currency	**freely floating exchange rate** = an exchange rate that is determined entirely by demand and supply of the currency, with no government intervention

How freely floating exchange rates are determined
Freely floating exchange rates are determined by demand and supply in the **currency market** (= market where currencies are bought and sold)

The special relationship between demand and supply of currencies

Buying and selling of currencies involves the direct exchange of one currency for another. In order to acquire or "buy" a currency, such as Indian rupees, one must give up or "sell" another currency, such as US dollars. Similarly to "buy" US dollars, one must "sell" Indian rupees.	✔ The demand for Indian rupees is equivalent to the supply of US dollars. ✔ The demand for US dollars is equivalent to the supply of Indian rupees.

Demand and supply of currencies

Consider two countries, India and the United States. **Demand for Indian rupees** arises when United States residents (consumers, firms, the government, banks and other financial institutions, and so on) wish to make payments to India in order to: • buy Indian goods and services (import) from India • buy stocks and bonds (make financial investments) in India • make **foreign direct investments** in India (see p 88) • travel to India ✔ To demand ("buy") Indian rupees, US residents must supply ("sell") US dollars. **Supply of Indian rupees** arises when residents in India wish to make payments to the United States for the same reasons as above (and for which they demand US dollars): • buy US goods and services (import) from the United States • buy stocks and bonds (make financial investments) in the United States • make **foreign direct investments** in the United States (see p 88) • travel to the United States ✔ Indian rupees are supplied ("sold") because US dollars are demanded ("bought"). ✔ **The equilibrium exchange rate for Indian rupees is determined by the intersection of S and D at e*.**	**The market for Indian rupees** 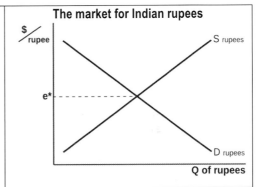 **Note how the axes are labeled** The horizontal axis measures the **Q of rupees**. The vertical axis, **$/rupee**, measures the "price" of rupees in terms of $, i.e. "the number of $ that must be paid to buy 1 rupee". ✔ Notice that **rupees appear in the denominator**.

Changes in exchange rates

currency appreciation = an increase in the value of a currency in a **freely floating exchange rate system**; may occur due to an increase in demand or decrease in supply of a currency	**currency depreciation** = a decrease in the value of a currency in a **freely floating exchange rate system**; may occur due to a decrease in demand or an increase in supply of a currency
¥ appreciation due to an increase in demand for ¥ 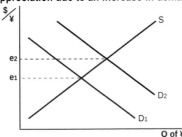	**¥ depreciation due to a decrease in demand for ¥** 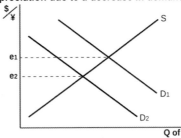
¥ appreciation due to a decrease in supply of ¥ 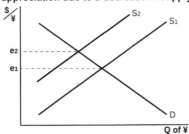	**¥ depreciation due to an increase in supply of ¥** 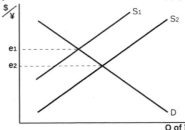

✔ Notice that in all diagrams, **¥** appear in the denominator of the label of the vertical axis. You can use any currency of your choice for the numerator.

Causes of exchange rate changes

✔ Exchange rates change whenever there is a change (increase or decrease) in the demand or supply of a currency.

Imagine a country called **Merryland** whose currency is the **Merryland $ (M$)**.

The M$ appreciates when there is:	The M$ depreciates when there is:
An increase in foreign demand for Merryland's exports ⇒ D for M$ increases ⇒ D curve for M$ shifts right ⇒ M$ appreciates	**A decrease in foreign demand for Merryland's exports** ⇒ D for M$ decreases ⇒ D curve for M$ shifts left ⇒ M$ depreciates
A decrease in Merryland's demand for imports ⇒ S of M$ falls (since less foreign exchange needed to pay for imports is demanded) ⇒ S curve of M$ shifts left ⇒ M$ appreciates	**An increase in Merryland's demand for imports** ⇒ S of M$ increases (since more foreign exchange needed to pay for imports is demanded) ⇒ S curve of M$ shifts right ⇒ M$ depreciates
A decrease in Merryland's incomes ⇒ Merryland's D for imports falls ⇒ S of M$ falls (since less foreign exchange needed to pay for imports is demanded) ⇒ S curve of M$ shifts left ⇒ M$ appreciates	**An increase in Merryland's incomes** ⇒ Merryland's D for imports rises ⇒ S of M$ increases (more foreign exchange needed to pay for imports is demanded) ⇒ S curve of M$ shifts right ⇒ M$ depreciates
A lower inflation rate in Merryland relative to other countries ⇒ Merryland's exports become more competitive abroad ⇒ D for exports increases ⇒ D curve for M$ shifts right ⇒ M$ appreciates; also Merryland's D for imports falls ⇒ S of M$ shifts left ⇒ M$ appreciates	**A higher inflation rate in Merryland relative to other countries** ⇒ Merryland's exports become less competitive abroad ⇒ D for exports falls ⇒ D curve for M$ shifts left ⇒ M$ depreciates; also D for imports increases ⇒ S curve of M$ shifts right ⇒ M$ depreciates
An increase in Merryland interest rates ⇒ Merryland becomes more attractive to foreign financial investors buying bonds in Merryland ⇒ D for M$ increases ⇒ D curve for M$ shifts right ⇒ M$ appreciates	**A decrease in Merryland interest rates** ⇒ Merryland becomes less attractive to foreign financial investors buying bonds in Merryland ⇒ D for M$ decreases ⇒ D curve for M$ shifts left ⇒ M$ depreciates
An increase in investment in Merryland from abroad (foreign direct investment (see p 88) **or financial investments)** ⇒ D for M$ increases ⇒ D curve for M$ shifts right ⇒ M$ appreciates	**A decrease in investment in Merryland from abroad (foreign direct investment** (see p 88) **or financial investments)** ⇒ D for M$ decreases ⇒ D curve for M$ shifts left ⇒ M$ depreciates
Currency speculation = buying or selling currencies to make a profit. **Expectations of M$ appreciation** ⇒ speculators buy M$ now to sell later at the higher exchange rate ⇒ D for M$ increases ⇒ D for M$ shifts right ⇒ M$ appreciates (note this may be a self-fulfilling process)	**Currency speculation: expectations of M$ depreciation** ⇒ speculators sell M$ now to buy later at the lower exchange rate ⇒ S of M$ increases ⇒ S curve of M$ shifts right ⇒ M$ depreciates (note that this may be a self-fulfilling process)
**Central bank intervenes by buying M$** (see p 69) ⇒ D for M$ increases ⇒ D curve for M$ shifts right ⇒ M$ appreciates	**Central Bank intervenes by selling M$** (see p 69) ⇒ S of M$ increases ⇒ S curve of M$ shifts right ⇒ M$ depreciates

Evaluating consequences of exchange rate changes

Appreciation of the M$ makes:	**Depreciation** of the M$ makes:
• Merryland's exports more expensive to foreigners (more foreign currencies must be given up per M$) ⇒ **exports fall** • Merryland's imports less expensive (the M$ can buy more of foreign currencies) ⇒ **imports increase** ✔ Appreciation causes net exports (X-M) to decrease.	• Merryland's exports less expensive to foreigners (less foreign currencies must be given up per M$) ⇒ **exports increase** • Merryland's imports more expensive (the M$ can buy less of foreign currencies) ⇒ **imports decrease** ✔ Depreciation causes net exports (X-M) to increase. (HL students: note the Marshall-Lerner condition and J-curve, p 73.)

Consequences for inflation

☑ **Appreciation** ⇒ net exports (X-M) ⇓ ⇒ aggregate demand shifts left ⇒ **demand-pull inflation** ⇓ ☑ **Appreciation** ⇒ imports less expensive ⇒ imported inputs (ex oil) cheaper so firms' costs of production ⇓ ⇒ **cost-push inflation** ⇓	☒ **Depreciation** ⇒ net exports (X-M) ⇑ ⇒ aggregate demand shifts right ⇒ **demand-pull inflation** ⇑ ☒ **Depreciation** ⇒ imports more expensive ⇒ imported inputs (ex oil) more costly, firms' costs of production ⇑ ⇒ **cost-push inflation** ⇑

Consequences for unemployment

☒ **Appreciation** ⇒ net exports (X-M) ⇓ ⇒ aggregate demand shifts left ⇒ **unemployment increases**	☑ **Depreciation** ⇒ net exports (X-M) ⇑ ⇒ aggregate demand shifts right ⇒ **unemployment decreases**

Consequences for economic growth

☒ **Appreciation** ⇒ net exports (X-M) ⇓ ⇒ aggregate demand shifts left ⇒ **negative effect on output and growth** ☑ **Appreciation** ⇒ imported inputs cheaper ⇒ lower costs of production increase SRAS ⇒ **positive effect on output and growth** ✔ Net effect on growth depends on which of the effects is stronger	☑ **Depreciation** ⇒ net exports (X-M) ⇑ ⇒ aggregate demand shifts right ⇒ **positive effect on output and growth** ☒ **Depreciation** ⇒ imported inputs more costly ⇒ higher costs of production decrease SRAS ⇒ **negative effect on output and growth** ✔ Net effect on growth depends on which of the effects is stronger

Consequences for the trade balance (current account balance)

☒ **Appreciation** ⇒ net exports (X-M)⇓ ⇒ trade deficit ⇑; trade surplus ⇓	☑ **Depreciation** ⇒ net exports (X-M) ⇑ ⇒ trade deficit ⇓; trade surplus ⇑ (HL: note the Marshall-Lerner condition and J-curve, p 73)

Consequences for foreign debt (see p 91)

☑ **Appreciation** ⇒ value of foreign debt ⇓ ⇒ easier for indebted countries to repay their debts	☒ **Depreciation** ⇒ value of foreign debt ⇑ ⇒ more difficult for debtor countries to reply their debts (a serious problem for some less developed countries; p 91)

Consequences for stakeholders

Consumers benefit from lower import prices and lower inflation **Firms** that depend on imported inputs benefit as costs of production ⇓ **Firms/workers** in export industries and import-competing industries lose **Foreign countries** exporting to Merryland gain from more exports	**Consumers** are hurt from higher import prices and higher inflation **Firms** that depend on imported inputs lose as costs of production ⇑ **Firms/workers** in export industries and import-competing industries gain **Foreign countries** exporting to Merryland lose from fewer exports

Government intervention: Fixed exchange rates

fixed exchange rate = an exchange rate fixed by a country's government or central bank at a certain level in terms of another currency (such as the US$ or €), hence not permitted to adjust to currency demand and supply; requires constant central bank intervention to maintain the fixed level	
devaluation = a decrease in the value of a currency in a **fixed exchange rate system**, achieved through the government or central bank which decides upon a new, lower exchange rate for the currency	**revaluation** = an increase in the value of a currency in a **fixed exchange rate system**, achieved through the government or central bank which decides upon a new, higher exchange rate for the currency

How the fixed rate is maintained

Suppose Merryland's currency, the M$, is fixed against the € at the rate of M$1 = €3. Initially the M$ market is at equilibrium at point a. Suppose foreigners' demand for Merryland's exports ⇓ so D for M$ shifts left from D_1 to D_2 ⇒ at the fixed rate of €3 there is excess S of M$ equal to a-b. In a free floating system the exchange rate would fall to €2 determined by D_2 and S_1 at point c.

✔ But at the fixed rate of €3, **D for M$ must be brought back to D_1 (hence to point a) or S of M$ must decrease to the dotted line S_2** (hence to point b) to maintain the fixed rate of €3.

✔ With freely floating exchange rates, the exchange rate adjusts to changes in D and S; **with fixed exchange rates, D or S are made to adjust in order to maintain the fixed rate**.

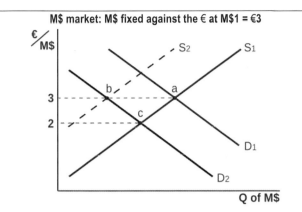

M$ market: M$ fixed against the € at M$1 = €3

Policies increasing D for M$: D for M$ curve shifts right to D_1:	Policies decreasing S of M$: S of M$ curve shifts left to S_2:
• The central bank can buy M$ in the foreign exchange market by selling reserves of foreign exchange (= foreign exchange held by the central bank) ⇒ D for M$ ⇑ and shifts right • The central bank can increase interest rates ⇒ financial capital is attracted to Merryland ⇒ D for M$ ⇑ and shifts right • The government of Merryland can borrow from abroad ⇒ funds flow into Merryland ⇒ D for M$ ⇑ and shifts right	• The government can use policies to limit imports: (i) contractionary fiscal and monetary policies ⇒ real GDP and incomes ⇓ ⇒ imports ⇓; and (ii) trade protection policies (tariffs, quotas, etc.) ⇒ imports ⇓. As imports ⇓ ⇒ S of M$⇓ and shifts left • The government can impose exchange controls (= limits on the amount of foreign exchange that can be bought by domestic residents) ⇒ S of M$⇓ and shifts left

However, each of these policies has disadvantages:

Policy	Disadvantages
Central bank buys M$ in foreign exchange markets	☒ Central bank eventually runs out of reserves of foreign exchange to sell
Central bank increases interest rates	☒ Higher interest rates cause recession in the economy
The government of Merryland borrows from abroad	☒ Repayment costs burden the economy in the future (see p 91)
Government limits imports through contractionary policies	☒ Contractionary policies cause recession
Government limits imports through trade protection measures	☒ Lead to resource misallocation and risks of retaliation
Government imposes exchange controls	☒ Lead to resource misallocation

✔ In the opposite situation, if foreigners' D for exports had increased, so D for M$ increased, the D for M$ curve would shift to the right. At the fixed rate of €3 there would be **excess D for M$**, leading to appreciation in a free-floating system. Appropriate policies to maintain the fixed rate would include central bank sales of M$ (by buying foreign exchange) so that S of M$ ⇑ or lowering the interest rate so that D for M$ ⇓.
✔ **It is easier to maintain a fixed rate for excess D of a currency than excess S**, as there are fewer negative consequences of policies.

Government intervention: Managed exchange rates

managed exchange rates (= managed float) = exchange rates determined largely by currency D and S, but where **the central bank intervenes at times** by buying and selling foreign exchange to avoid sharp short-term fluctuations and influence the value of the exchange rate	
✔ Most economically developed countries today have managed exchange rates. Exchange rates are determined mainly by market forces, with periodic intervention. Intervention takes the form of central bank buying and selling of reserve currencies, and sometimes interest rate changes.	✔ Some economically less developed countries **peg** (= fix) their currency to the US$, and float together with the US$. To maintain the pegged value of their currency, these countries use the policies discussed above in connection with fixed exchange rates.

Distinction between overvalued and undervalued currencies

overvalued currency = a currency whose value is maintained higher than its market equilibrium level; may occur in fixed or managed exchange rate systems		undervalued currency = a currency whose value is maintained lower than its market equilibrium level; may occur in fixed or managed exchange rate systems	
☑ makes imports less expensive; was used by less developed countries in the past to speed up industrialization, based on imports of cheap raw materials and capital goods (part of **import substitution** policies; see p 85)	☒ makes exports more expensive, hurting export industries and the economy ☒ worsens the current account balance and creates balance of payments difficulties (see p 71, 73) ☒ cheap imports create unfair competition for domestic producers ☒ the above lower domestic employment and economic growth	☑ makes exports less expensive to foreigners; used by some countries to promote growth of export industries ☑ promotes employment in export industries ☑ promotes economic growth	☒ creates an unfair competitive advantage for domestic industries, and so is known as a "dirty float" ☒ invites retaliation through competitive devaluations (one country devaluing after another) ☒ makes imports more expensive, causing cost-push inflation

Comparing and contrasting exchange rate systems

Freely flexible (floating) exchange rates

☑ no need for the central bank or government to intervene ☑ no need for the central bank to hold foreign currency reserves ☑ automatic correction of current account imbalances: a trade deficit (with excess S of the currency) through depreciation, a trade surplus (with excess D of the currency) through appreciation (see p 72) ☑ freedom for policy-makers to use monetary (and fiscal) policy to deal with domestic problems (inflation, unemployment) without having to respond to the need to maintain a fixed exchange rate ☑ there is usually a smooth adjustment to external shocks (barring sudden and abrupt exchange rate changes)	☒ uncertainty over future exchange rates for firms, importers and exporters, and investors, negatively affecting investment, the volume of trade, and the volume of investments ☒ large, sudden exchange rate changes may create instability, sometimes even leading to financial crises, requiring IMF intervention (see p 90) ☒ if there is inflation, the currency depreciates (since X ⇓ and M ⇑), but depreciation may lead to imported cost-push inflation, reducing export competitiveness and lowering economic growth ☒ there may be currency speculation

Fixed exchange rates

☑ high degree of certainty over future exchange rates for firms, importers and exporters, and investors, with positive effects on investment, the volume of trade, and the volume of investments ☑ inflation is kept low through fiscal policy; since there cannot be depreciation when there is inflation, a high inflation rate would create a large excess S of the currency (since X ⇓ and M ⇑), which would require major interventions with negative effects (see p 69) ; therefore fiscal policy is used to control inflation ☑ less room for currency speculation, as the exchange rate is fixed (except when currency revaluation/devaluation is expected, and speculation may hasten the revaluation or devaluation)	☒ need for constant intervention by the central bank to maintain the fixed exchange rate ☒ need for the central bank to hold foreign currency reserves to be able to intervene with purchases of the domestic currency when necessary ☒ loss of monetary policy to deal with domestic problems, since interest rates must be used to maintain the exchange rate ☒ in the event of large and persistent current account deficits, there must be contractionary fiscal policy to limit imports, with negative effects on the economy since recession results or becomes even deeper

HL topics Exchange rate calculations

Calculate the value of a currency in terms of another

Given the exchange rate £ 1 = US$ 1.65, calculate the value of 1 US$ in terms of £. US$ 1 = $\dfrac{1}{1.65}$ = **£ 0.61**	Given the exchange rate € 1 = Canadian $ 1.44, calculate the value of 1 Canadian $ in terms of €. Canadian $ 1 = $\dfrac{1}{1.44}$ = **€ 0.69**

Calculate the price of a good in different currencies using exchange rates

Given the £ - US $ exchange rate above, calculate the price in £ of 5 books that cost US$15 each. Total cost of books in US$ = 5 x US$15 = US$75. Since US$1 = £ 0.61 ⇒ 0.61 x 75 = **£45.75**	Given the Canadian $ - € exchange rate above, calculate the price in € of 7 pizzas that cost Canadian $10 each. Total cost of pizzas in Canadian $ = 7 x $10 = Canadian $70. Since Canadian $1 = €0.69 ⇒ 0.69 x 70 = **€48.30**

Interpret and calculate changes in a currency's value from a set of data

Average annual exchange rates: £ per US$1*	In which years did the £ appreciate? **2011**	In which years did the $ depreciate? **2011**	(a) Calculate the % change in the value of the US$ in 2007-2012.
2007 0.520 2008 0.567 2009 0.667 2010 0.673 2011 0.649 2012 0.656	In which years did the £ depreciate? **2008, 2009, 2010, 2012** ✔ Appreciation of one currency always implies depreciation of the other currency.	In which years did the $ appreciate? **2008, 2009, 2010, 2012**	$\dfrac{0.656 - 0.520}{0.520}$ x 100 = **26.15% appreciation of the US$** (b) Calculate the % change in the value of the £ in 2007-2012. (i) Find the value of £ in terms of US$ (£ price) in 2007 and 2012: **2007**: £1 = 1/.520 = **1.923** US$. **2012**: £1 = 1/0.656 = **1.524** US$ (ii) $\dfrac{1.524 - 1.923}{1.923}$ x 100 = **-20.75% depreciation for the £**

* These figures show the amount of £ that must be given up (sold) to buy 1 US$. They also show the amount of £ that can be bought by giving up (selling) 1 US$. In the period 2007-2012, an increasing amount of pounds was needed to get 1 US$ therefore the £ has been losing its value relative to the US$. At the same time, 1 US$ can get an increasing amount of £ therefore the US$ has been increasing its value relative to the £.

Linear demand and supply functions

Calculate the equilibrium exchange rate	Plot D and S to identify equilibrium exchange rate
Given demand and supply functions Qd = 12 -3P and Qs = -2 +4P, where Qd and Qs are in millions of M$ (Merryland's currency), find the equilibrium exchange rate of the M$ in terms of €, and the equilibrium quantity of M$. Since at equilibrium Qd = Qs: 12 – 3P = -2 +4P ⇒ 14 = 7P ⇒ P = 2 ⇒ **€2 per M$1** (i.e. M$1 is worth €2) To find equilibrium Q, substitute P=2 into the D or S equation and solve: Q = 12 – 3(2) ⇒ **6 million M$**	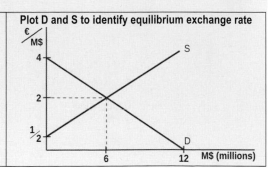

3.3 THE BALANCE OF PAYMENTS

The structure of the balance of payments

balance of payments = a record of all transactions between residents of a country with residents of all other countries, consisting of all payments entering into the country from abroad (Inflows) and all payments leaving a country to go abroad (outflows) over a period of time, usually a year; it consists of the **current account**, the **capital account** and the **financial account**, which in the course of a year add up to zero	
credit item = any item of the balance of payments involving an **inflow** of funds into a country, entered with a plus (+) sign	**surplus on an account** = an excess of credits over debits in any of the three accounts, meaning that inflows from abroad > outflows going abroad
debit item = any item of the balance of payments involving an **outflow** of funds from a country, entered with a minus (-) sign	**deficit on an account** = an excess of debits over credits in any of the three accounts, meaning that outflows going abroad > inflows from abroad

Components of balance of payments accounts

The current account is made up of four items:

1. Balance of trade in goods: value of exports of goods (a credit since payment is received from abroad) minus value of imports of goods (a debit since payments are made to foreigners). **The balance of trade is usually the most important item of the current account.**

2. Balance of trade in services: value of exports of services (a credit since payment is received from abroad) minus value of imports of services (a debit since payments for these are made to foreigners).

3. Income: receipts from abroad (credits) minus payments abroad (debits) of rents, interest and profits.

4. Current transfers: receipts from abroad (credits) minus payments abroad (debits) of items including pensions, remittances (= money sent home by workers living and working abroad), and gifts.

The capital account consists of two items, and is usually less important that the current and financial accounts:

1. Capital transfers: inflows (credits) minus outflows (debits) of a variety of items including debt forgiveness (when a foreign debt is cancelled), non-life insurance claims, and investment grants.

2. Transactions in non-produced, non-financial assets: inflows (credits) minus outflows (debits) of payments for purchase of natural resources that have not been produced (ex land, fishing rights, forestry rights), and purchase of intangible assets (ex copyrights, patents).

The financial account consists of three items:

1. Direct investment: inflows (credits) minus outflows (debits) of funds used for investments in physical capital, including factories and buildings (**FDI**, usually undertaken by **multinational corporations**; see p 88).

2. Portfolio investment: inflows (credits) minus outflows (debits) of funds used for investments in financial capital (stocks and bonds).

3. Reserve assets = foreign exchange held by the central bank that is bought or sold to influence the value of the country's exchange rate in a fixed or managed exchange rate system. Foreign exchange is **bought** when the central bank **sells the domestic currency** to lower its value (an outflow of domestic currency therefore a debit); foreign exchange is **sold** when the central bank **buys the domestic currency** in order to increase its value (an inflow of the domestic currency therefore a credit)

Errors and omissions: included to account for items that have not been included or for errors, forcing a zero overall balance

Merryland's Balance of payments, 2012, billion M$

1. Balance of trade in goods (goods exports minus imports)	-21
2. Balance of trade in services (services exports minus imports)	+5
3. Income (inflows minus outflows)	+3
4. Current transfers (inflows minus outflows)	- 4
(I) Balance on current account (= 1+2+3+4)	**-17**
1. Capital transfers (inflows minus outflows)	+3
2. Transactions in non-produced, non-financial assets (inflows minus outflows)	-5
(II) Balance on capital account (=1+2)	**-2**
1. Direct investment (inflows minus outflows)	+12
2. Portfolio investment (inflows minus outflows)	+4
3. Reserve assets	+2
(III) Balance on financial account (= 1+2+3)	**+18**
(IV) Errors and omissions	**+1**
BALANCE (I+II+III+IV)	**0**

✔ The overall balance of the balance of payments is always 0, because the sum of credits (+) is always balanced by the sum of debits (-) over a year: +M$30 ⇔ -M$30
+5+3+3+12+4+2+1 ⇔ -21-4-5

✔ The balance on current account is always balanced by the sum of capital account plus financial account balances plus errors and omissions: **- M$17 billion** ⇔ **+ M$17 billion** (= -2 + 18 +1)

✔ There is a **deficit on current account of M$17 billion** (debits > credits by M$17 billion), due mainly to a **trade deficit** (= X > M)

✔ There is a **deficit on capital account of M$2 billion** (debits > credits by M$2 billion)

✔ There is a **surplus on financial account of M$18 billion** (credits > debits by M$18 billion)

✔ In 2012, the Merryland central bank **bought M$2 billion** (by selling reserve assets) to make up for the shortage of credits needed to bring about a zero balance in the balance of payments.

The balance of payments in relation to exchange rates

Why the overall balance of the balance of payments is always equal to zero
A currency's exchange rate is always determined by currency D and S (this is true also for fixed exchange rates, where D = S is forced (see p 69). Notice that **D for a currency gives rise to credits (inflows of money into a country), and S of a currency gives rise to debits (outflows of money from the country)**. Since for any given exchange rate, D for the currency = S of the currency, it follows that **credits = debits**.

How credits equal debits in a freely floating exchange rate system
In a freely floating system, the equilibrium exchange rate is determined by market forces (D and S for the currency). Looking at the € market, at e₁, D for € < S of €, meaning that credits < debits in the eurozone, and so market forces push the value of the € downward to e*, where D for € = S of € and credits = debits. At e₂, D for € > S of €, meaning that credits > debits, and so market forces push the € upward to e*, where again S = D and credits = debits in the eurozone. Therefore market forces ensure that debits will always be equal to credits at the equilibrium exchange rate.

Credits = debits: freely floating exchange rates

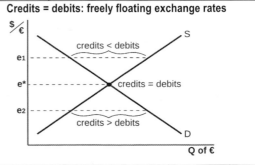

71

How credits are made to equal debits in a fixed exchange rate system	✔ If the exchange rate is fixed at a level where **D < S** and **credits < debits** the central bank must buy the currency (sell foreign exchange) or raise the interest rate (to attract foreign financial capital) ⇒ D for the currency ⇑ to the point where D = S hence credits = debits. **The increase in D for the currency creates the missing credits.**	✔ If the exchange rate is fixed at a level where **D > S** and **credits > debits** the central bank sells the currency (buys foreign exchange) or lowers the interest rate (foreign financial capital leaves) ⇒ S of the currency ⇑ to the point where D = S and credits = debits. **The increase in S for the currency creates the missing debits.**
In a fixed exchange rate system, since the exchange rate cannot change in the event of excess D or excess S of the currency, the central bank or government change D and/or S of the currency to make them produce the desired (fixed) rate (see p 69).		

The interdependence of the current account and financial account

Ignoring the capital account and errors and omissions (for simplicity and because they are relatively unimportant) it follows from the above that there is a close relationship between the current account and the financial account: a surplus in one account implies a deficit in the other. If there are excess credits in one account (a surplus) there must be excess debits in the other account (a deficit).

Current account imbalances and effects on exchange rates

Current account deficit and the exchange rate	Current account surplus and the exchange rate
✔ A current account deficit results in a downward pressure on the exchange rate because:	✔ A current account surplus results in an upward pressure on the exchange rate because:
The M$ is initially at equilibrium at e₁. Suppose there is a decrease in demand for Merryland's exports ⇒ D for the M$ falls ⇒ D for M$ curve shifts left to D₂ ⇒ at e₁ there is excess S of M$ and exports (credits) < imports (debits). If nothing changes in the capital and financial accounts to create the necessary amount of missing credits, **the exchange rate falls to e₂** ⇒ exports (X) increase and imports (M) decrease ⇒ **X (credits) = M (debits)** is restored.	The M$ is initially at equilibrium at e₁. If there is an increase in demand for Merryland's exports ⇒ D for the M$ increases ⇒ D for M$ curve shifts right to D₂ ⇒ at e₁ there is excess D for M$ and exports (credits) > imports (debits). If nothing changes in the capital and financial accounts to create the necessary amount of missing debits, **the exchange rate increases to e₂** ⇒ exports (X) decease and imports (M) increase ⇒ **X (credits) = M (debits)** is restored.
Current account deficit and falling exchange rate 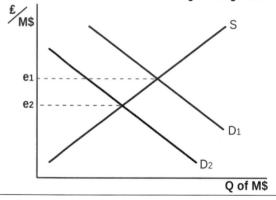	Current account surplus and increasing exchange rate 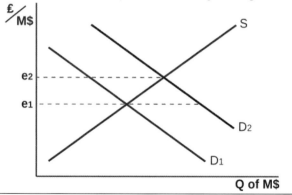

HL Topics The balance of payments

Calculate elements of the balance of payments

Fill in the missing figures below.	Use the following information on Country Y to present its balance of payments (2010, billion $) and fill in the missing figures.	
Country X Balance of payments, 2010, billion $	Balance on capital account	-8
Exports of goods ..... +105	Exports of services	+79
Imports of goods ..... -140	Balance	____
Balance of trade in goods ..... ____	Capital transfers	
Exports of services ..... ____	Balance of trade in services	-8
Imports of services ..... -34	Reserve assets	-14
Balance of trade in services ..... +14	Errors and omissions	-2
Income ..... -5	Balance on current account	
Current transfers ..... +3	Current transfers	-7
Balance on current account ..... ____	Direct investment	
Capital transfers ..... +2	Income	+25
Transactions in non-produced, non-financial assets ..... ____	Balance on financial account	
Balance on capital account ..... +3	Exports of goods	+410
Direct investment ..... + 17	Imports of goods	-325
Portfolio investment ..... ____	Balance of trade in goods	____
Reserve assets ..... +5	Imports of services	____
Balance on financial account ..... ____	Portfolio investment	-24
Errors and omissions ..... +2	Transactions in non-produced, non-financial assets	-3
Balance ..... ____		

Answers listed in the order of appearance of the blanks
First column: -35, +48, -23, +1, -4, +18, 0.   **Second column:** 0, -5, +95, -47, -85, +85, -87

Implications of persistent current account deficits

A current account deficit that persists over long periods of time can pose serious problems to an economy. It indicates that a country is **spending more to buy from abroad** (debits) than it is earning from selling abroad (credits). This excess of debits over credits must be balanced by credits (inflows) in the combined financial and capital accounts. Persistent current account deficits may result in:

☒ **Higher interest rates**, to attract financial investments (needed as credits), which are contractionary as they lead to recession	☒ **Increased borrowing from abroad**, leading to high **indebtedness** (= high debt levels) with its own set of problems (see p 91):
	• **poor international credit ratings** make it difficult to get more loans in the future
☒ **Contractionary fiscal policies**, to lower incomes and therefore imports, which also lead to recession	• **interest payments on loans**, that use up funds with alternative uses in the economy (investments, merit goods provision), i.e. opportunity costs
	• **fewer imports of capital and other resources**, needed for domestic production, since the ability to import is limited
☒ **Depreciation of the currency** may result (for reasons explained above, p 72), leading to cost-push inflation due to higher costs of imported inputs	• **increasingly higher interest rates** to attract financial capital
	• **lower future standard of living**, as future generations will have to reply the loans
☒ **Increased sale of domestic assets** to foreigners (stocks, real estate, factories), which may lead to loss of control of a country over its assets	☒ **Lower economic growth in the future**, in view of the above factors, including contractionary monetary and fiscal policies, interest payments with opportunity costs, and lower possibilities to import needed inputs

Methods to reduce current account deficits and evaluation

Expenditure-switching policies = policies that switch consumption away from imports and toward domestically produced goods. Include two main policies:	**Expenditure-reducing policies** = policies that reduce expenditures and aggregate demand, lowering imports and increasing exports. Include **contractionary fiscal and monetary policies**, with two effects:
• **trade protection policies** (tariffs, quotas, etc) ⟹ imports ⇓	• AD decreases ⟹ lower incomes ⟹ D for imports decreases
☑ trade deficit (X-M) hence current account deficit are reduced	• lower AD ⟹ rate of inflation falls ⟹ foreign D for exports increases
☒ prices of protected goods ⇑, consumption of protected goods ⇓	☑ trade deficit (X-M) hence current account deficit are reduced
☒ increased inefficiency of firms	☑ higher interest rates attract financial capital creating needed credits in the financial account
☒ greater domestic and global resource misallocation	☒ contractionary fiscal and monetary policy lead to recession ⟹ real GDP decreases and unemployment increases
☒ risk of retaliation by other countries	☒ higher interest rates ⟹ currency appreciation ⟹ exports decrease, imports increase ⟹ trade deficit and current account balance worsen (this partly cancels the effects of expenditure-reducing policies)
• **depreciation** ⟹ exports cheaper, imports more expensive	
☑ trade deficit (X-M) hence current account deficit are reduced	
☒ increased exports ⟹ AD⇑ ⟹ demand-pull inflation	
☒ higher import prices ⟹ cost-push inflation	
Supply-side policies Market-based supply-side polices, including policies to increase competition (p 61) and labor market reforms (p 62) as well as interventionist S-side policies (p 61), all of which aim to shift the LRAS curve to the right and lower inflationary pressures in the economy, thus increasing export competitiveness and leading to growth in exports.	
☑ lower inflation ⟹ firms more competitive in international markets ⟹ exports ⇑ ⟹ trade deficit (X-M) and current account deficit are reduced ☑ see p 61 - 62 for more details on the effects of supply-side policies	☒ need a long time to be effective ☒ see p 61 - 62 for more details on the effects of supply-side policies

Implications of persistent current account surpluses

A current account surplus that persists over long periods can pose some problems to an economy. It indicates that a country is **spending less to buy from abroad** (debits) than it is earning from selling abroad (credits). This excess of credits over debits must be balanced by debits (outflows) in the combined financial and capital accounts.

☑ **High rates of economic growth** may result from large volumes of exports and rapid export growth (ex China)	☒ **Lower consumption and hence lower standards of living** than necessary since X < M (therefore consumption < domestic production)
☒ **Appreciation of the currency** may result ⟹ reduced export competitiveness ⟹ X⇓, M⇑ ⟹ net exports (X-M) ⇓ ⟹ AD⇓	☒ **Lower domestic investment** than necessary since funds are leaving the country through the financial account (debits) to balance the credits

The Marshall-Lerner condition and the J-curve effect

The Marshall-Lerner condition

Depreciation or devaluation, by making imports more expensive to domestic residents and exports cheaper to foreigners, results in a fall in imports and a rise in exports, and hence a smaller trade deficit (or current account deficit). However, very often, the improvement in the trade deficit occurs only after a time delay. The reason lies in the price elasticity of demand (PED) for imports and exports, which is often quite low over short periods of time (price inelastic demand). The Marshall-Lerner condition states what must hold for a deprecation or devaluation to lead to a **smaller trade deficit**:

If $PED_{exports} + PED_{imports} > 1$, depreciation ⟹ smaller trade deficit.   But if $PED_{exports} + PED_{imports} < 1$, depreciation ⟹ larger trade deficit.

✔ Note that an **appreciation** or **revaluation** will lead to a **smaller trade surplus** provided $PED_{exports} + PED_{imports} > 1$.

| **The J-curve effect**
 Is a graphical representation of the effects of the Marshall-Lerner condition. In short periods of time (about six months for most manufactured products), $PED_{exports} + PED_{imports} < 1$, therefore depreciation initially leads to a larger trade deficit, shown in the diagram. After six months to a year, $PED_{exports} + PED_{imports} > 1$, therefore with depreciation the trade deficit starts to shrink and eventually becomes a trade surplus.
 PED for imports and PED for exports are low over short periods of time because consumers and producers need time to learn about and adjust to price changes, or to discover alternative products, or they may have prior contractual agreements. | 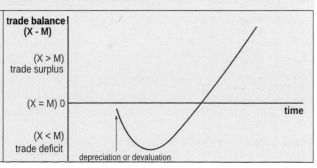 |

3.4 ECONOMIC INTEGRATION

economic integration = growing economic relations and cooperation between countries arising from trade or other agreements that link their economies together **preferential trade agreement** = according to the World Trade Organization (WTO), an agreement between two or more countries to give preferential access to particular products (access with low or no tariffs or other trade protection); often includes additional issues beyond trade such as services, investment, and intellectual property rights; they may be bilateral or regional agreements and they may involve **free trade areas** or **customs unions**	**trading bloc** = two or more countries that have agreed to reduce or eliminate trade barriers between them to encourage free trade **bilateral trade agreement** = an agreement between **two countries** to reduce or eliminate trade barriers to encourage free trade between them **regional grade agreement** = an agreement between **several countries in a geographical region** to reduce or eliminate trade barriers to encourage free trade between them **multilateral trade agreement** = an agreement between **many countries around the world**, as a rule under the leadership of the **World Trade Organization (WTO)**, to reduce or eliminate trade barriers to encourage free trade between them

Trading blocs

Free trade areas	Customs unions	Common markets
A **free trade area** is a group of countries that have agreed to reduce or eliminate trade barriers to achieve free trade between them. Each country retains the right to impose its own trade barriers toward non-members. Ex NAFTA (North American Free Trade Agreement)	A **customs union** is a higher form of integration than a free trade area because in addition to free trade between members there is also a common trade policy (common trade barriers) toward non-members. Ex SACU (South Africa Customs Union)	A **common market** is a higher form of integration than a customs union because in addition to free trade and a common trade policy toward non-members there is also free movement of labor and capital between the members. Ex EEC (European Economic Community, before this became the European Union)

Evaluating trading blocs

Trading blocs offer similar advantages as free trade:	Yet trading blocs also face a number of disadvantages:
☑ Increased competition among producers due to greater imports, forcing inefficient producers to close down and lowering production costs (efficiency improves) ☑ Lower prices for consumers, increased product variety and improved quality ☑ Provide opportunities for firms to expand into larger markets ☑ Increased internal or external investment by firms that want to benefit from the larger market size ☑ Increased exports to members of the trading bloc ☑ Greater economic growth ☑ Improved allocation of resources ☑ Reduced hostilities due to greater economic integration ☑ HL topic By growing in size due to expansion into larger markets, firms may benefit from **economies of scale** ☑ HL topic Possible benefits from **trade creation** = the replacement of higher-cost domestic products by lower cost imported products due to the formation of a trading bloc. Ex Clayland is an inefficient producer of ore compared to Rockland, but because of tariffs on ore it protects its high-cost ore producers. Clayland and Rockland then form a trading bloc and eliminate tariffs on ore ⇒ Clayland's domestic production of ore falls and is replaced by lower-cost imports from Rockland.	☒ Loss of national autonomy particularly in higher levels of integration ☒ Over the short term inefficient firms may go out of business, resulting in greater unemployment, increased poverty and greater income inequalities ☒ Trading blocs, often seen as an alternative to multilateral agreements under the WTO, may limit the role of the WTO as a forum to negotiate global free trade ☒ The break-up of the global economy into grading blocs rather global free trade through multilateral (WTO) agreements may increase inefficiency in global resource allocation ☒ Developing countries that sign preferential trade agreements with large countries (ex US) or country groups (ex EU) are unable to negotiate as effectively as they would if they negotiated together as a group under the WTO ☒ If member countries are not at a similar level of economic and technological development, the relatively less developed countries may be at a disadvantage as they may be unable to compete with the more advanced and often lower-cost producers of developed countries (see p 87 for more on economically less developed countries). ☒ HL topic Possible losses from **trade diversion** = the replacement of lower-cost imported products by higher-cost imports due to the formation of a trading bloc. Ex Woolland has a tariff on bricks, and imports bricks from Clayland, which is a lower-cost brick producer than Rockland. Woolland then forms a trade agreement with Rockland and eliminates tariffs on imports from Rockland, maintaining them on imports from Clayland, which now become more expensive. Therefore Woolland begins to import from Rockland, the higher-cost producer.

Monetary union

monetary union = members of a common market adopt a common currency and a common central bank responsible for monetary policy for all the members. Ex the Eurozone countries, that adopted the euro after giving up their national currencies, whose common monetary policy is the responsibility of the European Central Bank (ECB)

Evaluating monetary union

☑ No risk and uncertainty arising from exchange rate changes, as all countries have the same currency, benefitting firms, consumers, importers, exporters, leading to greater economic activity ☑ No transactions costs, or costs derived from having to convert one currency into another ☑ There is price transparency, making it far easier to compare prices and costs across countries ☑ Higher levels of investment due to lack of exchange rate risk ☑ Encourages efforts to maintain low inflation rate for export competitiveness since there is no possibility for currency depreciation ☑ Higher rates of economic growth due to all of the above ☑ A stronger influence in world affairs due to the much larger size of the combined economies of all the member states	☒ Loss of the ability to conduct monetary policy in accordance with domestic needs (to deal with inflation or recession and unemployment) ☒ Loss of own exchange rate and the ability of a country's own currency to appreciate/depreciate (revalue/devalue) to deal with trade imbalances ☒ Loss of economic sovereignty, as the responsibilities of national governments and national central banks are taken over by supranational bodies that moreover may be unelected (ex the European Central Bank) ☒ The single monetary policy impacts differently on each country depending on where it is in the business cycle, i.e. monetary policy may be too expansionary/contractionary for some countries ☒ Without a common fiscal policy, it is unlikely that monetary union can work; if a country/region experiences recession, centrally collected tax revenues could finance necessary investments in those regions

3.4 HL TOPIC TERMS OF TRADE

terms of trade = average price of exports divided by the average price of imports times 100; it is the ratio of two index numbers times 100:

$$\text{terms of trade (ToT)} = \frac{\text{index of average export prices}}{\text{index of average import prices}} \times 100$$

Understanding the terms of trade

Improvement in the terms of trade = the value of the ToT increases due to an increase in average export prices or decrease in average import prices (or both). ✔ A ToT Improvement indicates that the same amount of imports can be bought with a smaller amount of exports; or that more imports can be bought with the same amount of exports.	**deterioration in the terms of trade** = the value of the ToT decreases due to a decrease in average export prices or increase in average import prices (or both). ✔ A ToT deterioration indicates that a larger amount of exports is required to buy the same amount of imports, or that the same amount of exports can buy only a smaller amount of imports.

Calculations using the terms of trade

<table>
<tr><td colspan="5">Rockland's average export and import prices are shown below.</td><td>1. What is the base year? 2012 (index number = 100)</td></tr>
<tr><td></td><td>2011</td><td>2012</td><td>2013</td><td>2014</td><td rowspan="3">2. Calculate the terms of trade for each of the years.
2011: 98.72 / 97.53 x 100 = 101.22
2012: 100.00
2013: 105.43 / 104.27 x 100 = 101.11
2014: 109.7 5 / 105.17 x 100 = 104.35</td></tr>
<tr><td>Index of average export prices</td><td>98.72</td><td>100.00</td><td>105.43</td><td>109.75</td></tr>
<tr><td>Index of average import prices</td><td>97.53</td><td>100.00</td><td>104.27</td><td>105.17</td></tr>
<tr><td colspan="5"></td><td>3. In which year(s) did the ToT improve? In 2013 and 2014
4. In which year(s) did the ToT deteriorate? In 2012</td></tr>
</table>

Causes of changes in the terms of trade

Causes in the short term:	Causes in the long term:
• **changes in demand conditions** If global demand for a particular product increases (perhaps due to a change in consumer tastes) $\Rightarrow$ price of the product increases $\Rightarrow$ ToT improve for exporting countries and deteriorate for importing countries. If global demand falls the opposite will occur. • **changes in supply conditions** If global supply of a product increases (perhaps due to favorable weather conditions affecting agriculture or decreases in the global price of oil) $\Rightarrow$ price of the product falls $\Rightarrow$ ToT deteriorate for exporting countries and improve for Importing countries. If global supply decreases the opposite will occur. • **changes in relative inflation rates** If a country experiences higher inflation rates relative to other countries $\Rightarrow$ prices of exports increase $\Rightarrow$ its ToT improve and ToT of countries that Import from the high inflation country deteriorate. • **changes in relative exchange rates** Currency depreciation or devaluation $\Rightarrow$ import prices rise $\Rightarrow$ ToT deteriorate. Appreciation or revaluation $\Rightarrow$ import prices fall $\Rightarrow$ ToT improve.	• **changes in productivity** If productivity (output per unit of labor input) increases $\Rightarrow$ supply increases (S curve shifts right) $\Rightarrow$ prices of exports fall $\Rightarrow$ ToT deteriorate for exporting countries. • **technological improvements** Similar effects as productivity increases, since technological advances are often the cause of productivity increases; supply increases (S curve shifts right) $\Rightarrow$ prices of exports fall $\Rightarrow$ ToT deteriorate for exporting counttries. • **changes in income levels** Over long period of time incomes tend to increase, leading to demand increases, but the effects on countries' ToT depend on income elasticities of demand (YEDs) for exports and imports. Primary commodities, often produced and exported by developing countries, are income inelastic (YED<1) while manufactured goods and services, often produced and exported by developed countries, are income elastic (YED>1) (see p 11). Since D and hence P of income elastic goods rise faster than D and P of income inelastic goods, countries exporting goods with a high YED experience ToT improvements while countries exporting goods with low YEDs experience deteriorating ToT (see p 76 for more details).

Consequences of changes in the terms of trade

Effects of changes in the terms of trade on the current account

Points to note:
✔ Since the trade balance is the most important part of the current account, this examines the effects of ToT changes on the **trade balance**.
✔ Trade balance = **value of exports (export revenues) – value of imports (import expenditures)**.
✔ The effects of changes in the ToT on a country's trade balance **depend on the cause of changes in the ToT**.

| ✔ **If ToT changes are caused by changes in global demand**, the ToT and balance of trade change in the same direction: both improve or both deteriorate

 Suppose global D for corn increases from **D₁ to D₂** $\Rightarrow$ P⇑ from P₁ to P₂ and Q⇑ from Q₁ to Q₂ $\Rightarrow$ (P x Q)⇑

 For exporting countries: P⇑ means **ToT improve**, and (P x Q)⇑ means export revenues ⇑ $\Rightarrow$ **trade balance improves** (trade deficit ⇓ OR trade surplus ⇑)

 For importing countries: P⇑ means **ToT deteriorate**, and (P x Q) ⇑ means import expenditures ⇑ $\Rightarrow$ **trade balance worsens** (trade deficit ⇑ OR trade surplus ⇓)

 Suppose global D falls from **D₁ to D₃** $\Rightarrow$ P⇓ to P₃ and Q⇓ to Q₃ $\Rightarrow$ (P x Q) ⇓
 For exporting countries, **ToT deteriorate** and **trade balance worsens**
 For importing countries, **ToT improve** and **trade balance improves** | **When global D changes, ToT and trade balance both improve or both deteriorate**

 |

✔ **If ToT changes are caused by changes in global supply,** the effects on the balance of trade depend on the PED of the good that is exported or imported.	**When global S changes, the effects of ToT changes on the trade balance depend on PED**
Suppose global S of a good increases from S_1 to $S_2 \Rightarrow$ P⇓ to P_2 and Q⇑ to Q_2	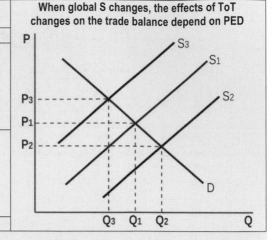
If PED < 1 (ex primary commodity) $\Rightarrow$ %⇑ in Q < %⇓ in P $\Rightarrow$ (P x Q) ⇓	
For exporting countries: since P⇓ $\Rightarrow$ ToT deteriorate; and P x Q (= export revenues) ⇓ $\Rightarrow$ trade balance worsens	
For importing countries: since P⇓ $\Rightarrow$ ToT improve; and $\Rightarrow$ P x Q (= import expenditures) ⇓ $\Rightarrow$ trade balance improves	
✔ **If PED < 1, the ToT and balance of trade change in same direction.**	
If PED > 1 (ex manufactured good) $\Rightarrow$ %⇑ in Q > %⇓ in P $\Rightarrow$ (P x Q) ⇑	
For exporting countries: since P⇓ $\Rightarrow$ ToT deteriorate; but P x Q (= export revenues) ⇑ $\Rightarrow$ trade balance improves	
For importing countries: since P⇓ $\Rightarrow$ ToT improve; but P x Q (= import expenditures) ⇑ $\Rightarrow$ trade balance deteriorate	
✔ **If PED >1, the ToT and balance of trade change in opposite directions.**	
✔ The same results hold for global supply decreases.	

✔ **If ToT changes are caused by exchange rate changes**, effects on the trade balance depend on the **Marshall-Lerner condition** (p 73)	
Depreciation/devaluation $\Rightarrow$ import prices ⇑ $\Rightarrow$ **ToT deteriorate;**	**Appreciation/revaluation** $\Rightarrow$ import prices ⇓ $\Rightarrow$ **ToT improve;**
If PEDx + PEDm >1 $\Rightarrow$ **trade balance improves** (trade deficit ⇓ OR trade surplus ⇑)	If PEDx + PEDm >1 $\Rightarrow$ **trade balance worsens** (trade deficit ⇓ OR trade surplus ⇑)
If the M-L condition does not hold (PEDx + PEDm < 1) $\Rightarrow$ **trade balance worsens** (trade deficit ⇑ OR trade surplus ⇓)	If the M-L condition does not hold (PEDx + PEDm < 1) $\Rightarrow$ **trade balance improves** (trade deficit ⇓ OR trade surplus ⇑)

Effects of short-term fluctuations in the terms of trade of developing countries

The ToT of developing countries whose exports are dominated by primary commodities tend to fluctuate much more than the ToT of countries that export manufactured products because of **inelastic D and S of primary commodities** (PED<1 and PES<1) (see p 10, 12).

Inelastic demand primary goods	Elastic demand manufactured goods	Inelastic supply primary goods	Elastic supply manufactured goods
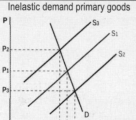	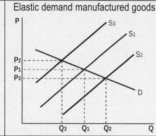	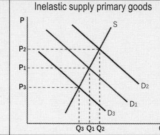	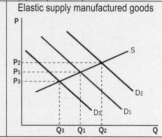

As S shifts along the D curve, price fluctuations are larger for primary goods with inelastic D (PED < 1) $\Rightarrow$ larger ToT fluctuations	As D shifts along the S curve, price fluctuations are larger for primary goods with inelastic S (PES < 1) $\Rightarrow$ larger ToT fluctuations
Consequences of ToT fluctuations for countries specializing in export of primary commodities	
☒ Fluctuating revenues of producers, leading to uncertainties with negative effects on investment ☒ Fluctuating government revenues, leading to unstable government spending, inappropriate fiscal policies, and difficulties in debt re-payment	☒ Fluctuating export revenues, preventing long-term planning of necessary imports of inputs for firms and food for consumers ☒ ToT improvements when prices rise prevent efforts to promote long-term diversification of the economy; instead help maintain dependence on commodity exports (see p 88 on the advantages of diversification)

Effects of long-term deterioration in the terms of trade of developing countries

Why developing countries specializing in export of primary commodities have been experiencing deteriorating ToT over many decades

• **Low income elasticity of demand (YED) for primary products compared to manufactured products** (see p 11). As incomes grow over time, a larger proportion of income is spent on goods and services with income elastic demand (YED>1) and a relatively smaller proportion on primary commodities with income inelastic demand (YED<1). With demand for primary commodities growing less rapidly, prices of these commodities also increase less rapidly, i.e. prices of commodities fall **relative to** prices of manufactured goods. Countries that export mainly primary commodities and import manufactured goods therefore face deteriorating ToT.	• **Technological advances in agriculture** shift the S curve to the right leading to a fall in price of agricultural products (important primary commodities) • **Monopoly power of oligopolistic firms producing manufactured products in developed countries** leads to higher prices than the prices of agricultural products whose markets are organized more competitively

Consequences of deteriorating terms of trade

A ToT deterioration over a long period of time means a country must keep exporting more to maintain the same quantity of imports (= increasing opportunity cost of imports). This leads to:

• Increasing difficulties to import necessary inputs for production • Growing and persistent balance of trade deficits • Increased need to borrow to finance trade deficits, leading to growing indebtedness • Reduced export earnings in agriculture, leading to greater rural poverty and income inequalities • Lower incomes and more poverty leading to lower government revenues, reducing the government's ability to provide merit goods and finance economic development	• The need to keep exporting primary commodities makes it difficult to pursue diversification • Lower economic growth and reduced possibilities for economic development • There is global redistribution of output and income over the long term, with growing income inequalities between developed and less developed countries; output and income are transferred from Country A to other countries, as A must give up more and more of its output in the form of exports in exchange for the same Q of imports

4.1 ECONOMIC DEVELOPMENT

The nature of economic growth and economic development

economic growth = increases in real GDP (real output) and/or real GNI (real income) over time; this is often measured in **per capita** terms (per person in the population), in order to determine how output or income are changing on average per person; economic growth may be negative, involving decreases in real GDP or real GNI	**economic development** = a process where increases in real GDP/GNI per capita occur alongside decreases in poverty, increased employment opportunities, lower income inequalities, increased access to merit goods including education, health care and infrastructure (sanitation and clean water supplies), increased gender equality, all generally leading to improvements in a population's standard of living
✔ Whereas economic growth occurs in a single dimension (increasing real GDP or GNI), **economic development is a multidimensional process**, as it includes change in many different areas of economic and social life.	

Sources of economic growth in economically less developed countries (ELDCs)

The most important sources of economic growth in economically less developed countries (ELDCs) are the following:

Increases in quantity of physical capital Increased quantities of machines, tools, equipment, roads and transportation systems, telecommunications, all of which are part of physical capital and are often in short supply in ELDCs, increase the **productivity** of labor (output per unit of labor) and therefore make economic growth possible.	**Improvements in appropriate technology** Technological change improves the quality of physical capital, contributing to increased labor productivity. However to be useful to ELDCs, the technology must be **appropriate** to local conditions relating to the environment, climate, quantities of labor supplies and levels of skills (see p 81).
Increases in quantity of human capital Improvements in the level of health and education, which are often relatively low in ELDCs, increase the quantity of human capital (see p 54), also raising labor **productivity** and making economic growth possible.	**Institutional changes** Economic growth requires the development of institutions allowing a market economy to function well, including an efficient and fair legal system and tax system, a banking system, protection of property rights, and protection against widespread corruption (see p 83-84).

The "curse of natural resources"

Whereas in theory, primary commodities (ex oil, natural gas, metals, minerals, timber) can make an important contribution to economic growth, in practice it is observed that many countries that have major resources of such commodities (ex Congo, Mexico, Nigeria, South Africa, Venezuela) have not been growing as rapidly as countries that are resource-poor (ex Hong Kong, Israel, Japan, Taiwan). One important factor behind this may be that reliance on commodities did not encourage efforts to achieve early **diversification** of the economy into manufacturing (p 88), while also burdening the economy with **volatility of export revenues** (p 84), **deteriorating terms of trade** (p 76), **trade deficits** and **current account deficits** (p 73), need for borrowing and **high levels of debt** (p 91). Resource-poor countries, being forced to diversify their economic activities and range of exports early on, were more likely to avoid these difficulties.

How economic growth relates to economic development

Growth in output and income per capita (economic growth), suggests that growth offers a greater capability for increases in consumption of goods and services and improvements in living standards. However, growth in output and income per capita is **only an average over the population**, hence revealing nothing about **how the increased output and income are distributed**. If the benefits of growth are concentrated in few high-income groups, while the bulk of the population remains without access to basic services (merit goods), without access to employment opportunities, living in squalid conditions in severe poverty, economic growth will not lead to economic development.

Economic growth may not lead to economic development if:	
• economic growth leads to a worsening distribution of income, often the result of market-based supply-side policies and trade liberalization (see p 86) • there are low levels of government investment in human capital, so that large parts of the population are left without adequate access to education and health care • there is widespread introduction of capital-intensive technologies leading to unemployment (see p 81) • improvements in infrastructure (clean water, sanitation) are concentrated in urban areas, with neglect of rural areas where many of the poor live	• within urban areas improvements in infrastructure are concentrated in the formal sector, with neglect of the informal sector of urban slums (see p 78) • there is discrimination against social groups on the grounds of religion, ethnicity, gender, race, etc • the poor live in remote geographical areas with limited access to growing economic activity • the poor are caught in a poverty trap/cycle (see p 78) • the poor have no access to credit (see p 82)

Country groups according to their level of economic development

Countries around the world are divided into groups by the World Bank according to **per capita income** (GNI) levels:

Economically less developed countries (ELDCs) are divided into three groups: (i) "low income", (ii) "lower middle income", and (iii) "upper middle income".	**Economically more developed countries** (EMDCs) consist of one group referred to as "high income".

✔ Income levels are adjusted each year to account for inflation. However, **classifying countries by income levels to determine their level of economic development can be highly misleading**. The multidimensional nature of development means that a low-income country may have greater achievements in areas other than income (education, health, income equality, gender equality, etc) than a high-income country. This problem is partially addressed by use of the **Human Development Index** (HDI, p 80).

Diversity of economically less developed countries (ELDCs)

ELDCs differ enormously from each other with respect to their:

natural resources	climate	type of political system
human and capital resources	history	degree of political stability

Common characteristics of economically less developed countries (ELDCs)

In spite of the great diversity between economically less developed countries, there are several characteristics they share in common (though it may be dangerous to generalize as there are often exceptions).

✔ **Low levels of GDP and GNI per capita** While there are very large variations in GDP and GNI per capita between ELDCs themselves, overall their levels of output and income are low, and in some cases extremely low. Moreover, the income per capita gap (or difference) between ELDCs and EMDCs on average has been growing in absolute terms. For the income gap to close, poor countries must achieve higher rates of growth than rich countries. This has been occurring in certain regions (ex East Asia), but other regions are falling behind (ex Africa).	✔ **High birth rates and population growth** ELDCs have higher birthrates than EMDCs, and this contributes to more rapid population growth. This may have negative effects on growth and development: the more children in a family, the less income is available for each child; mothers with lack of access to health care suffer poor health from many births; there may be environmental degradation as population pressures lead to unsustainable resource use, such as clearing forests to use land for agriculture (see p 23).
✔ **High levels of poverty** Low levels of output and income translate into high poverty levels. Roughly one in five households in the world live in **extreme poverty** (less than US$1.25 per person per day), and one in three live in **moderate poverty** (less than US$2.00 per person per day).	✔ **Low levels of health and education** Levels of health are low, due to several factors, including poor access to health care services and medications, malnutrition on account of poverty which does not allow families to buy sufficient amounts of food with essential nutrients, lack of access to clean water supplies, and lack of appropriate sanitation. Levels of education are also low, due to such factors as insufficient educational facilities, lack of access to schools, low priority attached by parents to education, especially in the case of girls, and the need to send children out to work to supplement family income.
✔ **High levels of unemployment and underemployment** Lack of employment opportunities result in high rates of unemployment and underemployment, where workers are occupied for only a part of the time. Unemployment is often 20% or more of the labor force.	
✔ **Large income inequalities** Whereas all countries in the world have income inequalities, these tend to be larger in ELDCs, where the poorer groups of the population often have much smaller shares of total income (leading to a relatively high gini coefficient; see p 55). This is an important reminder of why measures of income per capita, revealing nothing about distribution, are on their own, inadequate measures of economic development.	✔ **Low levels of physical capital and technology** Physical capital tends to be limited in quantities, in relation to very abundant labor supplies. Compared to rich countries, the amount of physical capital available per worker may be as little as one-twentieth. In addition, the level of technological development tends to be low, as the physical capital available often consists of relatively simple machines and equipment.
✔ **Large agricultural (and primary) sector** The share of the primary sector, including agriculture, in total output, and the proportion of workers in this sector, is high, often as much as 30% or more, compared to 1-3% in many EMDCs. In general, the lower the per capita income, the larger is this sector. This means that in some ELDCs there is a heavy reliance on agricultural (and primary) product exports, with a whole range of related difficulties (p 84 - 85).	✔ **Low levels of productivity** Low levels of health and education mean there are low levels of **human capital**. In combination with low levels of physical capital, these factors affect **productivity** (output per unit of labor input), which is also low. Low productivity in turn translates into low rates of economic growth.
✔ **Dual economies** These involve the simultaneous existence of two different systems that coexist in an economy, such as: • a formal (registered and regulated) and informal (unregistered, unregulated) urban sector • a technologically advanced agricultural sector based on the use of modern and advanced inputs side-by-side with subsistence agriculture based on labor and simple tools • very rich, highly educated people side-by-side very poor, illiterate and/or uneducated people	✔ **Large urban informal sector** An informal sector is one that is not regulated and not registered. While in EMDCs this is generally illegal, in poor countries it is a gray area that is not only permitted to continue to exist but is often even encouraged to grow. It is found especially in urban areas (cities) and consists of small-scale self-employed people in a very broad range of services and production, such as sale of food, clothing and various household items, mending of clothes, cobblers, barbers, and household cleaners. This sector is often encouraged because it absorbs a large part of the otherwise unemployed and underemployed workers who would have no alternative work. About one-third to one-half of non-agricultural workers in ELDCs work in this sector. Yet it remains highly problematic because being unregistered, informal sector workers have no social or legal protection, and often live in the most squalid conditions.

The poverty trap (poverty cycle)

The **poverty trap (cycle)** is shown in the diagram below. Low income and savings do not permit people to purchase (invest in) machines and equipment (physical capital), education and health care (human capital), or improved agricultural inputs to preserve soil nutrients or avoid overfishing, deforestation, etc (environmental capital). This leads to low productivity, and in turn to low income growth and hence low incomes, in a cycle or trap.

✔ The poverty cycle is transmitted across generations; children are caught in the trap along with their parents, growing up in poor health, with limited education and limited possibilities to live productive lives and earn higher incomes.

✔ Outside intervention, ex foreign aid and/or government investments in infrastructure and merit goods provision, are essential for a community to break out of the trap.

The poverty trap (cycle)

low growth ──────→ low savings

low income and poverty

low productivity ◄──── low investment in physical, human, and natural capital

The Millennium Development Goals

The MDGs grew out of the United Nations Millennium Declaration of September 2000, and aim to:
1. Eradicate extreme poverty and hunger
2. Achieve universal primary education
3. Promote gender equality and empower women
4. Reduce child mortality
5. Improve maternal health
6. Combat HIV/AIDS, malaria and other diseases
7. Ensure environmental sustainability
8. Develop a global partnership for development

The Millennium Development Goals (MDGs) are important tools in the efforts to promote economic development. Whereas some progress has been made toward achieving the targets, the reality remains far behind what had been originally hoped for. One difficulty is the large shortfall in funds that rich countries have made available for **foreign aid**, in spite of initial promises to the contrary (p 89).

4.2 MEASURING DEVELOPMENT

The difficulties of measuring development

Economic development is measured by use of **indicators** = variables indicating the state of what is being measured. Indicators allow us to:

• measure a country's performance with respect to reaching a goal	• measure progress made by a country over time
• compare the performance of different countries with each other	• design policies to help achieve specific goals (such as the MDGs)

Since economic development is multi-dimensional, there is no single indicator that can accurately measure it. To overcome this problem, development may be measured by groups of **single indicators used together**, or by **composite indicators**. Still, indicators have shortcomings:

☒ Inability to collect accurate data relating to indicators	☒ Data may not be available in some countries
☒ Definitions of some indicators may vary from country to country, so that indicators from different countries may not be directly comparable	

Single indicators

GDP per capita and GNI per capita

GDP measures total output produced in an economy over a year; **GDP per capita** measures the amount of output produced in a year that corresponds to each person in the population on average	GNI measures income received by residents of an economy over a year; **GNI per capita** measures the amount of income received by residents in a year that corresponds to each person in the population on average

✔ **GNI = GDP + income received from abroad minus income sent abroad** (see p 39 for more details)

✔ In EMDCs, GNI per capita and GDP per capita are often (though not always) similar because the inflows and outflows of income are not too different from each other, and tend to cancel out. In ELDCs the differences are sometimes greater, due mainly to (i) **profit repatriation** of multinational corporations (profits sent to the home country), and (b) **worker remittances** (wages of workers sent back to their home country).

☑ **GDP per capita is a better indicator of output produced per person** in an economy (than GNI per capita).	☑ **GNI per capita is a better indicator of standards of living** (than GDP per capita) because it measures **income received by each person on average**.

However, even **GNI per capita suffers from limitations as a measure of standards of living of a population** (see p 40). For example:

☒ It provides no indication of the distribution of income, and whether this is distributed relatively equally or unequally.	☒ It provides no indication of the composition of output (ex merit goods production versus military goods production).
☒ It does not account for achievements in standards of living, such as attainments in levels of health and education.	☒ It does not account for negative environmental externalities, unsustainable resource use and environmental destruction.
☒ It does not include incomes earned in the underground economy.	☒ It does not include output not sold in markets (ex food grown for own use).

GDP/GNI per capita and GDP/GNI per capita in purchasing power parities (PPPs)

Suppose there are two countries with identical GNI per capita of $5000, but with different price levels, Country A has low prices for goods and services and Country B has higher prices. This means that the GNI per capita of $5000 can buy more goods and services (has greater purchasing power) in Country A than in Country B. Therefore it is misleading to say that the two countries have identical GNI per capita, since the GNI of Country A is worth more in terms of what it can buy than the GNI of Country B.	This problem arises when market exchange rates (those explained in Part 3) are used to convert local currencies into US$ (or into other currencies). To resolve this problem, local currencies are converted into US$ by use of special exchange rates called **purchasing power parities (PPPs)** = **exchange rates** that convert local currencies into US$ in such a way that the influence of different price levels across counties is eliminated; the result is GDP or GNI per capita values expressed in US$ (PPP) directly comparable across countries.

✔ In general, high-income countries have higher price levels than low-income countries. This means that in terms of purchasing power, US$1 can buy more goods and services in a low-income country than in a high-income country. Therefore when we compare output and income levels between high- and low-income countries, GNI and GDP converted into US$ by use of market exchange rates exaggerate the differences. By contrast, when PPPs are used, the differences between higher- and lower-income countries become smaller.

✔ **Whenever an output or income indicator (ex GDP or GNI, total or per capita) is compared across countries it is very important to use PPPs in order for the comparison to have validity**.

Health indicators

health indicators = measures of the state of health of a population; three very commonly used health indicators are:

Life expectancy at birth measures the number of years a person can expect to live on average at the time of her/his birth.	**Infant mortality** measures the number of infant deaths each year, per 1000 live births, from the time of birth until the age of one year.	**Maternal mortality** measures the number of women who die each year from causes related to pregnancy, per 100,000 live births.

These **indicators of economic development** provide an indication of many factors that reveal information about a country's level of development:

• **The quality of public health services**, such as immunization and prevention of communicable diseases (ex malaria, tuberculosis)	• **Access of the population to health care services**, including doctors, hospitals, and medications
• **The quality of the environment**, including pollution levels and adequate infrastructure (sewerage, clean water supplies)	• **Access to sufficient food** in terms of both calories and essential nutrients, and absence of malnutrition
• **An adequate level of education for the whole population**; there is a close correlation between levels of education and levels of health.	

✔ Generally, the higher a country's income level, the higher the life expectancy and the lower the infant and maternal mortality. However, there are many exceptions to this, as many countries have achieved **far better health outcomes with lower incomes**. This indicates that **countries can often improve the health of their population by reallocating resources toward the provision of appropriate services**.

Education indicators

education indicators = measures of the level of educational attainment of a population; some very commonly used education indicators are:

The **adult literacy rate** measures the percentage of people in a population above age fifteen who can read and write.	**Primary school enrolment** measures the percentage of children who are of official school age who attend primary (elementary) school.	**Secondary school enrolment** measures the percentage of children of official school age who attend secondary school.	**Mean years of schooling** measures the number of years people aged 25 or more have attended school on average.

✔ Generally, the higher a country's income level, the higher the values of the measures provided by all the indicators above. However, as in the case of health indicators, there are major exceptions, as a number of countries have achieved very high literacy rates and primary school enrollment rates, in spite of having very low incomes per capita. For example, Uganda and Burundi, with very low incomes per capita, have primary school enrolment rates that are even higher than some very high-income countries. The reason behind this lies in government policies that have singled out primary school education as a major development goal that is pursued even though resources may be very limited.

Other single indicators

There are many hundreds of indicators that can be used to measure the widely different aspects of economic development. The World Bank compiles the World Development Indicators, of which there are over 900. Many of these can be accessed at http://data.worldbank.org/data-catalog/world-development-indicators. The indicators cover the following topics:

Agriculture and rural development	External debt	Private sector
Aid effectiveness	Financial sector	Public sector
Climate change	Gender	Science and technology
Economy and growth	Health	Social development
Education	Infrastructure	Urban development
Energy and mining	Labor and social protection	
Environment	Poverty	

Composite indicators

composite indicator = a group of single indicators used together to form a **single measure of development in several dimensions**; composite indicators are superior to single indicators of economic development, as they incorporate more than one dimension of development

The Human Development Index

The **Human Development Index (HDI)** measures development in **three dimensions**: • **The level of health**, measured by one indicator: life expectancy at birth. • **The level of education**, measured by two indicators: mean years of schooling (see above) and expected years of schooling (the number of years a five-year old child can expect to attend school). • **The standard of living**, measured by one indicator: GNI per capita. The HDI is an average over these three dimensions. It is presented as: • an index number from 0 to 1 for each country, and • an HDI rank, according to which all **countries are ranked from the highest in terms of their achievements in these three dimensions to the lowest**.	The **Human Development Index (HDI) is the most widely used composite indicator of economic development**, and is actually a measure of **human development**, a process defined in terms of human freedoms, including freedom from hunger, freedom from preventable diseases, freedom from ignorance, poverty and want, and freedom to live a full and productive life.

✔ The **HDI is far superior to GNI (or GDP) per capita as a measure of economic development** because it provides information on achievements in three dimensions simultaneously, i.e. health, education, and income per capita.	A comparison of **GNI per capita ranks** and **HDI ranks** across countries reveals that the two often do not go together, because: ✔ countries that attach a high importance to improving their health and/or education outcomes by allocating resources to the provision of health and education services have a higher HDI rank than GNI per capita rank, while a low priority to these areas appears as a lower HDI than GNI rank. ✔ This means that many countries in the world can achieve major health and education improvements by reallocating resources in favor of providing services in these areas.

Shortcomings of the Human Development Index

Over and above the shortcomings faced by all indicators, the Human Development Index is limited as an indicator of economic development in that it does not provide any indication of achievements in other important dimensions of development, such as income distribution, access to clean water and sanitation, employment, gender equality and others.

Additional composite indicators

The **Inequality-adjusted Human Development Index** (IHDI) is a measure that first appeared in 2010, which is the same as the HDI only that in addition it takes into account **inequalities** in each of the same three dimensions. The IHDI "subtracts" from the HDI to account for inequalities, therefore the greater the inequality, the lower the IHDI.	The **Gender Inequality Index** (GII), also first appearing in 2010, measures the losses women experience on account of inequalities in three dimensions: • **reproductive health**, measured by maternal mortality rates (seep 79) and adolescent fertility rate (the higher these are, the lower the GII); • **empowerment**, measured by the share of parliamentary seats held by women, and achievements in higher education (the higher these are, the higher the GII); • **labor market participation**, measured by women's participation in the labor market (the higher this is, the higher the GII).
The **Multidimensional Poverty Index** (MPI) measures poverty not just in income terms, but also in terms of deprivations experienced by poor people in three dimensions: health, education, and living standards (measured by access to water, electricity, cooking fuel, toilet, and others).	

4.3 THE ROLE OF DOMESTIC FACTORS

Education and health

Education and health are the building blocks of **human capital** (see p 54). ELDCs generally lag far behind EMDCs with respect to achievements in both education and health levels (though there are exceptions). Education and health are at one and the same time:

☑ **fundamental human rights** (according to the United Nations Declaration of Human Rights)	☑ **goals of economic development**, included in the **Millennium Development Goals** (MDGs, see p 78)	☑ **component parts of the Human Development Index**, widely used to measure economic development (see p 80)	☑ **major sources of economic growth**, through their contribution to labor **productivity** (output per unit of labor input, see p 54)	☑ **"goods"** leading to very significant **positive consumption externalities** (p 19)

Positive externalities of education and health care services

The market underallocates resources for the provision of education and health care services; the marginal social benefits (MSB) of consumption of education and health care are greater than the marginal private benefits (MPB), with the difference accounted for by **external benefits** (see p 19):

External benefits of education in ELDCs	**External benefits of health**
☑ Economic growth, arising from greater labor productivity ☑ Reduced unemployment ☑ More foreign direct investment (see p 88) as MNCs are attracted by an educated labor force ☑ Technological improvements due more R&D by skilled people ☑ Greater political stability, which contributes to more growth and development ☑ Education of women leads to higher labor force participation, reduced birth rates, lower population growth rates, and reduced poverty ☑ Education of women and mothers leads to a healthier female population and healthier children	☑ Economic growth, from increased labor productivity ☑ Lower risk of spreading diseases from a lower disease burden ☑ Lower risk of non-immunized people contacting a disease, arising from the immunization of a portion of the population ☑ Improved school attendance of healthier children and better school performance ☑ A longer life in which to use skills acquired and make contributions to society and the economy

✔ In view of the above, there are very strong justifications for government policies to promote access to education and health care services. Government policies may take the form of: • provision of schools that are attended free of charge • laws that make education compulsory up to a certain age • free immunization • access to government-provided health care services that are free of charge or have a very low charge ✔ Additional policies are the provision of infrastructure including clean water supplies and sewerage systems, as well as efforts to limit pollution, all of which contribute to improved health.	✔ The experiences of countries that have grown and developed rapidly over the last several decades shows that one important factor behind their successes has been major investments in education (ex China, Indonesia, South Korea, Thailand). ✔ Studies show that in low-income countries priority should be given to promoting universal literacy (the ability to read and write), which can be achieved by universal primary school education; this is, in fact, the second Millennium Development Goal (MDG; p 78). ✔ Note that three of the eight MDGs are directly related to improving health (Goals 4, 5, and 6; p 78).

Appropriate technology

The need for appropriate technology

appropriate technology = a technology that is well suited to a country's factors of production; this often refers to the quantities of **labor** relative to quantities of **physical capital** available, as well as **skill levels** needed in relation to skill levels available; in addition, technology must be appropriate in relation to a country's geographical, climate and ecological conditions	ELDCs are very often characterized by large quantities of labor in combination with relatively scarce quantities of physical capital, and large parts of the labor force are not highly skilled. This means they require technologies that are **labor-intensive**, meaning technologies that need large quantities of labor to run and maintain, and that are relatively simple to operate. Labor-intensive technologies should be contrasted with **capital-intensive technologies**, which require a relatively small amount of highly-skilled labor to run, maintain and operate.

In ELDCs with relatively abundant quantities of labor:

✔ use of **labor-intensive technologies** results in increased employment, increased use of local skills, more income for the workers employed, reduced poverty, and savings on foreign exchange (due to local production and maintenance of the equipment, as opposed to relying on imported capital goods).	✔ use of **capital-intensive technologies** results in greater unemployment, limited use of local skills together with skill requirements that may be difficult and costly to secure, reduced incomes and greater poverty, as well as increased use of possibly scarce foreign exchange to acquire costly imported capital equipment.

Appropriate technology is a major factor promoting growth and development, yet both historically and to the present, use is often made of inappropriate technologies, while not enough attention is paid to the development and use of appropriate technologies:

✔ One of the serious errors of **import-substitution** policies in the 1950s and 1960s (see p 85) was the use of imported capital-intensive technologies, that contributed to rising unemployment, the growth of an **urban informal sector** (p 78), and deficits in the current account (p 71) due to the need to import expensive capital equipment.	✔ The use of inappropriate technologies is one of the drawbacks of **foreign direct investment (FDI)** in ELDCs that relies on capital-intensive technologies (p 88).

✔ Most new technology originates in high-income countries, which tend to allocate far more resources to research and development than ELDCs. Since EMDCs have relatively abundant supplies of physical capital in relation to less abundant labor, much of this technology is capital-intensive and therefore inappropriate for labor-abundant ELDCs. Yet most ELDCs do not have the resources to develop their own technologies.

Credit and micro-credit

Why credit is important for economic growth and development

Banking and credit are important because they:

☑ provide a link between savers and investors; the savings of one household are made available for investors to borrow.	☑ provide an incentive for households to save, because they offer interest payments on the savings.	☑ provide funds for investors, who may be farmers, shop-owners, small business-owners, to borrow and finance (pay for) investments.	☑ offer a way out of poverty and the **poverty cycle/trap** (p 78); if poor people who lack savings can borrow they can create a profitable business

However, poor people are usually excluded from the possibility of borrowing to finance a business because:

☒ The credit system often is not well-developed and people do not have geographical access to bank branches.	☒ The banking sector is often dominated by foreign banks with an interest in lending large amounts to wealthy borrowers and large corporations.	☒ Banks require collateral for making loans, and poor people, lacking any property, have nothing to offer as collateral.

As a result of the above:

✔ Poor people are forced to borrow from illegal money-lenders who charge extremely high interest rates, and from exploitative pawnbrokers, obtaining far less than what they need to start or expand a small business.	✔ Poor people's lack of access to sufficient, reliable, low-cost sources of credit is a major obstacle to economic growth and development, preventing people from escaping their poverty.

The role of micro-credit: an evaluation

micro-credit = credit (lending) of very small amounts of money for short periods of time to poor people who have no other access to credit	The first micro-credit schemes began in the 1970s, initiated by Muhammad Yunus in Bangladesh, who received the Nobel Peace Prize in 2006 for his contribution to economic development.
Examples of micro-enterprises (businesses financed by micro-credit): carpenters, street vendors, seamstresses, knitting products, bicycle shops	

Accomplishments and challenges of micro-credit include:

☑ Micro-credit helps poor and unemployed people become self-employed in small businesses. ☑ It is not necessary to provide collateral to obtain a loan. ☑ The borrowers very often are women who have proven to have the highest repayment rates, and who use their business income to provide for the well-being of their children and family. ☑ The social status of women borrowers has improved. ☑ Micro-credit plays a key role in poverty reduction, as it results in higher and more stable incomes.	☒ There are far too few micro-credit schemes to cover the needs of billions of poor, and so only a very small proportion of poor people are benefitting from these. ☒ There is a risk that micro-credit schemes may become a substitute for badly needed government poverty-reduction policies. ☒ Many micro-credit borrowers end up working in the **urban informal sector**, in which workers are without social protection (p 78). ☒ Micro-credit has high interest rates, which are necessary to cover the high cost of the loans (administrative costs rise when loans are very small), but which may penalize very poor people struggling to earn a decent income. ☒ Excessive borrowing may lead to a debt trap (where the only way to repay is by borrowing more).

Empowerment of women

The meaning and importance of women's empowerment

✔ Serious gender inequalities in many countries, causing women to face discrimination that deprives them of numerous opportunities open to men, **have very significant consequences not only for the women themselves, but also for society, the economy, and economic development**.	**empowerment of women** = eliminating the discrimination faced by girls and women with respect to access to education and health care, in the labor market, inheritance rights and rights to property, access to credit, and in all spheres of social and economic life, with a view to achieving gender equality so that girls and women will have the same opportunities available to boys and men to achieve their potential to live a full and productive life

✔ The major significance of women's empowerment has made it Goal number 3 of the eight Millennium goals (MDGs, see p 78): "Promote gender equality and empower women", while the composite indicator "Gender Inequality Index" (GII, see p 80), allows gender inequalities to be measured and monitored over time in order to assess what progress is made in achieving this goal.

Positive consumption externalities of education for women

Education of women is perhaps the single most important route to their empowerment. The significance of women's education for economic development can be seen in the very important **external benefits** it provides (**positive consumption externalities**; p 19):

☑ **Improved health and nutrition of children** Educated women are more knowledgeable about good health and nutrition practices for their children, and so raise healthier children.	☑ **Higher participation of women in the labor force and higher income** Educated women are far more likely to have a job, making better use of human resources, and therefore a higher family income.
☑ **Improved education of children** Educated women are far more likely to appreciate the importance of education, and so support education for children (especially girls, whose education is often neglected).	☑ **Lower birth rates and lower population growth** Women who work are likely to have fewer children, thus improving the well-being of each child in the family, as the income available per child increases
☑ **Improved quality of the labor force** Higher levels of health and education of children lead to a more educated and healthier labor force in the future, and therefore to increased labor productivity.	☑ **Improved likelihood of breaking out of the poverty cycle** The higher incomes earned by work outside the home make it possible to break out of the poverty cycle.
☑ **Greater economic growth and development** All of the above contribute to greater economic growth and development.	

Income distribution

Income distribution tends to be more unequal in ELDCs than in EMDCs, but there are very broad regional variations within both groups of countries. Among the ELDCs, income distribution tends to be more equal in countries in East Asia, South Asia and the Middle East and North Africa, and less equal in countries in Latin America and sub-Saharan Africa (though there are exceptions within these geographical groupings as well).

Why a highly inequitable distribution of income is a barrier to economic growth and development

A highly unequal distribution of income (measured as a high gini coefficient) can act as a barrier to growth and development because:

☒ it may result in lower savings in the economy, partly because people on very low incomes have nothing to save, and partly because very high-income people often spend large amounts of money on expensive imported luxury goods; by contrast, middle-income people save the most.	☒ due to very low incomes of many people, it leads to lower demand for goods and services produced locally, depriving the local economy of opportunities to increase local employment, investment and incomes, and hence economic growth.
☒ it involves concentration of a large portion of total income in the hands of a few people, resulting in extensive political power and government policies that favor their own interests rather than policies to combat poverty.	☒ it involves greater poverty, which is associated with lower amounts of human capital, as very poor people have low levels of education and health, leading to lower economic growth.
☒ it means that a larger proportion of the population (the very poor) have no access to credit as they lack collateral, resulting in lower investment and fewer opportunities to break out of the poverty cycle.	☒ it is more likely to generate political instability due to widespread dissatisfaction, leading to lower economic growth.

Infrastructure

infrastructure = physical capital resulting from investments in socially and economically necessary goods and services, usually undertaken by governments; they include transportation systems (roads, railways, ports, airports), clean water supplies, sewerage systems, telecommunications (including telephones), and energy systems (electricity and gas).

The role of infrastructure in ELDCs

Infrastructure plays a very important role in both economic growth and development in very many ways. For example:

☑ Reliable transportation systems make it possible to transport goods and services to markets, they lower costs of transporting these, improve international competitiveness through lower costs, and allow easier access to schools and health care services.	☑ Energy systems increase the range of production methods that can be powered by electricity or gas, resulting in greater worker productivity; they lead to reduced indoor pollution arising from the burning of polluting fuels; they improve gender equality by freeing women's and girls' time otherwise spent collecting firewood and carrying water.
☑ Clean water supplies and sewerage systems improve the health of the population, reducing preventable illnesses, and contributing to improved standards of living.	☑ Telecommunications permit easier and faster communication, improving productivity, and allowing **diversification** of the economy (see p 88) into various activities including manufacturing and financial services.

Challenges faced by infrastructure in ELDCs

☒ **Governments run into financing difficulties** Governments often charge very low prices (below cost) for services provided (electricity, water, etc) in order to make them affordable to the poor, which results in insufficient revenues.	☒ **There is often a misallocation of resources between different types of infrastructure**. Too many resources may be spent on certain types of services for which there is low demand, and not enough on services that are badly needed.
☒ **Low revenues mean poor quality and maintenance** Insufficient budget resources and low revenues means many services are in poor condition.	☒ **Inefficient production resulting in high costs** For example, the use of capital-intensive production methods as opposed to labor-intensive result in higher production costs and lower employment.
☒ **Low revenues means lack of access by poor people** Due to low revenues, governments often do not provide services to remote rural areas and urban slums.	☒ **Environmental degradation and unsustainable development** Construction may involve high emissions of pollutants or may locate in ecologically sensitive areas, or there may be wasteful use of water, unsanitary landfills, poorly designed sanitation, etc

Additional domestic factors that affect economic growth and development

The topics in this section ("Additional domestic factors") are not listed explicitly in the current syllabus, but may be useful for a broader understanding of development issues and for answering HLP2 questions on economic development.

Ineffective taxation systems

The bulk of revenues needed by governments to make investments in health, education, infrastructure and other areas important for economic growth and development come from taxes. Yet taxes as a share of GDP collected in ELDCs on the whole are about half the levels found in EMDCs. Part of this difference is due to low levels of income in ELDCs, most of which goes to satisfy consumption needs among people on low incomes, but in addition, tax revenues are low due to the following:

☒ **Corruption in tax collection**, involving bribes of tax authorities to lower the amounts that must be paid in taxes.	☒ **Ineffective tax collection systems**, involving complicated procedures and a lot of bureaucracy resulting in inefficiencies and tax evasion.
☒ **Privileges and tax exemptions** offered to high income people who exercise a lot of political influence over the government.	☒ **Very low property taxes**, which on average are lower than in EMDCs, also due to political influence of high-income groups.

The legal system and property rights

The law and justice institutions must be efficient and fair, with laws protecting human rights, governing economic activities, and ensuring that property rights are secure. **Property rights** involve laws that ensure legal rights to ownership and sale/transfer of ownership from one owner to another. Legally secured property is very important for a market economy to be able to function well, as in the absence of this there is uncertainty over the use of property, creating a serious disincentive for economic activity, such as:

☒ **Lower investment** Investment is less likely to be undertaken if property rights are not secure, as there is a risk of loss of the business and the value of the investment.	☒ **Reduced access to credit** Secure property rights mean that the property can be used as collateral, thus increasing access to loans for investment purposes.	☒ **Lack of benefits for third parties** Insecure property rights to agricultural land may result in the land remaining fallow, instead of being rented out to landless farmers.

Lack of political stability

Political instability is associated with such events as frequent elections, frequent cabinet changes, demonstrations, strikes, riots, ethnic or religious tensions, and civil war. A stable government, which does not display the above characteristics, is very important because it creates favorable conditions for growth and development. Political instability results in:

☒ Absence of effective policy-making by the government, and instability, frequent changes and lack of continuity in the formulation of economic policies.	☒ Outflow of financial capital to other countries (= capital flight), which deprives the country of resources for growth and development.
☒ Lower domestic investment due uncertainty over future economic policy and the political situation.	☒ Lower investment by multilateral corporations, as these require some certainty over economic policy and the political situation.

Corruption

Corruption includes such activities as bribes, extortion, nepotism, fraud, and others. It is monitored by Transparency International (IT), which ranks countries around the world every year according to local perceptions of corruption. High corruption levels hold back growth and development because:

☒ **Money payments work like a tax**, reducing economic activity because it is a disincentive for investment.	☒ **Misallocation of resources** often results, as socially undesirable projects may be selected over important merit goods.
☒ **Money payments work like a regressive tax**, since payments are a higher fraction of incomes of the poor than incomes of the rich.	☒ **Environmental sustainability is weakened** as unsustainable projects go through due to the payment of bribes or other favors.
☒ **Money goes to private individuals rather than the government**, which would use tax revenues to provide social services, merit goods, etc; bribes involve money paid that is lost to society.	☒ **The people's confidence and trust in their government is weakened**, leading to disillusionment in the country and its institutions, and to disregard of legal institutions.

4.4 THE ROLE OF INTERNATIONAL TRADE

Trade problems facing economically less developed countries

Over-specialization on a narrow range of products

Many ELDCs tend to specialize in the production and export of a narrow range of products, which are usually **primary commodities** (= goods arising from the factor of production **land**, such as agricultural products, fossil fuels, minerals, etc). Such specialization has dangers and obstacles.

☒ **Export earnings are vulnerable to changes in conditions of world demand and supply** which determine price; whereas countries benefit in times of rising prices, they can be seriously hurt when prices of their main exports fall, resulting in lower incomes, increasing unemployment, increasing poverty, difficulties in buying needed imports, current account deficits, and possibly rising debt levels.	☒ **There is a lack of diversification of production and exports** (= an increased range of goods and services), which has numerous benefits that are entirely lost (see p 88).

Price volatility of primary products

Primary commodities have low PED and low PES, leading to highly volatile prices that cause short-term fluctuations in exporting countries terms of trade (see the diagrams on p 76; SL students should also see these diagrams to note the large fluctuations in primary commodity prices). Such volatile (fluctuating) prices can have serious consequences for countries whose exports are dominated by primary commodities:

☒ **Unstable export earnings** as prices of exports fluctuate	☒ **Negative effects of uncertainty on investment**, affecting economic growth
☒ **Unstable farmer's incomes**, due to fluctuating prices, creating uncertainty	☒ **Fluctuations in employment**, which increases as commodity prices rise and decreases when commodity prices fall
☒ **Unstable ability to import**, with negative effects on the current account and balance of payments	☒ **Inability of the government to plan economic development projects** and to carry out its plans and deliver on essential services

Inability to access international markets

Many ELDCs face serious problems in accessing international markets for their exports.

Reasons for ELDCs' poor access to international markets	Consequences of protection of rich-country farmers for the global economy and ELDC farmers
• **Protection of farmers: agricultural product price floors and/or subsidies in high-income countries** High-income countries provide their farmers with support in the forms of price floors and/or subsidies, resulting in over-production and lower prices (in the case of subsidies). This is one of the most important issues preventing ELDC access to rich-country markets. • **High tariff barriers imposed by EMDCs on ELDCs** The tariff barriers imposed by EMDCs on ELDCs are much higher than the tariff barriers EMDCs impose on each other. • **High tariff barriers imposed by ELDCs on each other** These are sometimes even higher than the tariff barriers imposed by EMDCs. • **Tariff escalation** = a practice sometimes used by EMDCs, involving the imposition of low tariffs on raw, unprocessed primary products (such as cocoa and coffee) and much higher tariffs on processed, final goods (ex chocolate from cocoa and processed coffee), thus preventing ELDCs from diversifying into processing and manufacturing of food products. • **Hidden trade protection** Recently, new forms of protection are appearing in the forms of increasing quality, food safety and environmental standards, as well as complicated customs procedures, intended to discourage imports from ELDCs (see p 65).	☒ **Resources are misallocated on a global scale** Overproduction of agricultural products in EMDC farms results in surpluses that are dumped into global markets through subsidies. Resulting low prices force some ELDC farmers out of business. Production is therefore shifted away from ELDC farmers and toward EMDC farmers. ☒ **Inefficiency on a global scale** ELDCs often produce agricultural products more efficiently than EMDCs, therefore the above shift in production toward EMDCs involves increasing inefficiency. ☒ **ELDCs lose export earnings** Lower volumes of agricultural product exports mean lower export earnings, possibly leading to current account deficits and increasing levels of debt. ☒ **Greater poverty of ELDC farmers** The above processes result in lower exports, lower incomes, lower investment, greater unemployment, and more poverty.

Long-term changes in the terms of trade

Deterioration in the terms of trade over long periods of time is an additional international trade barrier to growth and development in ELDCs. This has been explained on p 76.

Trade strategies for economic growth and development

Import substitution

import substitution = also known as **import substituting industrialization**, is a growth and trade strategy based on strong government intervention involving heavy protection of domestic industries (through tariffs, quotas, subsidies, etc) Intended to replace imports with domestic production	Having begun in Latin American countries in the 1930s, it was very widespread throughout most ELDCs by the 1950s and 1960s. Due to its numerous problems, it began to be abandoned by the 1970s and 1980s.

Potential advantages of import substitution	Weaknesses of import substitution
☑ Many newly independent countries in the 1950s considered this to be the way to modernize and "catch up" with rich countries. ☑ In the 1950s specialization in primary commodities was viewed with skepticism and rapid industrialization based on manufacturing was seen as the escape route. ☑ Use of the **infant industry** argument (see p 65) offered advantages of rapid growth of heavily protected industries. ☑ Protection of domestic industry was seen as the way to protect domestic employment, since trade barriers limit the quantity of imports. ☑ Placing limits on imports was considered to be a way to avoid current account deficits and balance of payments difficulties.	☒ **Serious inefficiencies and resource misallocation** resulted from • high trade barriers protecting domestic industries; • low competition domestically due to low levels of imports; • excessive government intervention in the economy, including considerable government ownership of many key industries, price controls, tax allowances, subsidized credit, wage subsidies. ☒ **Weak agricultural and other exports** due to **overvaluation of currencies** (p 69) in order to facilitate imports of capital goods needed for industrialization. ☒ **Capital-intensive production methods**, believed to foster rapid growth, led to unemployment, income inequalities, poverty, growth of the urban informal sector. ☒ **Disregard of technological improvements in agriculture**, leading to increasing food imports as well as rural poverty. ☒ **Balance of payments problems emerged**, due to imports of capital goods for industry, food imports and profit repatriation of multinational corporations. ☒ **Low rates of economic growth** due to the above problems.

Export promotion

export promotion = a growth and trade strategy based on strong government intervention intended to promote economic growth through the expansion of exports	Following the difficulties encountered by import substitution policies, many countries progressively turned toward export promotion, which was highly successful in promoting growth and development. Ex China, Hong Kong, Indonesia, Malaysia, Taiwan and others (the "Asian Tigers").

Export promotion policies included:

• **Targeting of specific export industries**; particularly those that were able to contribute higher value-added to the economy (see p 88). • **Support of export-oriented industries through industrial policies** (p 61) including subsidies, investment grants, tax exemptions, etc. • **Large investments by the government** in education, research and development and infrastructure (communications and transportation). • **Some trade protection of industries**, but only in certain areas, based on the **infant industry** argument.	• **Incentives for private sector R&D** were provided, intended to foster the development of high technology at the same time that the necessary complementary skills were being developed. • **Imposition of requirements on multinational corporations** ensuring the transfer of appropriate technology, the carrying out of R&D, promoting training and skill levels of local workers, and use of domestically produced inputs.

Strengths of export promotion strategies	Difficulties of export promotion strategies
☑ The use of appropriate, labor-intensive technologies led to effective use of local labor supplies and did not displace labor. ☑ Investments in education and skill improvements contributed to improved human capital, laying the grounds for broad-based growth, poverty alleviation and more equal income distribution. ☑ Targeting of industries for growth and export achieved **diversification** based on higher **valued-added** activities, contributing to increased employment, and higher levels of skills and technology (see p 88), while avoiding the dangers of excessive specialization. ☑ Increased exports allowed the expansion into new markets allowing achievement of economies of scale. ☑ Increased exports avoided current account deficits and balance of payments problems, providing foreign exchange for the purchase of necessary imported inputs.	☒ There is a possibility of resource misallocation due to strong government intervention in the economy. ☒ Strong dependence on exports makes the economy vulnerable to demand conditions in importing countries; if trading partners suffer a recession, the exporting economies are strongly affected ☒ The success of export promotion policies led to the erection of strong trade barriers, since the 1980s, in developed countries that are fearful of losing domestic output and jobs to foreign lower-cost competitor countries. ☒ The **World Trade Organization** (WTO, p 63, 87) and the **Washington Consensus** (see below) frown upon the use of industrial policies based on strong government intervention, therefore it is unlikely that the policies of the Asian Tigers can be broadly repeated in the present global economic climate.

Trade liberalization

trade liberalization = reduction or removal of trade barriers (tariffs, quotas, etc) aiming to achieve growth of international trade based on the principle of **free trade**; global trade liberalization is to be pursued through trade negotiations under the leadership of the **World Trade Organization** (WTO, see p 63 and 87)	The potential advantages of trade liberalization are the advantages of trade (see p 63)	
	☑ Specialization of production and exports according to comparative advantage increases production and consumption, resulting in greater global allocative efficiency. ☑ Opportunities for achieving economies of scale. ☑ Greater choice for consumers due to increased imports. ☑ Lower prices of imported goods due to removal of trade barriers.	☑ Greater efficiency in production due to increased competition. ☑ Ability of firms to acquire needed resources. ☑ More foreign exchange available, needed to pay for imports. ☑ Greater economic growth due to all of the above factors. ☑ Greater potential to reduce poverty and income inequalities due to economic growth.

There are two phases of trade liberalization:

The early phase, from the 1980s	Consequences
Trade liberalization became increasingly popular during the 1980s, when it began to be used as part of a growth and development strategy for ELDCs based on **market-based supply-side policies** (see p 61); these have included: withdrawal of government intervention from economic activities through such policies as privatization, deregulation, the imposition of limits on government borrowing, moving toward flexible exchange rates, reduction of restrictions on activities of multinational corporations. Many countries have moved toward liberalizing their trade and economies including Brazil, India, Kenya, Sri Lanka, Vietnam and many more. These policies have been heavily promoted by the **Washington Consensus** (World Bank, The international Monetary Fund (IMF), the US government, all based in Washington, D.C.).	✔ Trade liberalization, together with the introduction of highly pro free-market policies in ELDCs, are **highly controversial policies**. ✔ Countries that benefitted most from the potential advantages of free trade were middle-income ELDCs that already had an industrial base and had achieved some diversification of their economies. ✔ Low-income countries did not fare as well, because of: • their inability to compete in global markets • lack of access of their exports to foreign markets (see p 85) • lack of well-developed institutions needed for the effective functioning of markets (weak property rights, weak legal systems, weak banking and credit systems, weak tax systems) • low levels of human capital needed to take advantage of opportunities offered by trade and market liberalization. Such weaknesses led to: ☒ loss of export shares in world trade (ex African countries) ☒ inability to diversify into manufactured products ☒ increasing income gap (inequalities) between rich and poor countries ☒ increasing income inequalities within ELDCs ☒ limited effects on economic growth in many countries ☒ slow if any progress in reducing poverty, even in countries that experienced growth
The later phase, from the late 1990s to the present ✔ Growing recognition of the difficulties experienced by many countries in the early phase of trade liberalization that was accompanied by strong market liberalization, gave rise to a new perspective that to be effective, **trade liberalization must be accompanied by government intervention** focused on creating the conditions necessary for markets to work well, while at the same time focusing on alleviating poverty and improving income distribution.	**Policies for effective trade and market liberalization** ☑ ELDC governments should: • make investments in human capital formation (education and health), infrastructure, and R&D for the development of appropriate technologies • pursue policies for alleviating poverty and improving income distribution • pursue reforms of legal, tax, and banking systems; create regulatory frameworks for promoting private sector activities and reducing corruption, for more effective functioning of markets. • pursue more effective **governance** (see p 93) ☑ Rich countries (EMDCs) should: • remove the strong protection of their farmers • lower tariff and other barriers to imports from ELDCs • make funds available for the provision of **foreign aid** in order to (i) support poverty alleviation, (ii) achieve the MDGs (p 78,) and (iii) develop necessary institutions in ELDCs necessary for the growth of international trade (see p 90). ☑ The international community should: • support the WTO in arriving at decisions that are fair to ELDCs.

The role of the World Trade organization (WTO)

The WTO's functions and objectives were noted on p 63.

Potential advantages of the WTO	Criticisms
☑ It can help in the process of global trade liberalization. ☑ It can help in resolving disagreements and differences between trading partners, avoiding disputes that result in trade wars. ☑ It can provide a forum where all participating countries can voice their opinions and argue in favor of their interests. ☑ By achieving trade liberalization, it can help achieve a better allocation of resources globally. ☑ It can help countries around the world achieve lower costs (through removal of trade barriers), lower prices for consumers, and greater choice for consumers. ☑ If pursued together with appropriate policies for ELDCs, it can help achieve economic growth, higher incomes and reduced poverty.	✔ The "Uruguay Round" that ended in 1994, the last round of negotiations where agreements were reached, has been criticized for **favoring the interests of EMDCs**: ☒ There resulted larger tariff reductions in ELDCs, to the benefit of EMDCs, resulting in poorer countries facing substantially higher tariffs for their exports compared to EMDCs. ☒ Nothing was done about tariff escalation (see p 85), hurting ELDC exports. ☒ There was no agreement on reduction in support received by EMDC farmers, which create trade barriers for ELDCs. ☒ Agreements on intellectual property rights made it more costly for ELDCs to acquire new technology. ☒ No requirement that multinational corporations (MNCs) buy their supplies locally was imposed, eliminating a potential source of benefits for ELDCs that host MNCs (see p 88). ✔ The next round of negotiations, the "Doha Round", was begun in 2001, but since 2008 it has been apparent that WTO member states are unable to reach agreement in key areas including agricultural protection, tariffs on industrial products, and non-tariff barriers. ☒ This failure has created much pessimism on the WTO's role as a forum for global trade negotiations, and has given rise to the proliferation of **regional and bilateral trade agreements**, some of which **do not favor the trade, growth and development interests of ELDCs** (see below).

Regional and bilateral preferential trade agreements

Before reading this section you should review the **evaluation of trading blocs** (p 74). This section considers trade agreements from the specific perspective of ELDCs.	The failure of the WTO to conclude a new round of trade negotiations (see above) has resulted in a very rapid growth of regional and bilateral trade agreements by countries seeking to take advantage of the benefits of free trade.

✔ In order for participating countries to enjoy the benefits of free or freer trade offered by regional and bilateral trade agreements, while minimizing potential costs, they must have **similar levels of economic and technological development and similar market sizes**.	✔ Such similarities create conditions for **fair competition**. If one party to the agreement is economically or technologically stronger, the weaker party will be unable to compete due to the greater efficiencies, economies of scale, and technological superiority of the stronger party. In such situations, the weaker party may suffer firm closures, increased unemployment, increased poverty, increased income inequalities, lower exports, greater balance of payments difficulties, and lower possibilities for growth and development.

Regional trade agreements

These are usually formed between countries that are in regional groupings (geographically close to each other), for example ASEAN in southeast Asia, MERCOSUR in Latin America, CAIS in Central America, and many more.

☑ The great importance of regional trade agreements for ELDCs is that they offer them a way out of the dilemma of how to **increase their exports and enjoy the benefits of free trade** (see p 63), while **avoiding the obstacles to trade created by protectionist policies of rich countries** (see p 85). ☑ The advantages for all participating countries are greater, the more the conditions for **fair competition**, noted above, are met.	☒ Risks arise when the conditions for **fair competition** are not met, potentially resulting in the **numerous negative effects noted above**. ☒ Risks arise when the trade agreements encourage excessive specialization (see p 84), and prevent or discourage diversification of production and exports. ☒ Further risks are noted on p 86 under "Consequences" of trade liberalization.

Bilateral trade agreements

These usually involve **one high-income country** (EMDC), and **one low-income country** (ELDC). One or both of the two partners in the agreement may be a group of countries **acting as a unit**, such as the European Union (EU). Many of these agreements are between partners that are **not** geographically close to each other.

Bilateral trade agreements:	Bilateral agreements are commonly criticized for creating major risks for ELDCs:
☑ are of interest to ELDCs because they can gain access to the EMDC market, overcoming at least some of the barriers imposed by EMDCs. ☑ often come with conditions that the EMDC will provide the ELDC with funds for **foreign aid** (see p 89) in support of various growth and development objectives (ex building of schools, infrastructure, debt relief, and more).	☒ Tariff reductions on the imports of ELDCs from EMDCs are often greater than those required by WTO rules, creating risks that even efficient ELDC firms may close down, as EMDC firms are larger, technologically more advanced, hence more efficient. ☒ Tariff reductions made by EMDCs for ELDC exports may be greater for primary commodities, encouraging ELDCs to continue to specialize in primary good production and export, thus making it more difficult for them to diversify their production into processing and manufacturing. ☒ As a single EMDC (say the EU or US) forms many bilateral agreements with different ELDCs, these find themselves in competition with each other for the same market, and their growth of exports may be limited. ☒ Bilateral agreements prevent ELDCs from joining forces and presenting their interests in unity as they could within the WTO, greatly weakening their bargaining power. ☒ The agreements often impose conditions that are not in their favor (ex giving greater freedoms to multinational corporations originating in the EMDC). ☒ Bilateral agreements can work against the effective operation of regional agreements among ELDCs (ELDCs often make both regional and bilateral agreements). ☒ Unfair competition may result in the numerous negative effects noted above.

Diversification

diversification = a broadening of the range of goods and services produced and exported; it is the opposite of **specialization**, and provides protection against the drawbacks of excessive specialization (p 84) as well as advantages for growth and development

✔ Diversification of production and exports offers numerous advantages to ELDCs: ☑ it provides opportunities for increasing and maintaining higher export levels in products enjoying **sustained increases in demand**; these kinds of products are manufactured goods (not primary commodities) ☑ it avoids the problems of excessive specialization in primary commodities (see p 84) ☑ HL topic It avoids the problems of long-term deterioration in the terms of trade and short term fluctuations in the terms of trade (see p 76). ✔ Expansion into products **with higher value-added** (= value which is added to unprocessed goods after they undergo processing; ex cocoa in the form of chocolate has a higher value than raw cocoa) provides further potential benefits because it: ☑ creates new jobs as workers are needed to perform the processing ☑ creates new local businesses carrying out manufacturing activities ☑ encourages development of skills and technologies to support the broader range of production ☑ uses locally produced primary goods as the basis of expansion into processing and manufacturing.	Diversification of production and exports may lead to: ☒ loss of the benefits of specialization in production and export of goods arising from a country's ability to produce at lower relative costs than its trading partners (comparative advantage) ☒ loss of improvements in allocative efficiency arising from specialization ☒ there may be difficulties in overcoming barriers on manufactured products imposed by EMDCs (such as tariff escalation)

4.5 THE ROLE OF FOREIGN DIRECT INVESTMENT (FDI)
FDI and MNCs

foreign direct investment (FDI) = investment by a firm originating in one country (the home country) in **productive** facilities in another country (the host country), carried out by MNCs; **should be contrasted with** portfolio investment = financial investment (= purchase of stocks and bonds)	**multinational corporation (MNC)** = a firm that carries out foreign direct investment, thus having productive investment in more than one country

Why MNCs expand into ELDCs	ELDC characteristics that attract MNCs	
• expectation of greater sales and profits • avoidance of trade barriers imposed by ELDCs by producing within their boundaries • low costs of labor in ELDCs • use of raw materials that are locally produced, avoiding transportation costs • involvement with extraction of natural resources that some ELDCs possess (ex oil, minerals)	• large markets, because of the expectation of larger sales • political and macroeconomic stability • expectations of rapid economic growth • well-developed and well-functioning infrastructure (transportation and telecommunications systems) • a well-educated and skilled local labor force • low labor costs • weak labor unions	• a free-market economy with little government intervention • liberalized trade (to facilitate the use of imported inputs) • institutions advantageous to FDI: ex well-functioning legal system with strong property rights, favorable tax laws, freedom to repatriate profits, weak environmental protection

Advantages and disadvantages of FDI for ELDCs

How FDI can benefit ELDCs	Why MNCs may not benefit ELDCs, and may even harm them
☑ by increasing investment, which may be low in ELDCs due to insufficient savings. ☑ by increasing possibly low foreign exchange earnings, since the inflow of funds for FDI appears as a credit in the financial account of the balance of payments. ☑ by providing increased employment opportunities. ☑ by providing opportunities for training of the local labor force. ☑ by bringing in new technology, which can help in diversification into manufacturing and economic growth. ☑ by promoting local businesses and industry by buying locally produced inputs. ☑ by providing the domestic government with greater tax revenues. ☑ by improving infrastructure required for their functioning, thus also benefitting the domestic economy. ☑ by increasing exports. ☑ by increasing economic growth.	☒ There could be a greater outflow rather than inflow of foreign exchange, due to profit repatriation (p 39), as well as imports of inputs required for production. ☒ Employment opportunities may not increase significantly, in the event of use of capital-intensive technologies, and if managerial, administrative and technical staff are hired from the home country. ☒ Local skill levels may not improve if the links between the MNC and the local economy are very small, or if production makes use of only unskilled labor. ☒ If inputs are purchased from abroad, benefits for local businesses and manufacturing are unlikely to materialize. ☒ There may not be greater tax revenues for the government, due to tax breaks offered by the government, as well as the practice of **transfer pricing** (MNCs lower their declared profits by buying inputs from affiliates abroad and declaring highly inflated costs, making profits appear lower than they actually are). ☒ MNCs may have too much power, leading to inappropriate policies; MNC power over the host country government may lead to • use of domestic budget funds to build infrastructure needed by the MNC and not by the local population; • pass weak labor protection laws; • pass weak environmental protection laws. ☒ MNCs often engage in production methods that cause serious environmental destruction and lead to **unsustainable development** (p 22).

✔ In view of the above, FDI is a highly controversial topic. On the whole it is likely that it contributes to economic growth, and for this reason ELDCs compete among each other to make themselves attractive to MNCs.	✔ Because of the numerous potentially negative effects, this competition has been termed "the race to the bottom", suggesting that ELDCs could be sacrificing elements of economic development, as well as sustainable development, for the sake of achieving economic growth through the contributions of MNCs.

4.6 THE ROLES OF FOREIGN AID AND MULTILATERAL DEVELOPMENT ASSISTANCE

Foreign aid

foreign aid = transfer of funds in the form of loans or grants, or transfer of goods and services, as gifts, to ELDCs in order to help them achieve economic or social objectives; aid is **non-commercial** (the transfers don't involve buying and selling transactions) and it is **concessional** (loans involve lower than market interest rates, and are given for long periods of time)	**tied aid** = conditions on the borrowing country imposed by bilateral aid donors (see below) requiring that at least a portion of the borrowed amount must be spent to import goods and services from the donor country

Who are the providers of aid

Governments of donor countries; this aid is known as **Official Development Assistance (ODA)**, and reaches ELDCs in the form of: • **bilateral aid** = aid going from one donor to one ELDC recipient country, or • **multilateral aid** = aid going from donor countries to ELDCs through international organizations, such as various United Nations agencies, and many others	**Non-governmental organizations (NGOs)** = organizations concerned with promoting objectives that are in the public interest, ex OXFAM, Amnesty International. NGOs are increasingly important as providers of aid; they are involved in a very broad variety of development efforts, including technical assistance for farmers, education and health services, support for urban informal workers, micro-credit, rights of women, human rights, sustainable development, and many more. They have a strong anti-poverty perspective, they work closely with local people, have a clear understanding of their problems, and have generally earned the trust of those they try to help. NGOs in ELDCs number in the tens of thousands as they are small in size and mostly provide aid on a very small scale.

The distinction between humanitarian aid and development aid

humanitarian aid = aid extended in areas which are experiencing emergency situations due to crises caused by wars or natural disasters, and consist of **donations** of food, medical assistance, and emergency relief including provision of shelters and supplies	**development aid** = aid extended to ELDCs for the purpose of assisting them in development	
	Development aid consists of: • **concessional long-term loans** (below market interest rates, extended for long periods); • **grants** (gifts, that do not need to be repaid)	Development aid takes the form of: • **project aid** = aid for specific projects, ex building hospitals, irrigation systems, schools, etc • **programme aid** = aid in support of whole sectors of the economy, ex education, health care, banking, etc

Why EMDCs are motivated to provide aid

For political reasons Aid may be provided to support countries that are politically and ideologically friendly to EMDCs, such as the United States and the Soviet Union during the Cold War, which provided aid to their respective allies.	**For economic reasons** Aid may be provided to support economically less developed economies that have strong economic links with the donor country, such as trade and investment links; if the recipient country experiences rapid growth due to the aid, the donor country is likely to benefit due to the expansion of its own markets and exports to the recipient of aid.

For humanitarian reasons Aid may be provided out of feelings of compassion for the plight of poor people living under very harsh conditions.

Evaluating the contribution of foreign aid to economic development

Why aid is essential	Why aid may be ineffective	
☑ Aid can help very poor countries or very poor communities within countries to emerge from the **poverty trap** (p 78). ☑ It is quite impossible to achieve the **Millennium Development Goals (MDGs)** (p 78) without aid. ☑ According to United Nations organizations, there is strong evidence that by increasing investment, aid is linked with higher growth rates. ☑ Aid helps in poverty alleviation through • improvements in education and skills • reducing preventable diseases and improving levels of health • improvements in infrastructure, • development of simple appropriate technologies • empowering poor people by helping them find employment ☑ Aid helps highly indebted countries obtain debt relief (see p 91).	**Problems arising from the side of donor countries:** ☒ **Tied aid** is far less effective than untied aid because it: • does not allow recipient countries to search for low-price suppliers • does not allow them to import goods that best suit their needs • sometimes forces them to import inappropriate technologies. ☒ **Conditional aid** (= aid granted on condition that the recipient countries pursue particular policies, usually market-based supply-side policies) forces recipient countries to pursue objectives that may be more in line with donors' priorities, and that may be inappropriate for their economies. ☒ **Unpredictability of aid funds**, due to donors' changing budget priorities, makes it difficult for recipient countries to plan effective use of the funds. ☒ **Uncoordinated donor-financed activities**, due to very large numbers of donors and activities, mean that effective planning is not possible, while activities are a reflection of donor priorities. The result involves duplication of some projects with large gaps in others, and a significant waste of resources.	**Problems arising from the side of recipient countries:** ☒ **Use of aid funds in place of domestic budget funds** defeats the point of aid, which is to supplement domestic budget funds; may weaken governments' efforts to reform their tax systems, which would allow for increased domestic revenues. ☒ **Aid may not reach the intended beneficiaries**, particularly if governments are not committed to poverty alleviation, and the aid funds are spent elsewhere. ☒ **Corruption** in the case of aid is an additional reason why aid funds may not reach the intended beneficiaries.

The roles of aid and trade in economic development

Three strands of thought can be discerned in the debate over the merits of aid versus trade for economic development:

Trade not aid	Aid and trade	Aid for trade
This perspective focuses on the factors that limit the effectiveness of aid, claiming that it is a waste of resources because it has not succeeded in solving the problems of ELDCs, in spite of vast sums having been spent on aid over decades. Rather than rely on foreign aid, ELDCs should focus on expanding trade, which provides numerous benefits, through which it will be possible for them to achieve both economic growth and development.	This perspective focuses on the ideas that many of the factors that limit aid effectiveness are the responsibility of donors, and that while trade is important, it is not enough. First, there are difficulties in expanding trade due to rich country protectionist policies; second, even if rich countries were to abandon these policies, trade would still be unable to solve the problems of growth and development, because many very poor countries have little to export, and because some communities are so geographically isolated that they are unable to get their goods to markets due to prohibitive transportation costs. Therefore aid is necessary for many reasons including achievement of the MDGs, breaking out of the poverty trap, for poverty alleviation, etc.	This is a relatively newer perspective, according to which very poor ELDCs must be offered aid in order to help them build up their capacity to export. Difficulties in exporting that originate in the domestic economy include poor transportation systems, weaknesses in power generation (which increase production costs), inability to access sufficient credit, institutional weaknesses in the ability to meet hygiene and technical standards, complicated bureaucratic procedures, all leading to lower exports and therefore an inability to maximize the potentials that trade has to offer. Aid should be offered to help EMDCs overcome such problems. This aid should be in addition to, not in place of, aid funds for poverty alleviation, etc.

Multilateral development assistance

multilateral development assistance = lending to ELDCs by international organizations such as the World Bank to achieve development objectives on **non-concessional terms** (at market interest rates and market repayment periods); this should be distinguished from **foreign aid** (which is **concessional**)

Multilateral lending consists of:

Multilateral development banks, that lend to developing countries in order to assist them in their growth and development efforts; the best known of these is **The World Bank**; others include the African Development Bank, Asian Development Bank, Inter-American Development Bank.	**The International Monetary Fund (IMF)** that monitors the global financial system and lends to governments that are experiencing difficulties in making their international payments.

The World Bank	The International Monetary Fund (IMF)
Background The World Bank was established after World War II with the intention of lending to Europe for its reconstruction. In the 1950s it turned its attention to lending to ELDCs in order to support economic growth and development. Its lending in the early years focused on infrastructure development (ex transport, energy, irrigation, communications), followed in the 1970s by a partial turn to poverty alleviation (ex health, education, water supplies, sanitation, employment). Since then two broad phases can be distinguished in its approaches, corresponding very closely to the two phases of trade liberalization (see p 86):	**Background** The IMF was established at the same time as the World Bank, after World War II. At that time, the global economy had a system of fixed exchange rates (p 69) and the IMF's purpose was to lend to countries facing balance of payments problems (inability to maintain the fixed rate due to deficits). In more recent years the IMFs main responsibilities include monitoring the global financial system and macroeconomic policies of member states, and lending to countries that have difficulties making international payments, through short-term loans at market interest rates.
Market-based supply-side policies: Structural Adjustment Loans In the 1980s the program of "structural adjustment loans" (SALs), heavily influenced by market-based supply-side policies, had the objective to reduce government intervention and make ELDC economies market-based. Lending became **conditional** on adoption of policies that liberalize trade, privatize, remove price controls, cut government spending; these were the policies of the **Washington Consensus** (see p 86). SALs were sharply criticized because of **their ambiguous effects on growth, worsening income distribution, increasing poverty, negative effects on health and education (due to cuts in government spending) and on the environment (due to neglect of environmental sustainability) and generally, failure to promote development**.	**Stabilization policies** Lending by the IMF to help countries make international payments is also **conditional** on the adoption of specific policies, known as "stabilization policies". These policies are generally contractionary, and are intended to help countries that are unable to finance (pay for) their current account deficits or unable to make payments on their debts. As a rule they include the following: • Contractionary monetary policy, i.e. higher interest rates; the objective is to lower aggregate demand, reduce imports (hence the need for foreign payments), increase inflows of financial capital (hence improve ability to make foreign payments) • Contractionary fiscal policy: increases in taxes, imposition of fees for schools and health care, and cuts in government spending, including spending on education, health care and infrastructure • Currency devaluation/depreciation to reduce imports and increase exports • Wage cuts, to reduce spending • Market-based supply-side policies, ex trade liberalization, removal of price controls, etc.
Development of markets with government intervention In the mid-1990s the World Bank turned again toward poverty alleviation, with a focus on the Millennium Development Goals, along with a revised view on the role of government. In this view, government intervention is essential in (i) creating the necessary conditions and institutions for markets to work well, and (ii) providing support in areas including health care, education, infrastructure, credit, gender equity, sustainability, appropriate technology development, income redistribution.	✔ The IMF is more controversial than the World Bank, **because such policies have very serious negative effects on employment, poverty and income distribution**.

☒ Both the World Bank and IMF are criticized for the following: the policy of **conditionality**, where lending is conditional on the adoption of particular policies, which in effect deprive the borrowing country of control over its domestic affairs; the control over the governing bodies of both institutions by EMDCs, which control voting power; for the negative effects of the World Bank's SALs and the IMF's stabilization policies on economic development, the poor, and sustainability in ELDCs.

4.7 THE ROLE OF INTERNATIONAL DEBT

foreign debt = the amount of funds that have been borrowed by the government and the private sector from foreign sources and are owed; the problem of foreign debt arises mainly because of **government debt to foreign creditors**

The problem of foreign debt

When a government borrows from foreign sources, it must make interest payments in addition to repayment of the borrowed amount. These payments must be made in **foreign exchange**, which can come from greater exports, fewer imports, or more borrowing.	Governments borrow from foreign sources partly in the form of **foreign aid** (p 89) or **development assistance** (p 90), and also in order to acquire foreign exchange **to pay for a current account deficit**, usually arising when imports of goods and services are greater than exports of goods and services. **The problem of foreign debt arises from the need to finance current account deficits**.

How the debt problem in ELDCs originated

The debt problem began in 1973-74, when OPEC (the Organization of Petroleum Exporting Countries) abruptly and massively increased oil prices (the first oil price shock). Countries that were oil importers suddenly faced **huge import expenditures**. At the same time, they also had **lower export revenues**, because the oil price increases led to recessions due to **cost-push inflation**, causing EMDC imports from ELDCs to fall. The combination of lower export revenues with higher import expenditures led to very sizable **current account deficits**, and hence to the need to borrow to pay for the deficits.	The major actors and their roles at that time: • **OPEC countries** found themselves with huge oil export revenues, which they deposited in large commercial banks around the world. These banks, wanting to make use of the extra funds, began lending to ELDCs in a process that came to be known as "petrodollar recycling". • **EMDCs** encouraged petrodollar recycling, because they saw it as an opportunity to reduce their spending on **foreign aid** and **development assistance**. • **The commercial banks**, wanting to lend as much as possible, were careless in their lending practices and did not monitor the borrowers. • **ELDCs**, finding it easy to borrow from the banks, and having a free hand in how they spent the borrowed money, spent part of it unwisely (ex to maintain low tax rates and poor tax collection systems, to support inefficient public enterprises).

In 1979 there was a second oil price shock, whose contractionary effects were made much worse by high interest rates initiated by the United States to control inflation, and followed by other major countries, leading to a major global recession in the early 1980s. By then, the massive debt levels accumulated by a number of ELDCs (mainly in Latin America and sub-Saharan Africa) had become unsustainable. Almost bankrupt, these countries were forced request assistance form the **IMF**.	The 1980s were the time when **market-based supply-side policies** made their appearance (in fact their popularity was greatly increased by the inability of **demand-side policies** to effectively deal with **cost-push inflation**, or **stagflation**). These policies were the inspiration of the World Bank's "Structural Adjustment Loans" and the IMF's "stabilization policies" (see p 90), which were initiated during this period and were considered to be the cure to the problem of foreign debt.	However, as noted, these policies had highly damaging effects on ELDCs, as they worked to deepen the recession, increase unemployment, worsen poverty and income distribution, and cause a tremendous amount of human suffering.

Consequences of high level of debt

Over and above the effects of World Bank and IMF policies, high levels of debt have very serious consequences for highly indebted ELDCs:

☒ There are major opportunity costs of debt servicing, as the government has less funds available to invest in essential infrastructure, education, health care, and other important social services needed for poverty alleviation.	☒ Since debt repayments and payment of interest (debt servicing) must be made in foreign exchange, there less Is of It available to import essential goods and services and inputs for production.
☒ Private investment may be adversely affected due to uncertainty about the future of the economy, negatively affecting long term economic growth.	☒ A **debt trap** may arise, in which debt levels are so high that it is necessary to go on borrowing in order to repay prior debts.
☒ Lower economic growth results not only on account of lower private investment, but also lower government investment in human capital, and reduced ability to import needed inputs.	☒ Lower economic growth affects the ability to repay debts, as with lower growth fewer funds are available from which debt servicing can be made.

Debt cancellation in heavily indebted ELDCs

Debt rescheduling versus debt cancellation

debt rescheduling (= debt restructuring) = extending new loans with longer repayment periods and at lower interest rates, which are then used to pay back the older loans; this makes it easier for the debtor to make the loan repayments plus interest	**debt cancellation** (= debt forgiveness) = cancelling a portion of debts, so that the amount that must be repaid is reduced; debt cancellation is a stronger form of **debt relief** than debt rescheduling

The Heavily Indebted Poor Countries Initiative (HIPC)

This is an initiative begun in 1996 by the World Bank and IMF, intended to help very poor countries that are highly indebted, and was supplemented in 2005 by the Multilateral Debt Relief Initiative (MDRI), in cooperation also with the African Development Bank. Debt relief under these programs is available for countries with a GNI per capita below a particular level, and that are in a debt trap (have unsustainable debt). Debt relief is conditional upon (i) liberalizing their markets, and (ii) pursuing an anti-poverty strategy, i.e. the funds that become available through debt reduction must be spent on combatting poverty.

☑ These programs are an important contribution to providing debt relief.	☒ The level of debt reduction provided for may not be enough.	☒ Some very highly indebted countries do not qualify for assistance.
☑ The programs are commendable for their anti-poverty approach.	☒ The programs take a long time to take effect and countries slide more deeply into debt in the meantime.	☒ Some market liberalization conditions may not be appropriate (ex charging fees for hospitals and schools, cutting government spending on social services).

4.8 THE BALANCE BETWEEN MARKETS AND INTERVENTION

Evaluating market-oriented policies

Market-oriented policies are based on the idea that markets are the most effective way for ELDCs to grow and develop.

Strengths	Weaknesses
☑ The market allocates resources efficiently, maximizing social surplus, through the functioning of prices as signals and incentives.	☒ Market failures do not allow the market to achieve allocative efficiency; market failures tend to be far more prominent in ELDCs.
☑ Competition between firms forces them to be more efficient, lowering costs of production at the same time that quality is improved.	☒ The market fails to supply education, health care services and infrastructure (merit goods) that are in extremely short supply in ELDCs.
☑ Lower costs of production permit lower prices, which are in the interests of consumers, as well as firms because of lower input prices.	☒ The market fails to provide against environmental degradation and unsustainable development, which severely affect ELDCs.
☑ The market increases choice.	☒ The market cannot function well when there are weak market-supporting institutions, such as effective legal, tax, and financial (banking) sectors.
☑ The market provides incentives (such as higher incomes and profit) that encourage economic activity leading to greater growth.	☒ The market leads to the development of dual economies.
☑ Policies that encourage competition (privatization, deregulation, etc) allow firms to operate in a more competitive environment, lowering costs of production and increasing allocative efficiency.	☒ The market leads to large urban informal sectors, where workers live in squalid conditions and have no social protection by the state.
	☒ The market leaves very poor people without access to credit.
	☒ The market does not help communities break out of the poverty trap.
☑ Policies that promote labor market reforms encourage the working of demand and supply in the labor market, lowering unemployment and firms' costs of production.	☒ Competition-promoting policies (ex privatization) usually increase unemployment, adding to a very large unemployed labor force.
☑ Incentive-related supply-side policies (ex lower taxes) provide incentives to work more and invest more, increasing growth.	☒ Labor market reforms lead to greater worker insecurity and lower wages, when incomes are already very low.
☑ Trade liberalization policies allow firms to grow, achieving economies of scale, and increase competition, leading to all the benefits of increased competition noted above.	☒ Trade liberalization policies force ELDCs to remain excessively specialized, and do not encourage diversification.
	☒ Trade liberalization means that many firms, even efficient ones, will be forced to close down due to their inability to compete with larger, more technological advanced EMDC firms.
☑ Freely floating exchange rates (as opposed to fixed exchange rates) allow the market to solve balance of payments problems automatically by allowing exchange rates to respond to currency demand and supply.	☒ As a result of the above factors (loss of worker protection, higher unemployment, firms closures, very low levels of human capital, the poverty trap, inability to access credit) the market may lead to increasing income inequalities.
	☒ The market can do little to alleviate poverty.
	☒ The market may not lead to higher economic growth, especially in countries that are very poor and have relatively weak market-supporting institutions.

Evaluating interventionist policies

Interventionist policies are based on the idea that government intervention in the economy is necessary to achieve growth and development.

Strengths	Weaknesses
☑ Government policies are essential to correct market failures.	☒ Government policies require use of budge funds, which are usually in very short supply in ELDCs, entailing large opportunity costs in every kind of government expenditure.
☑ Government policies can be designed to increase the provision of merit goods (education, health care, infrastructure).	☒ The scarcity of budget funds means that governments run the risk of running up large budget deficits and debt in order to meet the demands being made upon them.
☑ Government policies are needed to prevent environmental degradation and to promote sustainable development.	☒ The scarcity of budge funds also means that it is very difficult, if at all possible, for governments to undertake all the activities that are socially desirable in ELDCs (health care, infrastructure, social safety net, etc).
☑ The government can engage in R&D for the development of appropriate technologies.	
☑ The government can take action to create institutions that are essential for the proper functioning of markets (property rights, effective tax and banking systems, etc).	☒ Governments are often inefficient as they do not face the incentive to be economical in resource use so as to reduce costs and maximize profit.
☑ Government policies can attempt to regulate the informal economy and provide protection to vulnerable workers.	☒ Excessive bureaucracy (too many complicated rules in administration) leads to further inefficiencies.
☑ The government can pursue macroeconomic policies that aim at achieving a favorable environment (low inflation, low unemployment) that is favorable to private investment.	☒ Government intervention in certain forms (trade protection, price controls in the form of price floors) can protect inefficient producers, leading to inefficiencies in the private sector.
☑ The government can provide a **social safety net** = transfer payments of various kinds to ensure that people do not fall below the poverty line.	☒ Excessive government intervention in the market (too many, or incorrectly applied industrial policies, overvalued or undervalued exchange rates, excessive government ownership of firms, etc) leads to major allocative inefficiencies.
☑ The government can provide income redistribution policies in favor of less income inequality.	☒ Macroeconomic policy may be imprudent, leading to high inflation and large public debts, which discourage private sector activity.
☑ The government can pursue **industrial policies** (a type of interventionist supply-side policy) in support of firms that need assistance to grow and become competitive (low-interest loans, subsidies, tax breaks, etc.)	☒ Governments are often susceptible to political pressures by elite groups that influence policy-making in their own narrow interests rather than the interests of society.
☑ The government can provide trade protection for infant industries, and to assist ELDCs diversify production and exports.	☒ Governments and government-provided services may be susceptible to corruption (ex bribes to pursue uneconomic projects, or bribes to receive health care services), resulting in major allocative inefficiencies, waste of resources, and unfair distribution of goods and services.
☑ The government can intervene in foreign exchange markets by fixing exchange rates and reducing uncertainty for private investment.	

Striking a balance

Three periods: three perspectives

Since the 1950s, when economic development first became a subject of interest in its own right, there have been three periods of time each marked by a different orientation on the appropriate roles of governments and markets:

1950s to the 1970s	1980s and 1990s	Late 1990s to the present
Import substitution policies, followed by export promotion, were both based on **very strong government intervention in the economy**, with a limited role for the market.	Trade liberalization policies, together with market liberalization, were founded on market-based supply-side policies, and focused on **limiting the government's role in favor of freeing market forces**.	The experiences of the past led to a consensus that the **government and markets must complement each other**. The private sector should be allowed to function largely according to market principles, with the government confining itself to what the market cannot do.

An appropriate role for governments in ELDCs

Areas that governments should be involved with include:

☑ correction of market failures	☑ provision of a social safety net
☑ provision of health services, education, infrastructure	☑ policies to reduce poverty and income inequalities
☑ promotion of R&D, development of appropriate technology	☑ provision of laws and policies to promote gender equality
☑ protection of the environment and support for sustainable development	☑ provision of selective industrial policies in support of small and medium-sized firms, and infant industries, including support for diversification

The role of good governance in economic development

governance = the process of governing, which involves the exercise of control and authority; according to The World Bank, good governance "is synonymous with sound development management".

Good governance is important in economic development because it promotes accountability, fairness and transparency of government activities. This ensures on the one hand that the government's objectives are likely to be carried out more effectively and efficiently, while at the same time it inspires respect for and confidence in the government and its institutions on the part of citizens and economic decision-makers, thus having a positive effect on the pace of economic activity.

GLOSSARY OF IMPORTANT TERMS

Microeconomics SL terms (core)

ad valorem tax = an indirect tax that is a percentage of the price of the taxed good, resulting in a steeper S curve: amount of tax ⇑ as P ⇑

allocation of resources = assigning particular resources to the production of particular goods and services; **reallocation** = changing the allocation of resources; **overallocation of resources** = too many resources are assigned to production, causing **overproduction**; **underallocation of resources** = too few resources are assigned to production, causing **underproduction**; **misallocation** = wrong allocation of resources, causing **lack of allocative efficiency**

allocative efficiency = the best allocation of resources from society's point of view, where **MB = MC**, or in case of externalities, **MSB = MSC**

cap and trade scheme = see **tradable permits**

capital (= physical capital) = machines, tools, equipment, factories, all construction including **infrastructure**

carbon tax = a tax on carbon dioxide emissions of fossil fuels

clean technologies = technologies that reduce negative environmental effects of production

common access resources = natural resources without ownership, that are not traded in a market, without a price, and can therefore be used freely by anyone; they are **non-excludable** yet **rivalrous**

competitive supply = when two goods use the same resources, ex onions and potatoes grown on the same agricultural land. If the price of potatoes ⇑, the Q of potatoes produced ⇑ (upward movement along potato S curve) and the S of onions ⇓ (S curve for onions shifts left)

complements (= complementary goods) = goods that are used together, ex sugar and coffee; tennis balls and tennis rackets: as P of good A⇑, D for good B⇓ (shifts left); as P of good A⇓, D for good B ⇑ (shifts right)

consumer surplus = benefit received by consumers who buy a good at a price lower than the price they are willing to pay = the area under the demand curve up to the price consumers pay

cross price elasticity of demand (XED) = responsiveness of demand for good X to changes in price of good Y = % change in Q_X demanded divided by % change in P_Y

demand (D) = the quantity of a good that buyers (consumers) are **willing and able to buy** at various prices over a time period, ceteris paribus; may involve **individual demand** = the demand of a single buyer, or **market demand** = the demands of all the buyers in a market, found by adding up all the individual demands for each price

demerit goods = goods whose consumption creates **negative consumption externalities**; are socially undesirable but are overprovided by the market and overconsumed

entrepreneurship = the human effort used to organize the other three factors of production, as well as risk-taking, innovation, management

excess demand = shortage = Q demanded > Q supplied

excess supply = surplus = Q demanded < Q supplied

excludable good = a good from whose consumption people can be excluded, i.e. prevented from buying it) by charging a price

externality = positive effect (benefit) or negative effect (cost) for third parties who are not part of a transaction and whose interests are not taken into account; the market fails to achieve allocative efficiency as **marginal social benefits (MSB) ≠ marginal social costs (MSC)**

factors of production (= resources) = inputs used to produce all goods and services that people need and want (**land, labor, capital, entrepreneurship**)

free rider problem = occurs when a good is used without payment; users take a "free ride"; closely related to **non-excludability**, where someone cannot be excluded from using a good (ex a lighthouse)

income elasticity of demand (YED) = responsiveness of demand for good X to changes in income (abbreviated as Y) = % change in Q demanded divided by % change in Y

indirect tax (= excise tax) = tax on spending to buy goods and services, paid indirectly to the government through the seller

inferior good = demand for the good ⇑ as consumer income ⇓, and vice versa; ex lower quality goods like used cars, used clothes: as income⇑, D⇓ (shifts left); as income ⇓, D⇑ (shifts right)

joint supply = when two or more goods, ex butter and skim milk, are derived from a single product (whole milk), it is not possible to produce **more** of one, ex butter, without producing **more** of the other, ex skim milk. If the price of butter rises, Q of butter produced increases (upward movement along the butter S curve) and S of skim milk increases (S curve for skim milk shifts right).

labor = all human effort, or work, that goes into producing goods and services (ex the work done by teachers, builders, lawyers, plumbers)

land = all natural resources that are above the ground (ex forests, rivers, agricultural land, fish in the sea) and all natural resources that are under the ground (ex oil, natural gas, minerals)

law of demand = a law stating that there is a negative causal relationship between **price (P)** and **quantity (Q)** of a good demanded: the higher the price, the lower the quantity demanded; the lower the price, the greater the quantity demanded

law of supply = a law stating that there is a positive causal relationship between **price (P)** and **quantity (Q)** of a good supplied: the higher the price, the higher the quantity supplied; the lower the price, the lower the quantity supplied

marginal benefits (MB) = the additional benefits derived by consumers from buying/consuming an additional unit of a good, equal to the demand curve

marginal cost (MC) = the extra cost to producers of producing an additional unit of a good, equal to the supply curve

marginal private benefits (MPB) = additional benefits for **consumers** arising from consumption of an additional unit of a good

marginal private costs (MPC) = additional costs to **producers** arising from production of an additional unit of a good

marginal social benefits (MSB) = additional benefits for **society** arising from consumption of an additional unit of a good

marginal social costs (MSC) = additional costs to **society** arising from production of an additional unit of a good

market failure = the failure of the market to allocate resources efficiently, resulting in overallocation, underallocation or no allocation of resources to the production of a good or service relative to what is socially most desirable

merit goods = goods whose consumption creates **positive consumption externalities**; are socially desirable but are underprovided by the market and underconsumed

minimum wage = a minimum price of labor (**price floor**) usually set by the government to protect low-skilled workers and ensure they can achieve a minimum standard of consumption; is a minimum price	**producer surplus** = benefit received by producers who sell a good at a higher price than the price they are willing to receive = the area above the supply curve up to the price received
nationalization = the transfer of ownership from the private to the public sector (the opposite of **privatization**)	**public good** = a good that is **non-rivalrous** and **non-excludable**
necessity = a good that is necessary to a consumer (to be contrasted with a **luxury** that is not essential)	**rational economic decision-making** = all economic decision-makers (consumers, firms, workers, etc) behave according to their best interests, and try to get more rather than less (more profit, more benefits from consumption, higher wages, etc)
non-excludable good = It Is not possible to charge a price and therefore exclude people from using the good (ex a lighthouse)	**rivalrous good** = its use by one individual makes it less available for use by others
non-rivalrous good = its use by one individual does not make it less available for use by others (ex a lighthouse)	**scarcity** = the condition of being limited in relation to the needs and wants of human beings; factors of production are scarce while human needs and wants are infinite; since there are not enough resources, goods and services are therefore also scarce
normal good = demand for the good ⇑ as consumer income ⇑; as income ⇑, D⇑ (shifts right); as income ⇓, D⇓ (shifts left)	
normative statement = a statement about something that **ought to be**, expressing a subjective opinion or value judgment; normative statements are used for making economic policy	**shortage** = see **excess demand**
	social surplus = the sum of producer and consumer surplus
positive statement = a statement about something that **is**, **was**, or **will be**; positive statements are used to describe events, and make hypotheses and theories	**specific tax** = an indirect tax that is a specific amount per unit of the good, and results in a parallel shift of the S curve to the left or upward;
opportunity cost = the sacrifice of the next best alternative as a result of making a choice; this concept is **central to economics**, because **scarcity necessitates choice**, and choice almost always involves an opportunity cost	**subsidy** = payment by the government to firms in order to lower costs and price, and increase supply
	substitutes (= **substitute goods**) = goods that satisfy a similar need, ex meat and fish; apples and oranges: as P of good A ⇑, D for good B ⇑ (shifts right); as P of good A⇓, D for good B⇓ (shifts left)
price ceiling = a maximum price on a good set by the government below the equilibrium price of the market, resulting in a **shortage**	
price elasticity of demand (PED) = responsiveness of Q demanded to changes in P = % change in Q demanded divided by % change in P	**supply (S)** = the quantity of a good that sellers (firms) are **willing and able to sell** at various prices over a time period, ceteris paribus; may involve **individual supply** = the supply of a single seller (firm), or **market supply** = the supplies of all the sellers in a market, found by adding up all the individual supplies for each price
price elasticity of supply (PES) = responsiveness of Q supplied to changes in P = % change in Q supplied divided by % change in P	
	surplus = see **excess supply**
price floor = a minimum price on a good set by the government above the equilibrium price of the market, resulting in a **surplus**	**sustainability** = the use of natural resources at a pace and in ways that do not decrease the quantity or destroy the quality of resources available for future generations
price control = setting of **price cellings (maximum prices)** or **price floors (minimum prices)** (usually by the government), preventing the market from reaching a market-clearing equilibrium price	**total revenue (TR)** = P x Q = a firm's total earnings from selling its output
primary commodities (or **products**) = goods arising from the factor of production **land**, including all agricultural products as well as fishing, forestry and extractive products (ex oil and diamonds)	**tradable permits** (= **cap and trade schemes**) = a maximum permissible amount of a particular pollutant is determined, and permits to emit this pollutant are distributed to firms by government (or international body), which can be bought and sold in a market
private good = a good that is **rivalrous** and **excludable**	**welfare loss** (= **deadweight loss**) = the benefits that are lost to society due to resource misallocation
privatization = the sale of public property by the government to private firms (the opposite of **nationalization**)	

Microeconomics HL terms

abnormal profit = positive economic profit, arising when total revenue (TR) > economic costs; it is profit over and above **normal profit**	**cartel** = an agreement between firms with the objective to maximize profits while behaving as if they were a monopoly and restricting competition between them, usually by fixing prices at a higher level and limiting output; cartels are formed by **collusive oligopolies**
allocative efficiency = producing the combination of goods and services that consumers mostly want; when P = MC (or MB = MC)	
	collusion = an agreement between firms to fix prices and share output; usually occurs in **oligopoly**
asymmetric information = a type of market failure occurring when one party to a transaction (buyer or seller) has more information than the other party, leading to allocative inefficiency	**concentration ratio** = a measure used to determine the degree of competition in an industry, and whether firms have too much **monopoly power**; it measures the percentage of output produced by the largest firms in the industry
barriers to entry = factors that prevent or make it very difficult for outsider firms to enter an industry and begin production	
break-even price = P where the firm makes normal profit, P = minimum ATC in perfect competition	**constant returns to scale** = as inputs increase, output increases in the same proportion: if inputs double, output also doubles

costs of production: total cost, total fixed cost, total variable cost; average total cost, average fixed cost, average variable cost; marginal cost = see p 29 for all cost definitions and formulas

decreasing returns to scale = as inputs increase, output increases less than in proportion: if inputs double, output less than doubles

diseconomies of scale = rising costs per unit of output (= rising average costs) that occur as the size of a firm increases when it varies all its inputs (in the long run)

economic costs = the sum of explicit and implicit costs; in economics "costs" refer to **economic costs**

economic profit = total revenue (TR) minus economic costs (explicit + implicit costs); economic profit may be positive, zero or negative

economies of scale = falling costs per unit of output (= falling average costs) that occur as the size of a firm increases when it varies all its inputs (in the long run)

explicit cost = a cost involving payment of money made by a firm to obtain a factor of production (input) for use in production

formal collusion = collusion (making an agreement) between firms leading to the formation of a cartel

game theory = a mathematical technique used to analyze behavior of interdependent decision-makers who use strategic behavior; the prisoner's dilemma game helps analyze behavior in oligopoly

implicit cost = a cost involving sacrificed income for the use of a factor of production (input) that is owned by the firm

increasing returns to scale = as inputs increase, output increases more than in proportion: if inputs double, output more than doubles

law of diminishing returns = as more and more units of a variable input (ex labor) are added to a fixed input (ex capital), the marginal product of the variable input (labor) at first increases, reaches a maximum, and then begins to fall; diminishing returns occur in the short run when at least one input is fixed

long run = period of time when all factors of production are variable (changing); there are no fixed factors

long-run average total cost curve = a cost curve showing the relationship between average cost of a firm and quantity of output it produces as it increases in size by varying all its inputs (in the long run); it is made up of a series of short-run average total cost curves

loss = negative economic profit : total revenue (TR) < economic costs

monopolistic competition = a market structure where there is a large number of firms, low barriers to entry, and product differentiation

monopoly = a market structure involving a single firm (or one dominant firm); it produces a good with no close substitutes; there are high barriers to entry

monopoly power = the ability of a firm to influence the price of the good that it produces and sells, due to a downward sloping demand curve; it is type of market failure because it results in an underallocation of resources to the production of the good in question, and hence in allocative inefficiency and welfare loss

natural monopoly = a firm with economies of scale so large that it satisfies demand of an entire market at a level of output where it still experiences falling average costs; two or more firms producing the same level of output would do so at higher average costs

non-price competition = competition between firms on the basis of non-price factors, through product differentiation

normal profit = arises when economic profit is zero, i.e. when total revenue (TR) is equal to total economic costs (TR = TC); it is the amount of revenue required by a firm to just keep it in business

oligopoly = a market structure where there is a small number of large firms; selling a homogeneous or differentiated product; with high barriers to entry; with interdependence among the firms due to their small number, causing them to face the conflicting objectives to compete or to collude

perfect competition = a market structure where there is a large number of small firms; there are no barriers to entry; all firms sell a homogeneous product; there is perfect information; and there is perfect resource mobility

price competition = competition between firms to attract customers away from the products of other firms by lowering the price of the product

price discrimination = selling a product at different prices to different consumer groups, where the price differences are not due to differences in costs of production

price leadership = a form of tacit collusion where a dominant firm sets a price, and also initiates price changes; the remaining firms accept the leader's price, becoming effectively price-takers

price maker = a firm that faces a downward sloping demand curve, thus having the ability to influence its selling price

price taker = a firm that sells all the output it wants at the price determined in the market; it has no influence over its selling price

price war = a situation where firms retaliate against each other by lowering prices to the point that they may end up making losses

prisoner's dilemma = a game in game theory showing how two rational decision-makers who try to make themselves as well off as possible by using strategic behavior, end up becoming worse off

product: total product, average product, marginal product = see p 29 for a summary of all product definitions and formulas

product differentiation = occurs when firms try to make their products different from others; products can be differentiated by appearance, taste, color, size, quality, packaging, branding, services (such as warranties), location (easy access by consumers); it forms the basis of **non-price competition**

productive efficiency = producing at the lowest possible cost; occurs where **production takes place at minimum ATC**

revenue: total revenue, average revenue, marginal revenue = see p 29 for a summary of all revenue definitions and formulas

short run = period of time when at least one factor of production is fixed (unchanging) and all other factors are variable (changing)

shut-down price = the price at which the firm will shut down; in the short run it is where P = minimum AVC

strategic interdependence = a characteristic of oligopolistic firms whereby they try to guess what the other will do, because the actions of one affect outcomes not only for themselves but also for the others

tacit collusion (= informal collusion) = cooperation between firms in oligopoly to restrict competition and fix prices without a formal agreement

tax incidence = the particular group bearing the burden of a tax, i.e. the group paying all or a portion of a tax

Macroeconomics SL terms (core)

absolute poverty = the number of people with an income level below a predefined "poverty line", which is the minimum income necessary to satisfy basic physical needs

aggregate demand (AD) = the total amount of real output (goods and services) that **all buyers** in an economy (consumers, firms, government and foreigners) are willing and able to buy at different possible **price levels**, in a year, ceteris paribus

aggregate supply (AS) = the total amount of real output (goods and services) produced in an economy in a year at different price levels; there are three kinds of AS curves: **short-run aggregate supply (SRAS), long-run aggregate supply (LRAS)** and **Keynesian AS**

automatic stabilizers = features in the economy that limit the size of economic fluctuations (recessionary and inflationary gaps) **without any government action**, thus stabilizing the economy; the most important are **progressive income taxes** and **unemployment benefits**

balanced budget = government revenues are equal to government spending, over the period of a year

budget deficit = government revenues < government spending, over the period of a year, usually made possible by government borrowing

budget surplus = government revenues > government spending, over the period of a year

business confidence = a measure of the degree of optimism of firms regarding the future of the economy

business cycle = short-term fluctuations (increases and decreases) in real GDP over time, consisting of four phases: **peak, contraction, trough,** and **expansion**

capital expenditures = spending by the government on public investments (roads, airports, public hospitals and schools, etc)

central bank = a financial institution concerned with carrying out **monetary policy** and exchange rate policy, as well as regulating commercial banks and acting as banker to both commercial banks and the government

consumer confidence = a measure of the degree of optimism of consumers regarding the future of the economy

consumer price index (CPI) = a measure of the cost of living of the typical household and how this changes over time; the CPI compares the cost of buying a fixed basket of goods and services from one year to the next; by calculating the value of the same basket from year to year, the CPI offers an estimate of how prices change on average from year to year

consumption = spending by consumers to buy goods and services

contractionary policy = policy carried out by the government (**fiscal policy**) or the central bank (**monetary policy**) intended to lower AD and close an **inflationary gap**

core rate of inflation (= underlying rate of inflation) = a measure of the rate of inflation based on a basket of goods and services that excludes goods with highly volatile prices (ex food and energy), in order to determine the underlying course of inflation

cost-push inflation = inflation caused by a decrease in SRAS, hence a leftward shift in the SRAS curve, resulting mainly from increases in costs of production or supply shocks

crowding out = a possible weakness of expansionary **fiscal policy** involving increases in government spending financed by borrowing, causing an increase in interest rates that reduces consumption and investment spending, thus counteracting the increase in AD

current expenditures = spending by the government for its day-to-day operations (wages of government workers, supplies, subsidies)

cyclical unemployment (= demand-deficient unemployment) = unemployment caused by decreases in AD, leading to the downward phase of the business cycle

deflation = a sustained decrease in the general price level

deflationary gap = occurs when short-run equilibrium GDP is less than potential GDP due to insufficient aggregate demand

demand-deficient unemployment = see **cyclical unemployment**

demand-pull inflation = inflation caused by an increase in AD, hence a rightward shift in the AD curve, resulting from an increase in any of the components of AD (C, I, G, X-M)

demand-side policies = policies that focus on changing AD for the purpose of reducing short-term economic fluctuations, i.e. close **deflationary** and **inflationary gaps**, and hence achieve low unemployment and a low and stable rate of inflation

deregulation = policies to eliminate or lower the amount of government regulation of an industry (ex regulation of prices or quantity of output produced, both used to protect firms from competition), thus exposing firms in the industry to greater competition

direct taxes = taxes on income and wealth, paid directly to the government (ex personal income taxes, corporate income taxes)

disinflation = a fall in the rate of inflation (ex 7% in 2010; 5% in 2011)

economic growth = growth in real GDP over a period of time, usually expressed as a percentage change in real GDP over time; is often calculated in **per capita** terms (per person in the population)

efficiency = the use of resources in the best possibly way, so that there is no waste of resources

equity = the condition of being fair, often interpreted to mean "equality" in the context of income distribution

expansionary policy = policy carried out by the government (**fiscal policy**) or the central bank (**monetary policy**) intended to increase AD and close a **deflationary gap**

expenditure approach = an approach to measuring GDP that adds up total spending of all buyers on all final goods and services within a year; includes C + I + G + (X - M)

fiscal policy = a type of demand-side policy by the government in order to manipulate AD (by changing taxes and/or government spending) to achieve price stability and low unemployment

frictional unemployment = unemployment including workers who are in between jobs

full employment output (= potential output) = the level of real output produced by the economy when unemployment is equal to **natural unemployment**

gini coefficient = a measure of income inequality derived from the **Lorenz curve** = area between the Lorenz curve and line of perfect income equality, divided by entire area under line of perfect equality

government budget = a plan relating government revenue to government spending, usually for a period of a year

green GDP = a measure of GDP that takes into account environmental destruction due to production or consumption activities; green GDP = GDP – value of environmental destruction

gross domestic product (GDP) = the total value of all final goods and services produced within the boundaries of a country, in a year

gross national income (GNI or GNP) = the total income received by the residents of a country in a year, regardless where the factors of production owned by the residents are located

hidden unemployment = people without a job not included in official unemployment figures because they are not actively seeking a job (ex "discouraged workers") as well as underemployed people counted as fully employed in official unemployment figures

income approach = an approach to measuring GDP that adds up all income earned by the factors of production in the course of producing total output within a year; includes wages, rent, interest and profits

indirect taxes = taxes on spending to buy goods and services, paid indirectly to the government through the sellers (ex sales taxes, VAT)

industrial policies = a type of interventionist supply-side policy intended to promote specific industries; include tax reductions, tax exemptions, low-interest loans, subsidies and grants for industries that are held to be important to support growth

inflation = a sustained increase in the general price level

inflation targeting = a policy pursued by some central banks focusing on targeting a particular rate of inflation and carrying out monetary policy (manipulation of interest rates) to achieve the targeted rate

inflationary gap = occurs when short-run equilibrium GDP is greater than potential GDP due to excess aggregate demand

injection = money that enters the circular flow of income in the form of investment spending, government spending or export revenues (spending by foreigners)

interest rate = payment for borrowed money over a certain time period, expressed as a percentage of the borrowed amount; the "price" of money services

investment = spending by firms or the government to buy capital goods (machines, equipment, as well as infrastructure)

Keynesian AS = an AS curve with a horizontal section (when the economy is in recession), an upward-sloping section (when the economy approaches full employment output) and a vertical section (when the economy has reached maximum capacity output)

leakage = money that leaves the circular flow of income in the form of saving, taxes, and spending on imports

long run aggregate supply (LRAS) = an AS curve showing real output produced as being independent of the price level; the LRAS is vertical at real GDP where **unemployment = natural unemployment**

Lorenz curve = visual representation of income shares received by percentages of the **population**; the further away a Lorenz curve is from the line of perfect equality, the more unequal the distribution of income; forms the basis of computing the **gini coefficient**

monetary policy = a type of demand-side policy undertaken by the central bank in order to manipulate AD (by changing interest rates) to achieve price stability and low unemployment

natural unemployment = the sum of **frictional**, **seasonal** and **structural unemployment**; is the unemployment level of the economy when it is producing **potential output** (= **full employment output**)

net exports = the value of exports minus the value of imports

nominal GDP (or nominal GNI) = a measure of output and income in terms of **current prices** (prices at any given moment in time)

output approach = an approach to measuring GDP that adds up the value of each good and service (PxQ) produced in the economy within a year, thus obtaining the value of all final goods and services

potential output (= full employment output) = the level of real GDP produced when the economy is on its long-term growth trend, where **cyclical unemployment** = 0 and unemployment = **natural unemployment**

poverty = the inability to satisfy basic physical needs (ex, food, clothing, shelter, etc) due to low income

producer price index (PPI) = a measure of changes in costs of production based on average prices of factors of production; since the PPI measures price level changes at early stages in production, it is useful in predicting changes in future inflation (measured by the CPI)

productivity = output per worker; it increases as a result of investments in physical, human and natural capital; a major cause of **economic growth**

progressive tax = the percentage of income paid as tax (average tax rate) increases as income increases

proportional tax = the percentage of income paid as tax (average tax rate) remains constant as income increases

real GDP (or real GNI) = a measure of output and income in terms of constant prices that prevail in one particular year; therefore real values eliminate the influence of price level changes over time

recession = falling real GDP over a period of at least two consecutive quarters (six consecutive months)

regressive tax = the percentage of income paid as tax (average tax rate) decreases as income increases

relative poverty = the number of people with an income level below a predefined level that changes over time, defined as a percentage of society's median income; poverty is "relative" to other people's income; reflects the idea that people should be able to afford a lifestyle typical of their society

seasonal unemployment = unemployment including workers who are unemployed on a seasonal basis, ex ski instructors in the summer

short run aggregate supply (SRAS) = an AS curve showing the total amount of real output produced in a year to be directly related to the price level; as the price level □ the amount of real output produced □

structural unemployment = unemployment that is usually long-term, arising from changing demand for different labor skills (due to technological change or structural changes in the economy), changes in the geographical location of industries, and labor market rigidities

supply-side policies = policies that focus on the supply side of the economy, aiming to promote long-term economic growth and hence increase potential output (increase LRAS or Keynesian AS); may be **interventionist** (involving government intervention in the economy) or **market-based** (based on development of free competitive markets)

transfer payments = transfers of income from taxpayers to vulnerable groups who are people in need, including unemployment benefits, child allowances, pensions, housing benefits and others

underemployment = people who are employed, but who (i) work part-time when they would rather work full-time, and (ii) work at a different skill or lower skill level than what they were trained for (ex an engineer working as a waiter)

unemployment rate = the number of people in the labor force actively looking for work but without a job, expressed as a percentage of the labor force (= number of unemployed / labor force x 100)

Macroeconomics HL terms

average tax rate (ATR) = tax paid / taxable income x 100	**marginal tax rate (MTR)** = tax rate applied to an individual's income in the highest tax bracket
marginal propensity to consume (MPC) = $\Delta C/\Delta Y$ = fraction of additional income spent to consume (buy) domestic products	**multiplier** = a multiplied effect on AD, and hence on real GDP (= real income), due to a change in spending caused by an **injection**
marginal propensity to import (MPM) = $\Delta M/\Delta Y$ = fraction of additional income (Y) spent on buying imports (M)	**Phillips curve** = a curve showing the relationship between the rate of inflation (vertical axis) and rate of unemployment (horizontal axis); **short-run Phillips curve** shows an inverse relationship; **long-run Phillips curve** is vertical at the natural rate of unemployment, indicating that unemployment is independent of the price level
marginal propensity to save (MPS) = $\Delta S/\Delta Y$ = fraction of additional income (Y) that goes toward saving (S)	
marginal propensity to tax (MPT) = $\Delta T/\Delta Y$ = fraction of additional income (Y) paid as taxes (T)	**stagflation** = short for "stagnation" and "inflation", arising from a decrease in **SRAS**, which causes a rising price level (**cost-push inflation**) and a fall in real output

International economics SL terms (core)

administrative barriers = a variety of obstacles to imports imposed by governments as a form of **trade protection**, intended to limit the quantity of imports and protect domestic producers from foreign competition; ex complicated bureaucratic procedures, unnecessary packaging, health, safety, and environmental standards with which imports must comply in order to be admitted into the country

anti-dumping tariffs = tariffs imposed by an importing country on goods by another country to raise the price to pre-**dumping** levels

appreciation of a currency = an increase in the value of a currency in a **freely floating exchange rate** system; may occur due to an increase in demand or decrease in supply of a currency

balance of payments = a record of all transactions between residents of a country with residents of all other countries, consisting of all payments entering into the country from abroad (Inflows) and all payments leaving a country to go abroad (outflows) over a period of time, usually a year; it consists of the **current account**, the **capital account** and the **financial account**, which in the course of a year add up to zero

balance of trade in goods = value of exports of goods minus value of imports of goods

balance of trade in services = value of exports of services minus value of imports of services

bilateral trade agreement = an agreement between two countries to reduce or eliminate trade barriers to encourage free trade between them

capital account = an account in the **balance of payments** consisting of "capital transfers" and "transactions in non-produced, non-financial assets"; it is usually less important that the **current account** and **financial account**

common market = a type of trading bloc where members have free trade between them, a common trade policy toward non-members, and free movement of labor and capital between the members; ex EEC (European Economic Community, before this became the European Union)

credit item = any item in the balance of payments involving an inflow of funds into a country, entered with a plus (+) sign

current account = an account in the **balance of payments** consisting of the sum of the balance of trade in goods, balance of trade in services, income (inflows minus outflows), and current transfers (inflows minus outflows)

customs union = a type of trading bloc where members have free trade between them and common trade barriers toward non-members; ex SACU (South Africa Customs Union)

debit item = any item in the **balance of payments** involving an outflow of funds from a country, entered with a minus (-) sign

deficit on an account = an excess of debits over credits in any of the three accounts of the **balance of payments**, meaning that outflows going abroad > inflows from abroad

depreciation of a currency = a decrease in the value of a currency in a **freely floating exchange rate** system; may occur due to a decrease in demand or an increase in supply of a currency

devaluation = a decrease in the value of a currency in a **fixed exchange rate** system, achieved through the government or central bank which decides upon a new, lower exchange rate for the currency

direct investment = an item in the **financial account** of the **balance of payments** showing inflows minus outflows of funds used for investment in physical capital (undertaken by **multinational corporations**, or **MNCs**)

dumping = selling goods (exports) in international markets at a price lower than average cost of production; it is against WTO rules

economic integration = growing economic relations and cooperation between countries arising from trade or other agreements that link their economies together

exchange rate = the value of one currency expressed in terms of another; can be thought of as the "price" of a currency

financial account = an account in the **balance of payments** consisting of the sum of **direct investment**, **portfolio investment** and **reserve assets** (in all cases, inflows minus outflows)

fixed exchange rate = an exchange rate fixed by a country's government or central bank at a certain level in terms of another currency (such as the US$ or €), hence not permitted to adjust to currency demand and supply; requires constant central bank intervention to maintain the fixed level

free trade = international trade with no government intervention imposing restrictions of any kind on imports or exports

free trade area = a group of countries that have agreed to reduce or eliminate trade barriers to achieve free trade between them; each country retains the right to impose its own trade barriers toward non-members; ex NAFTA (North American Free Trade Agreement)

freely floating exchange rate = an exchange rate that is determined entirely by demand and supply of the currency, with no government intervention

infant industry = an industry that is just starting to be set up and is unable to compete in international markets with well-established firms that have experience and economies of scale; one of the strongest arguments in ELDCs favor of protection on the grounds that these industries must be protected until they grow and "mature"	**revaluation** = an increase in the value of a currency in a **fixed exchange rate system**, achieved through the government or central bank which decides upon a new, higher exchange rate for the currency
managed exchange rates (= **managed float**) = exchange rates that are determined by currency demand and supply, but where the central bank intervenes at times in order to avoid sharp short-term fluctuations and to influence the value of the exchange rate	**reserve assets** = an item in the **financial account** of the **balance of payments** showing inflows minus outflows of foreign exchange held by the central bank, corresponding to domestic currency sales and purchases in order to influence the value of an exchange rate
	speculation (currency)= buying or selling currencies to make a profit
monetary union = members of a common market adopt a common currency and a common central bank responsible for monetary policy for all the members; ex the Eurozone countries, that adopted the euro after giving up their national currencies, whose common monetary policy is the responsibility of the European Central Bank (ECB)	**subsidy** = payment by the government to firms to lower costs of production and price and increase supply; often used as a form of **trade protection**
	surplus on an account = an excess of credits over debits in any of the three accounts; inflows from abroad > outflows going abroad
multilateral trade agreement = an agreement between many countries around the world, as a rule under the leadership of the World Trade Organization (WTO), to reduce or eliminate trade barriers to encourage free trade between them	**tariff** = a form **of trade protection** involving a tax on the value of imported goods; is a type of **indirect tax**
overvalued currency = a currency whose value is maintained higher than its market equilibrium level; may occur in **fixed** or **managed exchange rate** systems	**trade liberalization** = removal of import barriers and trade restrictions between countries, in order to bring about **free trade**
portfolio investment = an item in the **financial account** of the **balance of payments** showing inflows minus outflows of funds used for financial investments (ex buying bonds and stocks)	**trade protection** = government intervention in international trade involving the imposition of trade barriers intended to limit the quantity of imports and protect the domestic economy from foreign competition; ex **tariffs**, **quotas**, **subsidies**
preferential trade agreement = according to the World Trade Organization (WTO), it is an agreement between two or more countries to give preferential access to particular products (access with low or no tariffs or other trade protection); often includes additional issues beyond trade such as services, investment, and intellectual property rights	**trading bloc** = two or more countries that have agreed to reduce or eliminate trade barriers between them to encourage free trade
	undervalued currency = a currency whose value is maintained lower than its market equilibrium level; may occur in **fixed** or **managed exchange rate** systems
quota = a form of **trade protection** involving restriction on the quantity of imports	**World Trade Organization** = an international organization involved with multilateral trade negotiations aimed at liberalizing global trade; with resolving trade disputes between member countries; and with overseeing the global system of trade rules
regional trade agreement = an agreement between several countries in a geographical region to reduce or eliminate trade barriers to encourage free trade between them	

International economics HL terms

absolute advantage = a country has an absolute advantage in the production of a good if it can produce it with fewer resources (= more efficiently) than another country	**J-curve** = a curve showing what happens to a country's trade balance following a currency **depreciation** (or **devaluation**); initially the trade balance worsens (because the **Marshall-Lerner (M-L) condition** is unlikely to hold) but after a period of time begins to improve (when the **M-L condition** is satisfied)
comparative advantage = a country has a comparative advantage in the production of a good if it can produce it at a lower **opportunity cost** than another country	**Marshall-Lerner (M-L) condition** = a condition specifying what must hold for a **deprecation** / **devaluation** to lead to a smaller trade deficit: If $PED_{exports} + PED_{imports} > 1$, **depreciation / devaluation** □ smaller trade deficit
expenditure-reducing policies = contractionary **monetary policies** and **contractionary fiscal policies** used to reduce persistent **current account deficits** by lowering AD and the price level, so that imports □ and exports □	
	terms of trade = average price of exports divided by the average price of imports times 100; it is the ratio of two index numbers times 100
expenditure-switching policies = include trade protection policies and **depreciation** used to reduce persistent **current account deficits** by switching consumption away from imports and toward domestically produced goods	**trade creation** = the replacement of higher-cost domestic products by lower-cost imported products due to the formation of a trading bloc
factor endowments = natural resources, factors of production, and technology possessed by a country, that determine its **absolute and comparative advantage**	**trade diversion** = the replacement of lower-cost imported products by higher-cost imported products due to the formation of a trading bloc

Development economics SL terms (core)

appropriate technology = a technology that is well suited to a country's factors of production; often refers to quantities of labor in relation to physical capital, as well as skill levels needed in relation to skill levels available

bilateral aid = **foreign aid** going from one donor country to one ELDC recipient country

composite indicator = a group of single indicators used together to form a single measure of development in several dimensions; the best known is the **Human Development Index (HDI)**

concessional long-term loans = **foreign aid** consisting of loans with below-market interest rates, extended for long periods of time

development aid = **foreign aid** extended to ELDCs for the purpose of assisting them in their development efforts

diversification = broadening the range of goods and services produced and exported; protects against excessive specialization and provides advantages for growth and development

dual economy = two different systems that coexist in an economy; ex a formal (registered and regulated) and informal (unregistered, unregulated) urban sector

economic development = a process where increases in real GDP/GNI per capita occur alongside decreases in poverty, increased employment opportunities, lower income inequalities, increased access to merit goods including education, health care and infrastructure, all leading to improvements in standards of living

economic growth = increases in real GDP (real output) and/or real GNI (real income) over time; often measured in **per capita** terms

export promotion = a growth and trade strategy based on strong government intervention intended to promote **economic growth** through the expansion of exports

foreign aid = transfer of funds in the form of loans or grants, or transfer of goods and services, as gifts, to ELDCs in order to help them achieve economic or social objectives; aid is **non-commercial** (the transfers don't involve commerce) and it is **concessional**

foreign debt = the amount of funds borrowed by the government and private sector from foreign sources; the problem of foreign debt arises mainly because of **government debt to foreign creditors**

foreign direct investment (FDI) = investment by a firm originating in one country (the home country) in **productive** facilities in another country (the host country), carried out by MNCs

governance = the process of governing, which involves the exercise of control and authority; according to The World Bank, good governance "is synonymous with sound development management"

human capital = skills, knowledge, education and good health acquired by people that make them more productive

humanitarian aid = **foreign aid** extended in areas experiencing emergency situations due to crises caused by wars or natural disasters; consist of donations of food, medical assistance, etc

Human Development Index (HDI) = a **composite indicator** measuring development in three dimensions: the level of health; the level of education; and the standard of living

import substitution = a growth and trade strategy based on strong government intervention involving heavy protection of domestic industries (through **tariffs**, **quotas**, **subsidies**, etc) intended to replace imports with domestic production

infrastructure = physical capital (from investments usually by governments) in social necessary items; ex transportation systems (roads, railways, ports, airports), clean water supplies, sewerage systems, telecommunications (including telephones), energy, etc

International Monetary Fund (IMF) = an international financial institution that monitors the global financial system and lends to governments experiencing difficulties in making their international payments

micro-credit = credit (lending) of very small amounts of money for short periods of time to poor people who have no other access to credit (such as though commercial banks)

Millennium Development Goals (MDGs) = a set of eight goals for ELDCs emerging from the United Nations Millennium Declaration of September 2000; ex eradicate extreme poverty and hunger; achieve universal primary education; improve maternal health

multilateral aid = **foreign aid** by donor countries to ELDCs through international organizations, such as various United Nations agencies

multilateral development assistance = lending to ELDCs by international organizations (ex World Bank) to achieve development objectives on **non-concessional terms** (at market interest rates and repayment periods); to be distinguished from **foreign aid**

multinational corporation (MNC) = a firm that carries out **foreign direct investment**; has productive investment in more than one country

non-governmental organizations (NGOs) = organizations concerned with promoting objectives that are in the public interest, ex OXFAM; are involved in a broad variety of development efforts, ex technical assistance for farmers, education and health services, support for urban informal workers, micro-credit, rights of women, human rights, sustainable development, etc

Official Development Assistance (ODA) = **foreign aid** provided by governments of donor countries

poverty trap (cycle) = a cycle where low income and savings lead to low investment in physical, human and natural capital, in turn leading to low productivity and low income growth, hence to low income once again; it is often transmitted from generation to generation

programme aid = **foreign aid** in support of whole sectors of the economy, ex education, health care, banking, etc

project aid = **foreign aid** for specific projects, ex building hospitals, irrigation systems, schools, etc

purchasing power parities (PPPs) = **exchange rates** that convert local currencies into US$ so that the influence of different price levels across counties is eliminated; therefore GDP or GNI per capita values expressed in US$ (PPP) are directly comparable across countries

social safety net = **transfer payments** of various kinds to ensure that people do not fall below the poverty line; ex child benefits

tied aid = conditions on the borrowing country imposed by **bilateral aid** donors requiring that at least a portion of the borrowed amount is spent to import goods and services from the donor country

urban informal sector = an unregulated, unregistered sector in many cities in ELDCs; includes small-scale self-employed people in a broad range of activities, ex sale of foods, clothing and various household items, mending of clothes, cobblers, barbers, and household cleaners

World Bank = an international financial institution involved in **multilateral development assistance** (as distinct from **foreign aid**); it lends to ELDCs to assist them in growth and development efforts

INDEX